Linking Teacher Preparation Program Design and Implementation to Outcomes for Teachers and Students

A volume in
*Contemporary Issues in Accreditation, Assessment,
and Program Evaluation Research in Educator Preparation*
Joyce E. Many, *Series Editor*

Linking Teacher Preparation Program Design and Implementation to Outcomes for Teachers and Students

edited by

Jennifer E. Carinci

*American Association for the
Advancement of Science*

Stephen J. Meyer

RMC Research Corporation

Cara Jackson

Bellwether Education Partners

INFORMATION AGE PUBLISHING, INC.
Charlotte, NC • www.infoagepub.com

Library of Congress Cataloging-in-Publication Data

A CIP record for this book is available from the Library of Congress
http://www.loc.gov

ISBN: 978-1-64113-957-1 (Paperback)
      978-1-64113-958-8 (Hardcover)
      978-1-64113-959-5 (E-Book)

Printed in the United States of America

CONTENTS

PREFACE

Improving the use of evidence in teacher preparation is one of the greatest challenges and opportunities for our field. The chapters in this volume explore how data availability, quality, and use within and across preparation programs shed light on the structures, policies, and practices associated with high quality teacher preparation. Chapter authors take on critical questions about the connection between what takes place during teacher preparation and subsequent outcomes for teachers and students—which has remained a black box for too long. Despite the emergence almost two centuries ago of formal teacher preparation in the United States and a considerable investment in preservice and in-service training, much is still to be learned about how preservice preparation impacts teacher effectiveness.

A strong empirical basis that informs how specific aspects of and approaches to teacher preparation relate to outcomes for graduates and their preK–12 student outcomes will provide a foundation for improved teaching and learning. Our book responds to stakeholders' collective responsibility to students and teachers to act more deliberately. Issues of data availability and quality, the uses of data for improvement, priorities for future research, and opportunities to promote evidence use in teacher preparation are discussed throughout the volume to inspire collective action to push the field towards more use of evidence. Chapters present research that uses a variety of research designs, methodologies, and data sources to explore important questions about the relationship between teacher preparation inputs and outcomes.

INTRODUCTION

Despite agreement that some teachers have more positive impact on student learning than others (e.g., Aaronson, Barrow, & Sander, 2007; Kane, McCaffrey, Miller, & Staiger, 2013; Rivkin, Hanushek, & Kain, 2005; Rockoff, 2004), much is still to be learned about the factors that affect teacher effectiveness, especially in terms of how preservice preparation influences teacher effectiveness. Despite a long history of teacher preparation in the Unites States and a considerable national investment in preservice training, there have been few comprehensive attempts to understand the diverse landscape of teacher preparation providers, the varied programs offered by them, and their effectiveness (Corcoran, Evans, & Schwab, 2004; Crowe, 2007; Goodlad, 1990, 1994).

The National Research Council (2010), in a congressionally mandated review of research, reported that "there is little firm empirical evidence to support conclusions about the effectiveness of specific approaches to teacher preparation," and, further that, "the evidence base supports conclusions about the characteristics it is valuable for teachers to have, but not conclusions about how teacher preparation programs can most effectively develop those characteristics" (p. 4). Since the 2010 National Research Council report, there has been continued focus on better understanding the effects of teacher preparation, though the evidence base for guiding development of programs and policies remains thin.

Linking Teacher Preparation Program Design and Implementation to Outcomes for Teachers and Students, pages ix–xvi
Copyright © 2020 by Information Age Publishing

In light of disagreement around how best to prepare teachers (Wilson, Floden, & Ferrini-Mundy, 2002) in the quantity and quality demanded by the increasingly diverse U.S. school population, developing an evidence base for teacher preparation program policies and practices is one of the greatest challenges for our field. Teacher preparation providers and the programs they offer are "extremely diverse along almost any dimension of interest: the selectivity of programs, the quantity and content of what they require, and the duration and timing of coursework and fieldwork" (NRC, 2010, p. 2). Heightened concerns among U.S. policy makers around uneven preparation of teacher candidates and teacher quality has led to new—though largely untested—approaches for ensuring the quality of teacher preparation and guiding program improvement (CAEP, 2013; Cochran-Smith, Piazza, & Power, 2013). Research could inform the development and improvement of these programs, guiding their design and implementation in ways that reflect best practice, ultimately benefiting students in the classrooms of new teachers.

CONTRIBUTION OF THIS VOLUME

This second volume in the series *Contemporary Issues in Accreditation, Assessment, and Program Evaluation in Educator Preparation* seeks to improve the knowledge base about how to prepare effective teachers. The chapters in this volume explore how data availability, quality, and use within and across preparation programs can help develop evidence and shed light on the structures, policies, and practices associated with high quality teacher preparation. Chapter authors discuss research and continuous improvement cycles conducted in a variety of contexts. These chapters further our collective thinking about the data, research designs, and methodologies needed to conduct studies of teacher preparation programs and policies; methodological and other challenges to identifying effective practice; and approaches for linking aspects of teacher preparation to outcomes for teacher candidates, practicing teachers, and PreK–12 students.

Chapter 1, "Improving Teacher Preparation: The Promise, Challenges, and Research Needs of State Accountability Systems," written by Saroja Warner, Michael Allen, and Charles Coble, discusses the history of accountability in teacher preparation, including various large-scale efforts to ensure the quality of teacher preparation and state accountability policies. The authors discuss their experiences working with 15 states that were part of the Network for Transforming Educator Preparation (NTEP), a group convened by the Council of Chief State School Officers between 2013 and 2017 to develop model strategies and resources that could be adopted for improving teacher preparation. The chapter focuses on challenges experienced by NTEP states in working to improve the quality of state agency data, highlighting *key effectiveness indicators* examined across states and the research that guided their work. Taken together, the experiences of these states provide a set of considerations for how information about teacher preparation program implementation and effectiveness may be collected and used. The chapter concludes with a discussion of implications for future research, for developing data infrastructure and capacity, and for improving program review and accountability systems.

The relationship between teacher preparation program features and student achievement outcomes in one state is examined by Courtney Preston in Chapter 2, "Learning to Teach: Optimizing Coursework and Fieldwork Requirements in Traditional Teacher Preparation." The chapter begins with an overview of research related to coursework and field experiences in teacher preparation. Next, results from a study of secondary English/language arts and mathematics teacher preparation programs at 15 public universities in North Carolina are presented. Results include an analysis of requirements for coursework and field experiences across the programs and of the relationship between these requirements and achievement outcomes for the Pre–K students of program graduates. Preston concludes by discussing the study limitations and suggestions for future research.

An approach for using case study data to drive program improvement is described in Chapter 3, "Using Case Study Data of Completers as Evidence in a Continuous Improvement Model." In this chapter, Bruce Weitzel, Hillary Merk, Jacqueline Waggoner, James Carroll, and Randy Hetherington begin with a discussion of accountability in teacher preparation, including requirements for national accreditation and associated challenges related to available data. Next, the chapter describes a case study approach implemented at a small university in Oregon that offers both undergraduate and graduate level teacher preparation programs. The case study approach was guided by requirements for national accreditation and uses a diverse array of data sources and measures, including surveys of program graduates and their principals, interviews with principals, graduate classroom observation, and assessments of student learning by both beginning teachers and by candidates during clinical experiences. The authors describe the data collection and analysis, the findings from the case study, how findings were used to guide improvement, and study limitations. The chapter concludes with discussion of the utility of the case study approach and the importance of using data to inform continuous improvement.

The authors of Chapter 4, "Educating Effective Science Teachers: Preparing and Following Teachers Into the Field," examined several questions related to the preparation of secondary-level science teachers. Elizabeth Lewis, Ana Rivero, Aaron Musson, Lyrica Lucas, Amy Tankersley, and Brian Helding begin with an overview of literature related to science teacher preparation that informs the study's conceptual framework. The review includes discussion of teacher subject matter and pedagogical knowledge in relation to student misconceptions and teacher curricular choices, the importance of inquiry-based instruction and assessment practices, and the instructional practices of beginning science teachers. Next, the chapter describes two secondary science teacher preparation programs (an undergraduate and a graduate program) at a large university in Nebraska. Findings from a study of program candidates and beginning science teachers are presented, including common discipline-specific misconceptions (in chemistry, physics/physical science, and life science) among science teacher candidates and factors associated with those misconceptions. The study also examines the self-efficacy of beginning teachers, the extent to which their instructional practices are inquiry-based, and variation by preparation program type. The chapter concludes with discussion of implications for science teacher preparation program design and implementation, and recommendations for future research instrumentation and evidence-based policy.

In Chapter 5, authors Zafer Unal, Yasar Bodur, and Aslihan Unal examine an approach for understanding the diversity of teacher candidate field experience placements and the relationship of placement diversity to program graduate outcomes. "Measuring Diversity in Teacher Candidate Practicum Placements and its Relationship to Outcomes" begins with a discussion of the importance of preparing teachers to work with diverse student populations, definitions of diversity, related expectations for national accreditation and state program approval, and the importance of clinical experiences. Next, the chapter describes how teacher preparation programs at a Florida institution of higher education measured the diversity of student demographics in field experience placements. The authors describe the school diversity index and its use as part of a quality assurance system. Next, the authors present findings from analyses linking the diversity of candidate placements to relevant outcomes: program graduates' evaluation scores as practicing teachers, the diversity of schools in which they are subsequently employed, graduates' satisfaction with their preparation, and the satisfaction of graduates' employers. The chapter concludes with discussion of study limitations, the utility of examining field placement diversity to guide program improvement, and implications for future research.

In Chapter 6, "Signature Practices in an Urban Residency Program: How Are These Practices Evident in the Graduates' Classrooms?" Jennifer Collett, Nancy Dubetz, Harriet Fayne, Anne Marie Marshall, and Anne Rothstein examine the instructional practices of beginning teachers who completed a graduate residency program focused on elementary mathematics teaching. The authors begin with a discussion of the challenges that motivated the development of the Mathematics Achievement with Teachers of High-Need Urban Populations (MATH UP) program, a partnership between a teacher preparation program in New York City and five elementary schools. Next the chapter describes the MATH UP program and its emphasis on signature instructional practices related to formative assessment, standards-based mathematics instruction, and effective instruction of English learners. Interview and observation data collected from program graduates were used to assess the extent to which these signature instructional practices were evident during graduates' first 2 years of teaching. The chapter concludes with a discussion of how tailored data collection and analysis approaches can be used to examine different types of instructional practices, and implications for teacher preparation programs and future research.

Preservice teacher quality ratings are the focus of Chapter 7. In this chapter, "Preparing and Keeping Our Best: Linking a Measure of Preservice Teacher Quality to Professional Outcomes," authors Margarita Pivovarova, Robert Vagi, and Wendy Barnard begin with a discussion of the importance of teacher preparation and need to better understand preservice teacher quality and its relationship to subsequent outcomes. Next, the chapter presents findings from analysis of data collected from multiple cohorts of graduates of a traditional preparation program at a large state university, including observation-based quality ratings during their year-long student teaching residency. Employment data from the state department of education are also used to examine subsequent entry and retention in teaching. Notably, the authors use discrete-time hazard and latent growth modeling—quantitative methods novel to teacher preparation research—to understand the relationships. Study findings focus on changes in preservice teacher quality ratings during student teaching, the relationship between teacher characteristics and growth in quality ratings, and the relationship between preservice teacher quality ratings and subsequent entry and retention in teaching.

In Chapter 8, "Toward Causal Evidence on Effective Teacher Preparation," authors Dan Goldhaber and Matthew Ronfeldt present an approach for using experimental research to provide causal evidence about how teacher preparation affects the quality of teacher candidates. The chapter begins with a discussion of the importance of teacher quality and effective teacher preparation and the limited research to inform understanding of how teacher preparation contributes to outcomes for teachers and students. Next, the authors provide a summary of research that links teacher preparation programs and program features to outcomes for practicing teachers and their students, highlighting its limitations. The chapter continues with a description of the Improving Student Teaching Initiative (ISTI), developed by the authors to examine the impact of aspects of student teaching experiences on various outcomes including candidate perceptions, the likelihood of entry into teaching, teacher performance, and teacher retention. The authors describe how they implemented randomization to assign teacher candidates to differential student teaching experiences, as well as various challenges they faced. The chapter concludes with a discussion of the importance of continued experimental research, suggesting that the approach used in ISTI may be adapted to explore additional questions about the impact of teacher preparation, and that additional studies of this type will generate a much needed evidence base to improve teacher preparation.

Concluding the volume, Editors Cara Jackson, Jennifer Carinci, and Stephen Meyer explore themes across chapters and implications for developing evidence that links teacher preparation program design and implementation to outcomes for students and teachers; they discuss issues of data availability and quality, the uses of data for improvement, priorities for future research, and opportunities to promote evidence use in teacher preparation.

—**Stephen J. Meyer**
Jennifer E. Carinci
Cara Jackson

REFERENCES

Aaronson, D., Barrow, L., & Sander, W. (2007). Teachers and student achievement in the Chicago public high schools. *Journal of Labor Economics, 25*(1), 95–135.

Cochran-Smith, M., Piazza, P., & Power, C. (2013). The politics of accountability: Assessing teacher education in the United States. *The Educational Forum, 77*(1), 6–27.

Corcoran, S., Evans, W. N., & Schwab, R. M. (2004). Changing labor-market opportunities for women and the quality of teachers 1957–2000. *American Economic Review, 94*(2), 230–235.

Council for the Accreditation of Educator Preparation. (2013). *CAEP accreditation standards and evidence: Aspirations for educator preparation.* Washington, DC: Author.

Crowe, E. (2007). *An effective system of data collection on teacher preparation.* Paper prepared for the Committee on Teacher Preparation Programs, Division of Behavioral and Social Sciences and Education, National Research Council, Washington, DC.

Goodlad, J. I. (1990). *Teachers for our nation's schools.* San Francisco, CA: Jossey-Bass.

Goodlad, J. I. (1994). *Educational renewal: Better teachers, better schools.* San Francisco, CA: Jossey-Bass.

Kane, T. J., McCaffrey, D. F., Miller, T., & Staiger, D. (2013). *Have we identified effective teachers?* Seattle, WA: Bill & Melinda Gates Foundation.

National Research Council. (2010). *Preparing teachers: Building evidence for sound policy.* Committee on the Study of Teacher Preparation Programs in the United

States, Center for Education. Division of Behavioral and Social Sciences and Education. Washington, DC: The National Academies Press.

Rivkin, S. G., Hanushek, E. A., & Kain, J. F. (2005). Teachers, schools, and academic achievement. *Econometrica, 73*(2), 417–458.

Rockoff, J. E. (2004). The impact of individual teachers on student achievement: Evidence from panel data. *American Economic Review, 94*(2), 247–252.

Wilson, S. M., Floden, R. E., & Ferrini-Mundy, J. (2002). Teacher preparation research: An insider's view from the outside. *Journal of Teacher Education, 53*(3), 190–204.

CHAPTER 1

IMPROVING TEACHER PREPARATION

The Promise, Challenges, and Research Needs of State Accountability Systems

Saroja R. Warner
Council of Chief State School Officers

Michael B. Allen
Teacher Preparation Analytics

Charles R. Coble
Teacher Preparation Analytics

Improving the quality and efficacy of the data collected on teacher preparation in this country has been a longstanding concern of the field. Data-driven accountability has been a primary focus of the Council for the Accreditation of Educator Preparation (CAEP) as it develops new standards for preparation providers and new accompanying data collection and reporting requirements (CAEP, 2013). Similar concerns motivated both the

Linking Teacher Preparation Program Design and Implementation to Outcomes for Teachers and Students, pages 1–31
Copyright © 2020 by Information Age Publishing

initial effort of Congress and the U.S. Department of Education to include teacher preparation program reporting requirements in the Higher Education Act (HEA) Title II legislation beginning in 2001 and several efforts subsequently to revise those requirements (U.S. Department of Education Office of Postsecondary Education, 2017).

The focus of this chapter, however, is on the role of state agencies, including departments of education and professional standards boards, in improving teacher preparation data. The discussion in this chapter draws on a good deal of related literature, but it draws even more on the authors' work with a unique initiative of the Council of Chief School Officers (CCSSO), the Network for Transforming Educator Preparation, or NTEP. From 2013–2017, this initiative provided a veritable laboratory of 15 diverse states all seeking to improve their accountability-related practices and policies concerning teacher preparation to strengthen teacher preparation program outcomes.

The chapter begins with a brief history of recent efforts to improve preparation program accountability and the motivation behind the NTEP initiative. We then summarize the NTEP initiative itself and some of the data work that helped guide this initiative. Following that is a discussion of the challenges the states faced in their efforts to strengthen program accountability and the lessons learned. Finally, we conclude with the implications for the future of such efforts and for the education research community.

THE PUSH FOR BETTER PERFORMANCE DATA

The quality of teacher education in the United States is a longstanding concern (Labaree, 2004), and concerns persist despite the development of policies to regulate teacher preparation. The continued poor outcomes of so many of our nation's P–12 students over the past several decades, and particularly those who have been historically marginalized by society in general and in our education system, have led some critics to question whether traditional programs of teacher education are of any value at all (Walsh, 2001). Even leading teacher educators have been strongly critical of the status quo and have called for substantial reform in the way teachers in the United States are prepared (Darling-Hammond et al., 2017; Levine, 2006; National Commission for Teaching and America's Future, 1996; National Council for the Accreditation of Teacher Education, 2010). These and other reports have led to numerous efforts to reform teacher education through increased focus on clinical preparation in university/college programs; the proliferation of district-run residency programs, such as the Boston Teacher Residency program; and the spread and continuing proliferation of "alternate routes" into the profession (Woods, 2016).

The variation in preparation program design increases the onus on states to ensure that all approved pathways to teacher licensure produce effective teachers. There are significant differences, however, between states' specific requirements and standards for teacher licensure. This state-to-state variation includes differences in the examinations required for teacher licensure and different passing scores on common licensure examinations. An additional concern is the practice of weakening entry standards into the profession to increase teacher supply—a practice now adopted by numerous states that have reported shortages in recent years (Associated Press, 2017; Herron, 2017; Holland, 2017; Sutcher, Darling-Hammond, & Carver-Thomas, 2016; Truong, 2017).

The establishment of the National Council for Accreditation of Teacher Education in 1954 was intended to provide a bulwark against poor-performing educator preparation programs (Christensen, 1984). In 2010, the National Council for Accreditation of Teacher Education (NCATE) and the Teacher Education Accreditation Council (TEAC) merged and formed a new accrediting agency, the Council for the Accreditation of Educator Preparation (CAEP). Now operating as CAEP, the national accreditor seeks to ensure that all accredited preparation programs demonstrably satisfy standards of program quality and that their graduates have solid teaching knowledge and skills as well as demonstrated preservice teaching success. However, even if national accreditation accomplished that goal in every case, states have not required all preparation programs to seek national accreditation. As a result, approximately half of the 1,700 teacher preparation programs in the United States (1,500 based at institutions of higher education) are nationally accredited (Sawchuk, 2016; U.S. Department of Education, 2016a).

Several high-profile attempts to provide effective and convincing criteria for evaluating teacher preparation programs have not gained wide traction or appeared to have much impact on program providers. Since 1998, Title II of the HEA has required the states to gather data on every teacher preparation program and report these data to the U.S. Secretary of Education, who through 2016 issued an annual summary based on the state reports (U.S. Department of Education, 2016b). Among other information, the Title II data include the number of enrollees and completers for every teacher certification program in the states by race/ethnicity/gender and by program type (traditional, alternative, baccalaureate, and post-baccalaureate, based at an institution of higher education and not based at an institution of higher education). The Title II reports include hundreds of data points, including data on admission and completion criteria for all preparation programs, state licensure criteria, completer certification examination pass rates, and the list of programs states deemed *low-performing*. Critics of the Title II data accuse the process of being too formulaic and imprecise to provide an accurate assessment of preparation program quality, and many state officials and teacher educators have reported that the federal reporting requirements are onerous and largely unhelpful in determining the effectiveness of their preparation programs (Allen, Coble, & Crowe, 2014; Crowe, 2010).

The only other large-scale effort to provide a national picture of the quality of teacher preparation programs is that of the National Council for Teacher Quality (NCTQ). The NCTQ provides a biannual assessment of the extent to which state policies serve to strengthen preparation programs in each state (Ross, 2017). The NCTQ also maintains an online database of ratings of individual teacher preparation programs throughout the United States that it updates every year (Drake, Pomerance, Rickenbrode, & Walsh, 2018). Lauded by some for its audacity and its attempt to shake up the status quo, the NCTQ program assessments also have been widely criticized for the criteria and evidence they employ to assess program quality, which are largely based on review of course syllabi, texts, and candidate assessments (Darling-Hammond, 2013; Fuller, 2013).

Increasing the urgency to develop effective measures and mechanisms to strengthen quality control in teacher preparation are higher expectations of new teachers coming from the profession itself. These expectations are evidenced by the new accreditation standards developed by the CAEP Commission on Standards and Performance Reporting, which was comprised of a broad range of stakeholders including teacher education professionals and prominent critics of teacher education (CAEP, 2013). It is no longer sufficient that new teachers be *highly qualified*, as reflected by obtaining a bachelor's degree, successful passage of licensure examinations, or evidence of subject matter knowledge; there is a growing expectation among state education leaders that new teachers, regardless of their route into the profession, will be *learner-ready* on day one as the teacher of record (CCSSO, 2012).

These higher expectations require assessments of programs and their completers to be much more grounded in evidence of actual teacher performance rather than in programs' compliance with input standards, coursework requirements, or time spent in P–12 classrooms. Many state education agencies have begun to identify and collect more outcomes-oriented data on both practicing teachers and their preparation programs— in some cases in response to the Obama administration's requirement that states receiving Race to the Top funding construct an educator preparation data and accountability system that focused on various candidate outcomes (Crowe, 2010). The Obama administration attempted to require all states to follow this path, but new Title II rules intended to accomplish that goal were never enacted (Iasevoli, 2017).

State Interest in Improved Programs and Program Data

In addition to the developments described above, a key driver of states' interest in the improvement of preparation programs has been the need to ensure that teachers are able to teach more rigorous college-and career-ready standards adopted in response to the Common Core State Standards initiative launched in 2009 (CCSSO, 2012). On the one hand, state education leaders assumed teachers and school leaders would take responsibility for developing additional knowledge and skills necessary to keep up with the changing nature of their work as professionals. On the other hand, state education leaders realized that they also have a responsibility to ensure that teachers are adequately prepared to improve student achievement and growth under a more rigorous set of standards (CCSSO, 2012).

This policy and practice context prompted more than twenty states to collect, analyze, and report data on preparation program performance—moving from inputs to outcomes where possible (CCSSO, 2016). Individual states' constitutional responsibility for P–12 education and the associated regulatory obligations are the primary drivers to collect better data on preparation program outcomes. State officials need to know that the programs they approve are producing successful beginning teachers and that the overall production capacity of state-approved programs meets the need for teachers across the state. Prospective teachers, who will invest their time and financial resources in professional preparation, ideally should know which programs can best ensure they are ready to teach P–12 students effectively on day one in the classroom.[1] Similarly, districts should have reliable information about which preparation programs are consistently able to produce teachers who will be effective in teaching the subjects for which they have current or projected vacancies. If preparation programs themselves are to improve, program administrators and faculty need to have solid information about how candidates are performing as they move through the programs and how completers perform once they are in P–12 classrooms. To achieve this level of systemic, data-informed decision-making, states have had to re-examine the data they collect and determine what information they need to help improve and strengthen preparation programs and their individual certification programs.

THE COUNCIL OF CHIEF SCHOOL OFFICERS' NETWORK FOR TRANSFORMING EDUCATOR PREPARATION

To aid state leaders, in 2011, CCSSO created the Task Force on Educator Preparation and Entry into the Profession. The task force was composed of seven serving chief state school officers and three former chiefs. Members of the National Association of State Boards of Education and the National Governors Association also contributed to the task force discussions and recommendations. The task force wanted to make salient the importance of investing in strong educator preparation—that the entry point into the profession is the foundation for cultivating the knowledge and skills necessary for effective teaching and leadership over an educator's career. Underlying the work of this task force was the belief that, as candidates enter educator preparation programs, they should begin a career-long journey of continuous improvement of knowledge and skills, understanding of students' needs and backgrounds, and ability to use data to drive instruction (CCSSO, 2012).

The task force report, *Our Responsibility, Our Promise,* called on state leaders to make educator preparation a top priority (CCSSO, 2012). The report identified three policy levers for strengthening teacher preparation over which state chief school officers in most states have significant authority: (a) teacher licensure; (b) state program approval; and (c) data collection, analysis, and reporting. The report also offered ten related policy recommendations and a call for action by state education leaders to act on these recommendations in their own states.

Appreciating that this work is complex and that states committed to implementing the recommendations from the task force report would greatly benefit from information, technical assistance, and the opportunity to share ideas, challenge conventional wisdom, and learn from others, CCSSO launched the Network for Transforming Educator Preparation (NTEP) in October 2013.[2] States were invited to join NTEP based on demonstrated commitment to innovative and aggressive reform of educator preparation. The network's mission was to work together to ensure new teachers are ready to teach each learner from the first day they enter the classroom as the teacher of record.

The NTEP launched with a cohort of seven states that were already taking steps toward reforming educator preparation along the lines of the task force report or had the documented commitment to move forward in that direction.[3] Two years later, a second cohort of eight states signed on.[4] Together, these 15 states became visible and credible national leaders in the effort to reshape the landscape of teacher preparation policy. The network's overarching goal was that these states would produce model policies, program designs, lessons, tools, and resources to share with all states by the end of the initiative in September 2017.

Developing Teacher Preparation Data Systems

Of the three policy levers in the CCSSO task force report, the related concerns of state program approval and improved state data systems drew the greatest attention among NTEP states. All participating states appreciated that improving data systems to more strategically collect, analyze, and report data about teacher preparation programs and their completers was a high priority. State officials and teacher educators on the NTEP state teams[5] were particularly eager to use these data for program accountability decisions and to support continuous improvement efforts. In addition, NTEP members thought that the data could be useful to P–12 districts in recruiting and hiring decisions, and for prospective teacher candidates to use in selecting a preparation program (e.g., by looking at consumer information such as completers' job placement data).

From the very start, however, making progress in improving educator preparation performance data and accountability systems presented formidable challenges. Some states quickly realized that they did not have adequate data to evaluate past and present performance of educator preparation programs. Other states realized that they didn't know exactly what data would be required to undertake a more rigorous assessment of teacher preparation programs and whether the necessary data were currently available.

The delay—and ultimate demise—of the anticipated new Title II federal regulations for educator preparation program state data collection (Iasevoli, 2017) slowed progress as states waited in vain for clarity about reporting requirements. Ultimately, however, one of the biggest obstacles for states was a lack of clarity about the precise goals and objectives for the system they sought to develop and a solid implementation plan. Nevertheless, several NTEP states made notable progress.

The authors of this chapter spent considerable time with the 15 state teams over the life of the NTEP project. Most contact time was in quarterly conferences attended by all state teams, but there were also webinars that engaged all of the states, as well as opportunities to meet with state team members and other stakeholders on visits to the states themselves. Assistance was provided to state teams in analyzing their current data systems and developing strategies for improving those systems. Consultations covered the development of program performance indicators and measures, improving data quality, and establishing effective data accountability policies and continuous improvement practices. The analysis and recommendations that constitute the bulk of this discussion are derived overwhelmingly from what we observed and learned during our work with the NTEP project.

State Policies for Program Accountability

All NTEP states shared the goal of having a robust annual or biannual program review system that would provide some assurance of adequate program performance and ultimately lead to program improvement. Building such a system, however, is an iterative, multi-year process and requires fine-tuning various indicators and improving the quality of the data. If the system is to be long-lasting and effective, leaders must attend to the delicate task of building and maintaining stakeholder support—especially the support of the teacher preparation professionals whose work will be most directly impacted.

The distinctive function of the annual review process differed somewhat among the states. One of the key differences was the nature of the accountability implications of the review and the relationship between the annual review process and any other accountability process, such as the 5- to 7-year program reapproval decision that is common in many states. In Tennessee and Washington, for example, the two-fold purpose of the annual review was: (a) to provide an indication to state officials of whether teacher preparation programs have deficiencies in need of remediation and, if necessary, state intervention; and (b) to provide data to programs that can guide continuous improvement (Washington Professional Educator Standards Board, 2015; Tennessee Department of Education, 2017). For Washington, the annual review was the only state accountability mechanism once a preparation program was initially approved; there was no multiyear state reapproval cycle. Tennessee, on the other hand, required that all programs pass a comprehensive program review every 7 years in addition to the annual review process (Tennessee State Board of Education, 2018).

Delaware's regular program review was biennial and focused heavily on state accountability. Delaware sorted programs into four performance levels to provide the state education agency with evidence of the need for intervention to address identified program deficiencies (Delaware Department of Education, 2016b, 2016c). All university providers and their programs were required to maintain national accreditation and program approval.

In sharp contrast, the annual review in Massachusetts had no accountability function. The review was intended only to be an early indicator for state officials and preparation programs that some elements of the program may need remediation if the program was to be unconditionally reapproved when that decision was next made in the state's 7-year approval cycle (Comb, 2018).

The Challenges of Reliable Program Assessment Data

The NTEP states not only differed in the accountability ramifications they attached to their program review systems, but also in the data systems they had begun to develop. Working in isolation prior to joining NTEP, most states had already adopted their own indicators of program performance, and there were significant differences between the states in the quality, rigor, and comprehensiveness of states' data. Virtually all the indicators and many of the measures that incoming states had chosen, however, were reflected in a set of recommended indicators and measures developed by Teacher Preparation Analytics, dubbed the Key Effectiveness Indicators (KEI).[6] The KEI was developed very close in time to the inauguration of the NTEP initiative and became a common framework for discussions among NTEP states as they worked to strengthen their data systems (Allen et al., 2014; Teacher Preparation Analytics, 2016). Although no states had adopted a majority of the indicators by the close of the initiative, states were sufficiently influenced by the KEI that clear similarities between the states' data systems could be perceived by the time NTEP ended.

In developing the KEI, Teacher Preparation Analytics attempted to meet a specific challenge: to identify a limited set of essential indicators—and ultimately measures—that would (a) be useful for program improvement, (b) be equally applicable to all programs in a state (traditional and nontraditional) without prescribing program content and structure, (c) be focused principally on program outcomes rather than inputs, (d) be compelling and transparent for a variety of stakeholders, and (e) respond to the concerns that both experts and the greater public have expressed about the effectiveness of programs and the caliber of individuals entering the teaching profession. The KEI framework uses four categories (or domains) of program assessment data, 12 performance indicators, and a set of proposed measures for each indicator. The latest iteration of the KEI appears in the Appendix.

The KEI represents an attempt to distill both the experience of several states in the vanguard of efforts to build preparation program data systems and the relevant empirical research. There is a body of research literature that directly or indirectly addresses many of the methodological issues that states face in developing educator preparation program accountability systems. Much of that literature illuminates the evidence (or lack thereof) for the adoption of various kinds of measures of preparation program performance. The evidentiary basis for the KEI is reviewed in the *Building an Evidence-Based System* report (Allen et al., 2014) and in the *Guide to the Key Effectiveness Indicators* (Teacher Preparation Analytics, 2016).

The National Academy of Education report, *Evaluation of Teacher Preparation Programs: Purposes, Methods, and Policy Options* (Feuer, Floden, Chudowsky, & Ahn, 2013), is perhaps the most thorough and cautious review of the relevant literature. The report concludes that the research supports the importance of asking several questions in any process of developing assessment measures for preparation programs. The authors also caution, however, that the research is not adequate to support the adoption of any specific performance measures. This limited conclusion of the National Academy of Education report may indeed be empirically justified, but does not offer the guidance needed by states—like the NTEP states—whose program evaluation trains are already far down the track in building more evidence-based performance assessment systems.

In going beyond the evidence in the research literature, the efforts of the NTEP states to develop preparation program review and accountability systems take on a certain degree of arbitrariness. They are guided by experience and wisdom of practice, but are in some respects experimental. This does not mean, however, that states don't value the findings of research in their efforts to develop their systems. Many NTEP state leaders had genuine interest in knowing what performance measures the existing body of research might support and what the limitations of that support might be. Massachusetts, for example, specifically commissioned its own review of the relevant literature in developing its annual program review system (Massachusetts Department of Elementary and Secondary Education, 2016).

CHALLENGES RELATED TO STATE EDUCATION DATA

The states in the NTEP network faced several additional challenges: (a) improving the quality of their states' education data, (b) collecting placement and performance data on program completers, (c) ensuring the quality of measures used, and (d) using measures to then assure program quality and support program improvement. Each of these challenges is discussed in detail below.

Improving the Quality of State Agency Data Systems

Improving the quality and breadth of the data available for preparation program assessment was the greatest challenge facing the NTEP states and often the biggest limitation to the potential effectiveness of state program performance review systems. Many states have high-quality P–12 data systems based on individual student records that track students' course taking and performance throughout their (in-state) elementary and secondary education careers. Such systems serve the needs of P–12 accountability. Fewer states, however, have adequate statewide postsecondary data systems that can serve similar accountability needs for educator preparation. Ideally, states would also make it possible to track employment outcomes by merging employment data with education data. A 2003 publication from the State Higher Education Executive Officers provides a detailed description of the data and database communication that would be necessary to build a rigorous teacher data system (Voorhees, Barnes, & Rothman, 2003). A more recent publication from WestEd draws on several discussions of the current state-of-the art postsecondary education databases and the challenges facing efforts to improve and standardize them (Cubarrubia & Perry, 2016).

Improving candidate data maintained by preparation programs, particularly in institution-based programs, is a continuing challenge. Based on our experience with the NTEP states, we conclude generally that institutional research offices in higher education need to work more closely with colleges, schools, or departments of education to ensure that the appropriate data on teacher preparation candidates are available for state and national accreditation purposes and to support program improvement. Gathering good-quality data can be a significant challenge for small colleges and universities and even for small preparation programs in larger institutions, which have more limited staff capacity to focus on this work. We also found, especially in smaller institutions, that preparation programs may lack the necessary expertise to assess the quality of the data they do have, and to use those data effectively for program improvement.

Collecting Placement and Performance Data on Completers

State officials in the NTEP states—as in most other states—were especially interested in tracking the placement and retention of teachers produced by in-state preparation programs. This was a function both of program faculty curiosity about the fate of their completers and a recognition that where (and especially how) completers end up teaching is prima facie an important indicator of program success. However, it is a challenge for states—and even more for preparation programs—to obtain data on program completers that are truly representative of the completer population. Sometimes the problem is a lack of staff resources that hinders the systematic tracking of program completers after graduation. In addition, although state employment databases provide information on program completers who are teaching in the state, tracking of completers who leave the state is generally infeasible.[7] And even within a state, tracking data on teachers employed in private schools rather than in the public schools is difficult because the former have fewer reporting requirements. Still, even data restricted to completers working in the state's public schools would be of value to preparation programs by providing some indication of where their candidates end up and how long they stay in education.

Beyond the issues of placement and retention, obtaining data on completer performance as teachers is also a very desirable goal for many states and for forward-looking teacher preparation programs as well. Some states, like North Carolina, have state-approved teacher performance evaluation instruments that are used in all school districts across the state and include required training protocols to help ensure effective implementation. Other states, like Illinois, require annual teacher performance evaluations but give districts a good deal of discretion in developing their own evaluation tools and standards.

The holy grail of data on teacher performance is the actual impact on their P–12 students' learning gains or other important learning-related outcomes (Blazar & Kraft, 2017). There is an extensive literature on the promises and pitfalls of using value-added or student growth data to evaluate teachers, as well as a smaller body of research on the validity of attributing teachers' impact scores back to the programs that prepared them (Ehlert, Koedel, Parsons, & Podgursky, 2014; Goldhaber, 2013; Goldhaber, Liddle, & Theobald, 2013; Henry, et al., 2013). At the state level, Louisiana piloted the connection between teacher preparation programs and their completers' impact on P–12 student learning. Several other states (e.g., Tennessee, Ohio, Washington, North Carolina, and Delaware) have since attempted to use that connection as key element of a larger preparation program performance assessment system (Gansle, Noell & Burns, 2012; Noell & Burns, 2006; CCSSO, 2016).

The great majority of states, however, are not currently able to follow suit. In some states, the data are simply not adequate to permit this (CCSSO, 2016; Aragon, 2016). No state has assessments in all teaching subjects that are adequate to ground reliable teacher impact measures. Other states simply have not chosen to link student outcomes to teachers, sometimes because of an inadequate database and sometimes for philosophical or political reasons (e.g., strong opposition from teacher unions; Sawchuk, 2014). Still other states use teacher impact data as part of their annual teacher evaluation but are prohibited by privacy restrictions or labor agreements from using these data for any other purpose—even if data are aggregated and anonymous as they would be in data on preparation program performance (Doherty & Jacobs, 2015). Without data on teacher impact, however, the preparation program review system lacks a true connection to student learning—the core outcome teacher preparation programs are intended to promote.

Ensuring the Quality of Measures Used

Another critical consideration in building a teacher preparation program data system is the granularity of the data. We found that many NTEP states, especially during the early stages of development when the states were trying to gain clarity about what data were most readily available or within relatively easy reach, were focused on provider-level data rather than data on individual certification programs. That made data collection easier and tended to avoid the sensitivities involved in displaying data on so few program candidates or completers that those individuals might be identifiable. However, this practice masks differences in the performance of individual programs and severely compromises the accountability and program improvement value of the data collected. Effective program improvement and credible accountability require data to be disaggregated to the program level, and the states most advanced in the development of their data systems were able to provide that.

Adopting specific program performance *indicators* is relatively easy conceptually and technically compared to the far more difficult task of developing and implementing valid and reliable *measures* that define those indicators. An *indicator* simply denotes a feature or outcome of a preparation program that is to be measured on the assumption that it will provide a good indication of key program strengths or weaknesses (e.g., the *academic strength* of incoming candidates or the *demonstrated teaching skill* of program completers). A *measure*, however, is a numerical value that is intended to affirm (in the present context) whether or not the preparation program feature or outcome is strong or weak. In the case of demonstrated teaching skill, a measure may be the mean performance of program candidates on a classroom observation assessment such as the Danielson Framework for Teaching. The validity and reliability of a measure frequently come into question due to concerns about data quality, about the rigor of assessments used, or about the validity of complex mathematical models that may be employed (e.g., to determine completers' impact on their K–12 students).

When the focus of state action is on indicators—as it principally was during the NTEP project—states' efforts to develop program review and performance systems may be attributed more success than is really warranted. All states have good intentions in adopting indicators and developing appropriate measures, but there is significant variability in the validity and reliability of measures employed, variability in the specific values reported in the measures—and thus in the information communicated, and variability in the acceptable performance levels both between states and sometimes within an individual state (because of district-level inconsistencies). In some cases, these differences reflect the quality of data available for the different indicators or measures. In other cases, they result from flaws in the design of the measures that compromise validity and reliability. Even if the indicators adopted are the same, such differences in measures—however subtle—make cross-state comparisons of teacher impact virtually impossible and even within-state comparisons problematic.

Ultimately, the quality of the measures will make or break the program performance review system. Measures such as licensure examination pass rates are not likely to provide much discrimination between the performance of different programs in states where cut scores for determining passing scores on such assessments are low. Several NTEP states employ—or plan to employ—program completers' scores on their annual teacher performance assessments as an indicator of program performance. This is reasonable if the assessments are comparable across school districts and differences in measured performance are a product of actual variations in performance rather than of disparities in how the assessments measure performance. In states with which we've worked, however, that inter-district comparability is not always present. And in some cases, it is not only an issue of variation in assessments but of a lack of uniformity in how districts weight the several components of the overall annual assessment (e.g., a classroom observation assessment, a teacher self-assessment, a supervisor survey, or a teacher impact measure).[8] Even in states deploying standardized teacher performance assessments across districts and uniformly weighting assessment components, achieving sufficient levels of inter-rater reliability is a challenge and remains a significant issue for data quality assurance.

One particularly important difference among states is that some states— Tennessee and Delaware, for example—provide not only mean scores for candidate or completer outcome measures, but also distribution scores that reveal what percentage of candidates or completers fall significantly above or below the mean or a designated benchmark. There is an important difference between a program whose candidates all score very near a statewide or national mean, and a program with the same mean score but with a significant number of candidates who fall well below (and above) it. The first program at least demonstrates consistency in candidate performance, whereas the inconsistency of the second program and the fact that many of its candidates fail to perform at an average level (even if many other candidates are well above average) raise initial concerns about program consistency and/or program recruitment strategies. The fact that a good number of candidates in a program may be outstanding does not make up for a significant number of candidates in that same program performing below average and potentially being sent into the teaching profession inadequately prepared.

Still another important difference between states that otherwise may appear to have similar performance measures is in the benchmarks they set for satisfactory (or exemplary) program performance. Two states may use the same assessment of candidates' knowledge of their teaching subject, for example, but require different passing scores. Or, one state may set a performance benchmark at the national median score on the assessment while another state with a very similar measure sets it at a specific score that denotes mastery. Thus, although there may be isomorphism between states in some of the measures they employ, actual inter-state comparability of measures is likely to be limited.

Two indicators included in the KEI, *subject-specific pedagogical knowledge* and *teaching promise*, were not adopted by any of the NTEP states. The KEI justification for a subject-specific pedagogical knowledge indicator, separate from either *mastery of teaching subject* and *completer teaching skill*, was that the importance of this sort of knowledge had been demonstrated convincingly by Deborah Ball and her associates (Ball, Thames, & Phelps, 2008). Furthermore, none of the common tests of candidate content knowledge or teaching skill—including the edTPA and the similar Praxis Performance Assessment for Teachers—adequately assess subject-specific pedagogical content knowledge (Allen et al., 2014; Educational Testing Service, 2018; Stanford Center for Assessment, Learning, & Equity, 2018).[9] Since the development of the KEI, the Educational Testing Service has developed a Content Knowledge for Teaching test that is intended precisely to provide the sort of broad and deep assessment of subject-specific pedagogical knowledge the KEI emphasizes (Phelps, Weren, Croft, & Gitomer, 2014). However, we did not observe significant interest among the NTEP states in adopting a new licensure examination. Furthermore, the Educational Testing Service contends the Content Knowledge for Teaching test requires the same level of basic content knowledge as is assessed in the Praxis II series, which obviates the need to administer a separate pure content knowledge assessment (J. DeLuca, personal communication, February 18, 2016; Phelps et al., 2014).

Many more NTEP states expressed interest in pursuing the adoption of a *teaching promise* assessment. The justification from Teacher Preparation Analytics for including *teaching promise* as a measure of program performance is that, just as programs should seek to require solid academic skills for entering teacher candidates, so should they require candidates to demonstrate solid interest and aptitude for teaching in 21st century classrooms (Allen et al., 2014). Several related assessments have already been developed to screen prospective teachers, such as the Gallup Teacher Insight Assessment, the Haberman Star Teacher Prescreener, and an intensive Teach For America selection process (Dobbie, 2011; Gallup, 2014; Hill-Jackson, Stafford, James, & Hartlep, 2018). The state of Missouri has worked with Pearson to develop a teaching aptitude profile for all entering teacher candidates that is intended to identify deficiencies on 16 teaching-related habits or dispositions that need to be addressed before candidates complete their program (NCS Pearson, 2013). The Missouri assessment has been standardized and tested for both construct and predictive validity, but neither this assessment nor any other assessment of *teaching promise* or dispositions was designed to be used in an accountability context. Whether this interest in assessing *teaching promise* results in a related program performance measure that can be legitimately used as part of a program performance accountability system or whether the assessment of *teaching promise* remains an internal program and candidate improvement tool is to be determined.[10]

USING ACCOUNTABILITY TO ENSURE PROGRAM QUALITY

For most of the NTEP states, the core motivation for collecting performance data on teacher preparation programs is program accountability.[11] The measures are intended to provide state authorities—and usually also the public—with an indication of the adequacy of programs' performance as signaled by the scores on the measures chosen. In its quality assurance role, the state agency responsible for program approval would then be expected to take some sort of corrective action in cases where program performance appears to be deficient.

The NTEP states differ significantly in what that corrective action is and in the extent to which the accountability data are also intended to provide information that can guide program improvement efforts. In some states, the accountability function is quite strong. Delaware, for example, utilizes a weighted measures system for program review that places programs into four groups based on aggregate scores. Programs that end up in the two lowest performance tiers are subject to state intervention, and could be placed on probation or have candidate admissions suspended (Delaware Department of Education, 2016a; Delaware Department of Education, 2016b).

At the other end of the accountability spectrum is the state of Washington, which flags any indicator score deemed low for two consecutive years, and then launches an inquiry with the preparation program to determine if a program deficiency might be responsible. More severe action can be taken with programs that fail to raise performance scores to a satisfactory level. This annual program review system is the only ongoing review process the state of Washington employs once a program receives initial approval to operate (Washington Professional Educator Standards Board, 2015). That means that the annual review system has the strongest possible accountability role to play. The intervention process itself, however, is much more cautious than the process Delaware employs. The other NTEP states tend to fall between these two extremes, and all other states have a multi-year program reapproval cycle in addition to the annual review (CCSSO, 2016).

Adequate Data Strength

Critical issues raised by the accountability function of the annual program review process are the quality of the data and whether the measures that ground the review in any given state are up to the task. These issues are complex, and require confronting questions such as those discussed immediately below.

Are the Data Valid and Reliable and Genuinely Comparable Between Programs?

If, for example, a state employs data on teacher impact in its accountability system, does the fact that completers from some programs teach overwhelmingly in affluent schools while completers from other programs teach overwhelmingly in high-poverty schools confound the comparability of the two programs, or is this confound overcome by the regression models or calculations used to determine the program scores?

Are the Data Used Representative of the Candidate/Completer Population?

This is particularly a challenge in the case of programs with significant numbers of completers who are difficult to track post-completion because they end up teaching in multiple states or in private schools. A related issue is small sample size, which especially plagues very small programs. Even if the small cohort is the actual population and not a potentially unrepresentative sample, there could be a large enough deviation between individual cohort member scores to make an average score highly misleading. Moreover, small sample sizes raise privacy concerns; identifying the specific individuals included in a small population or sample may be relatively easy, and this could run afoul of Family Educational Rights and Privacy Act (FERPA) laws or other privacy protection policies. Most NTEP states addressed this issue by adopting a policy of reporting out scores only on a sample size of at least 10 or 15 candidates or completers. Another work-around that states employ is using three consecutive years of data for measures, adding the newest cohort data each year and dropping the oldest. This poses other problems, however; because such a process can mask a marked drop or increase in performance between years, and some data used to make corrective decisions could be several years old and less relevant to current program conditions.[12]

Do The Individual Measures Genuinely Distinguish Between Program Performance?

Attempting to implement a measure of teacher impact on student achievement in Missouri's program accountability system, for example, researchers found that the measure failed to distinguish between the performance of different programs and that there was as much diversity among the performance scores of completers from the same program as there was between completers from different programs (Koedel, Parsons, Podgursky, & Ehlert, 2015). Similarly, benchmarks employed by states to distinguish satisfactory from unsatisfactory performance may be of questionable validity (i.e., they may not denote meaningful differences between performance levels). Some measures may be notoriously prone to fail on this count; some researchers, for example, note that cut scores on licensure examinations do a mediocre job of predicting effective from ineffective teachers—and even more so after a year or two of experience in the classroom (Goldhaber, 2007; Shuls, 2016).

Can the Measures be Meaningfully Weighted?

A key issue for the states is how to handle multiple measures in an accountability context. Most states would like some way of triaging programs so that they can place greater attention on those with the lowest performance scores. Some states (e.g., Delaware) have attempted to weight the measures in order to derive an overall performance score for each program and then rank the programs from highest to lowest performing. Weighting the measures, however, poses significant strategic and methodological challenges. In general, measures that count more for accountability also will be taken more seriously by the programs, and measures that count for relatively little may be given much less attention. In addition, providing weights to measures is ultimately an arbitrary exercise, and the recognition of that fact can undermine stakeholder confidence in the system. Prima facie, teacher impact or teacher performance in the classroom seem to be among the most important indicators, but how does that translate into the defensible assignment of a specific weight? Moreover, some measures differentiate program performance more than others, and assigning a large weight to a measure with little differentiation will narrow the range of overall performance scores and make the grouping of programs into performance levels appear more arbitrary.

Stakeholder Confidence in the System

Such shortcomings and potential compromises in the program review data and performance measures pose challenges to stakeholder confidence in the measures and in the accountability system. Many teacher educators, for example, have solid research backgrounds and can perceive quite clearly any limitations in the data used to evaluate their programs. Our experience with the NTEP states and others indicates that stakeholders will be tolerant of less-than-perfect program review data during the early stages of system development in the expectation that problems will be remedied and that, until that time, any judgments about program performance based on deficient data carry an asterisk and limited accountability consequences. All the NTEP states engaged in some sort of pilot in their development of program review and accountability systems precisely to gain a better understanding of the limitations of their data and to fine-tune system features before the accountability measures were invested with consequences for programs.

If shortcomings in the data and performance measures persist, however, or if they are endemic and not completely fixable, state officials proceed at their own risk in attaching strong accountability consequences to program performance scores. Not only might judgments of program performance simply be incorrect, but the combination of strong accountability and weak data and measures undermines stakeholder confidence in the accountability system. Teacher educators may see the accountability system as unfair and treat related reporting requirements as just an exercise in compliance, rather than as an opportunity to use data for program improvement.

Additionally, program performance indicator systems being developed by states are inherently and intentionally limited in the data they provide. Unlike long-term program approval or national accreditation processes, the annual state preparation program review systems are developed with a priority on data parsimony.[13] Nevertheless, the indicators and measures included are intended—at least in the KEI model system—to provide some redundancy and triangulation such that low performance scores on several different measures may yield clues about the source of the problems behind those scores. A low teacher impact score, for example, coupled with a high score in demonstrated teaching skill but a low score in teaching subject knowledge might indicate that a program's standards for their candidates' content knowledge are insufficiently rigorous. These annual review systems are not likely to provide all the data programs would like to have for improvement efforts, but they will fulfill their primary accountability function if they accurately signal problematic and exemplary program performance.

A decision to require a low-scoring program to undertake corrective action or to assign all relatively low-scoring programs to a group that denotes their inadequacy ultimately may be justified, but it remains to be seen whether such a decision can be made confidently based on data from performance review indicators alone. Performance reviews may fail to include information about specific program context, for example, that a high percentage of completers from one program traditionally take teaching jobs in a neighboring state, or that another program addresses its mission to increase the number of minority teachers in area schools by lowering academic admissions standards but requiring all completers to perform at a high level. A precise diagnosis of the problems that may account for a program's low performance scores, as well as a prescription for correcting them, almost certainly requires additional information beyond what is needed for the state's annual program review process. This information would include qualitative data that can provide important context and nuance and finer-grained quantitative data that focuses more on specific candidate sub-skills, or even candidate-level data that enable program faculty to better understand how specific candidate strengths and weaknesses may impact overall teaching performance.

USING DATA FOR PROGRAM IMPROVEMENT

All the NTEP states that had made substantial progress in developing program review systems were committed to using the program review data for purposes beyond issuing annual program performance reports. At the very least, this involved the expectation that programs would use the data reports for improvement. And one of the frequent discussions among the NTEP state teams was what role the state agencies could play in the continuous improvement efforts of teacher preparation programs. The relationship between state expectations that preparation programs use data to inform program improvement and the actual and successful use of data to improve varied among states. Among those states where data were used to improve, the successful use of data was partially attributed to the existence of effective partnerships and collaboration between the state and the teacher preparation community. In states like Connecticut, Georgia, Louisiana, and Missouri, changes to program review and approval that required the collection, analysis, and use of data for both accountability and program improvement were designed to include all the relevant stakeholders in the decision-making process (CCSSO, 2017).

Recent reports issued by Bellwether Education Partners (Mitchel & Aldeman, 2016), the CCSSO (2018), the Data Quality Campaign (2017), and Deans for Impact (2016) indicate that a key requirement for program improvement data is that they be of sufficiently fine grain size. In the first instance, this means data must focus on candidate and student outcomes at the individual program level, or possibly subject certification level. In some cases, an adequately clear identification of the possible sources of program deficiencies may require data on the performance of individual candidates or completers—and not just as measured by composite assessment scores but by specific domains within an assessment. Tennessee, for example, provides data to preparation programs on recent completers' observed classroom performance scores not only overall but by specific skill (e.g., planning, motivating students, etc.; Tennessee Department of Education, 2017). As we noted previously, however, releasing data to programs that can permit the identification of individual candidates or completers may violate FERPA or other privacy rules. And some states are already struggling to disaggregate data to the individual program level, let alone to the individual candidate or completer level.

In our experience, many teacher preparation programs are awash in data, particularly from formative assessments of candidates. The quality of those data is often questionable, however, because the data may be derived from non-rigorous assessments, highly subjective evaluations (and self-evaluations) of candidate performance, or partial and anecdotal information (e.g., about the teaching performance of recent program completers). And with multiple sources of data (some required to be collected by the state education agency), programs may be uncertain about which data are most strategic for improvement purposes. Augmenting the accountability review data, which should meet a high standard, with formative data that address the various accountability review measures may be an effective strategy. A program that has low annual performance review scores on candidate teaching skill, for example, may be able to gain important context from looking at other assessments of candidate teaching skill that help identify the underlying causes of the problem. Accreditation review also can be an important source of information relevant to program improvement, and has the added advantage that some information derives from the observations and reports of trained outside evaluators.

IMPLICATIONS FOR RESEARCH AND FUTURE EFFORTS

State program performance and review systems—even those that have the longest history—are still relatively new and untested. These systems have yet to demonstrate the promise that many in the education community (including the authors) hold out for them, although there are currently empirical studies underway in Massachusetts and Tennessee that may provide some initial evidence and perspective in that regard. The Massachusetts study, expected to be completed in 2019, explores the predictive validity of several measures of candidate teaching skill and performance on those candidates' later effectiveness as classroom teachers (Theobald, Conaway, Cowan, & Peske, 2020). The Tennessee study, which released an initial report on 183 certification programs, has found statistically significant differences between teacher education programs based upon observational ratings of program graduates—differences that are also correlated with achievement gains of those graduates' students (Ronfeldt & Campbell, 2016).

Such studies provide just a glimpse of the vital roles that the education research community can play in helping state officials and teacher educators build more rigorous and effective approaches to preparation program improvement and accountability. One role is to continue to produce empirical studies that will be valuable to the field. This includes studies that examine the relationship between various measures of educator preparation program candidates' performance on preservice assessments and the performance of those candidates after they become teachers in the classroom. The research community could also produce studies that attempt to determine whether differences in programs' performance scores on different measures can be traced to differences in program practices or other factors internal to preparation programs or to the higher education institutions that may house them.

In addition to strategic empirical studies, the entire field of teacher preparation—not only the program review systems—will benefit from continued research and development efforts to improve assessments of teachers' and candidates' knowledge and skills and of other competencies and dispositions that may influence overall effectiveness in the classroom or ability to work successfully with specific populations of P–12 students. This includes continued efforts to improve models and measures of teacher impact on P–12 student learning.

Also important is evaluation of the accountability and program improvement systems themselves. What impact, if any, have they had on the policies, practices, and performance of the programs in the states? How does the impact of the annual program review systems on programs compare to that of multi-year national reaccreditation and state program reapproval? Case study, as well as correlational, research can be valuable in this context, as case studies can identify contextual factors (the political climate or economic factors, for example) that may play a role.

Finally, state officials and teacher educators have a continual need for expert guidance in the technical development of program review systems and in the analysis, interpretation, and use of data. Some of this expertise may already exist within various state agencies, but much of it will likely have to come from outside agencies as contracted support. Technical tasks include (a) improving the quality of data—constructing valid and reliable measures of various candidate or completer outcomes and other program performance measures; (b) selecting or, if necessary, developing valid and reliable assessments of candidate or completer outcomes that can be standardized across preparation programs in the state; (c) clarifying and confronting the weaknesses and limitations of system data and performance measures and exercising appropriate caution about the conclusions and actions that can be based on these measures; (d) developing reporting templates that provide effective visualizations of program performance data to maximize impact and understanding for all consumers of the data reported; and (e) helping state officials and teacher educators evaluate the impact the accountability policies and practices have had on the practices and performance of teacher preparation programs in the state.

The better the research becomes, the more the promise and the limitations of various preparation program review and accountability strategies can be illuminated. These systems, of course, ultimately may fail to live up to expectations. States may be unable to overcome fiscal constraints or the limited ability of state officials or teacher educators to devote the time required for accountability systems to achieve full effectiveness. Even now, the greater effort to ensure the quality of the United States teacher workforce is threatened by new policies in many states that lower the bar for entry into the profession to address shortages of teachers (Associated Press, 2017; Herron, 2017). The support for accountability systems by key stakeholders may dwindle, or they may be legislated out of existence or give way to a superior method of preparation program evaluation. In large part, however, the success or failure of accountability policies and practices will be dependent upon the kinds of data and methodological improvements that can only come about through the efforts of the education research community.

NOTES

1. There is good evidence suggesting that for teachers who receive their certification through undergraduate programs at public universities, quality considerations may not have played a predominant role in their choice of preparation program. A recent study from the American Council on Education finds that students who enroll as undergraduates in public universities select those schools more on the basis of proximity to home than because of financial and academic factors (Hillman & Weichman, 2016).

2. Philanthropic support provided by the Bill and Melinda Gates Foundation and the Charles and Lynn Schusterman Foundation.

3. The NTEP's first cohort of states included Connecticut, Georgia, Idaho, Kentucky, Louisiana, Massachusetts, and Washington.

4. The NTEP's second cohort of states included California, Delaware, Missouri, New Hampshire, Oklahoma, South Carolina, Tennessee, and Utah.

5. Each state team was made up of SEA staff with influence over one or more of the three key policy areas (licensure, program approval and data collection, analysis, and reporting), representatives from the teacher preparation community in their respective state and other key stakeholders.

6. Two reports comparing states' accountability indicators and measures to those in the KEI show progress in state implementation of similar program performance measures over several years' time—although only 15 states were surveyed in the earlier report. For the most part, however, the state systems employed a limited number of the KEI indicators, and the actual measures states constructed generally lacked the rigor of the measures proposed in the KEI. (See Allen et al., 2014; Council of Chief State School Officers, 2016).

7. In the last few years, the National Association of State Directors of Teacher Education and Certification has been working with the state of Georgia to develop a Multistate Educator Lookup System that would provide the instantaneous transfer of information between states about teachers' credentials and employment. The system is not yet up and running, however (National Association of State Directors of Teacher Education and Certification, n.d.).

8. The state of Massachusetts attempts to mitigate this potential district variability by "norming" teachers' annual performance assessment scores by district (Comb, 2018).

9. The edTPA and the PPAT are commercially available assessments of teacher candidates' general teaching skill, using videos of actual classroom teaching as part of the data for assessment. They are increasingly supplanting paper-and-pencil assessment of preservice teaching, such as the Principals of Learning and Teaching. However, the edTPA and PPAT assess a narrow range of subject-specific pedagogical knowledge that arguably is not sufficient to demonstrate the broader and deeper grasp a teacher candidate needs to be effective across his or her teaching field.

10. For a thorough, though slightly dated discussion of teacher assessment—including preservice assessment—see Kennedy, 2010.

11. This is not the case in Massachusetts, where the annual program measures serve only to provide an early warning that programs may have weaknesses in need of attention and do not by themselves trigger any sort of state intervention (Comb, 2018). And although it is now the case in Tennessee that the annual review is accountability-focused, the original function of the annual program reports was to draw media and public attention that hopefully would pressure low-performing programs into taking corrective action (Allen et al., 2014, p. 146).

12. Taking into consideration the additional likelihood that data used for performance measures already are based on performance from a year earlier (because of the lag in reporting time and the need to clean the data), a 3-year sample of data could include data that is from 4 years ago.

13. One of the goals of states in developing annual program review systems is to identify a limited number of key measures that can give state officials and programs a relatively quick assessment of potential program problems that may need to be addressed before they become worse.

APPENDIX

Key Effectiveness Indicators

Assessment Categories	Key Indicators	Measures [Note: EPP=Education Program Provider (a.k.a. "Unit"); TPP=individual Teacher Preparation Program]
I Candidate Selection and Completion	Academic Strength	PRIOR PROFICIENCY—1. Average GPA of candidates in most recent coursework (high school or college) prior to program entry—TPP. 2. Overall entering cohort average percentile score in national distribution on standardized entrance tests required by IHE or EPP (SAT, ACT, GRE, MAT, or College Skills Test (e.g., Praxis Core)—TPP, EPP. COMPLETER PROFICIENCY— Completer GPA in required subject major courses compared to all university students in same major—EPP.
	Teaching Promise	ATTITUDES, VALUES, AND BEHAVIORS SCREEN—Percent of accepted program candidates whose score on a rigorous and validated "fitness for teaching" assessment demonstrates a strong promise for teaching—TPP.
	Candidate/ Completer Diversity	DISAGGREGATED COMPLETIONS COMPARED TO ADMISSIONS—Number & percent of completers in newest graduating cohort AND number and percent of candidates originally admitted in that same cohort: overall and by race/ethnicity, age, gender, etc.—TPP, EPP.

Assessment Categories	Key Indicators	Measures [Note: EPP=Education Program Provider (a.k.a. "Unit"); TPP=individual Teacher Preparation Program]
II Knowledge and Skills for Teaching	Mastery of Teaching Subjects	CONTENT KNOWLEDGE TEST—Program completer mean score*, tercile distribution, and pass rate on rigorous and validated nationally normed assessment of college-level content knowledge used for initial licensure—TPP. *Validated proficiency benchmarks may be substituted for mean scores on these assessments
	Subject-Specific Pedagogical Knowledge	PEDAGOGICAL CONTENT KNOWLEDGE TEST—Completer mean score*, tercile distribution, and pass rate on rigorous and validated nationally normed licensure assessment of comprehensive pedagogical content knowledge—TPP. *Validated proficiency benchmarks may be substituted for mean scores on these assessments
	Completer Teaching Skill	TEACHING SKILL PERFORMANCE TEST—Program completer mean score*, tercile distribution, and pass rate on rigorous and validated nationally normed licensure assessment of demonstrated teaching skill—TPP. *Validated proficiency benchmarks may be substituted for mean scores on these assessments
	Completer Rating of Program	COMPLETER PERCEPTIONS OF PROGRAM QUALITY—State- or nationally-developed program completer survey of program quality and teaching preparedness, by cohort, upon program completion and at end of first year of full-time teaching—TPP.

Assessment Categories	Key Indicators	Measures [Note: EPP=Education Program Provider (a.k.a. "Unit"); TPP=individual Teacher Preparation Program]
III Performance as Classroom Teachers	Impact on K-12 Student Learning	**TEACHER CONTRIBUTION TO STUDENT LEARNING**— Success of program completers in 2nd and 3rd most recent cohorts or of alternate route candidates during their first two years of full-time teaching based on valid and rigorous student learning measures, including value-added or other statewide comparative evidence of K-12 student growth overall and in high-need schools. Average student growth score for completer cohort and percentage of completers in cohort scoring below the 33rd and above the 67th percentile compared to the average score and distribution for all <u>novice</u> teachers statewide and for <u>all</u> teachers statewide—TPP.
	Demonstrated Teaching Skill	**ASSESSMENTS OF TEACHING SKILL**—Annual assessment based on observations of program completers' or alternate route candidates' first two years of full-time classroom teaching, using valid, reliable, and rigorous statewide instruments and protocols—TPP.
	K-12 Student Perceptions	**STUDENT SURVEYS ON TEACHING PRACTICE**—K-12 student surveys about effectiveness of completers' or alternate route candidates' teaching practice during first two years of full-time teaching, using valid and reliable statewide instruments—TPP

Assessment Categories	Key Indicators	Measures [Note: EPP=Education Program Provider (a.k.a. "Unit"); TPP=individual Teacher Preparation Program]
IV Contribution to State Workforce Needs	Entry and Persistence in Teaching	**EMPLOYMENT**—Percent of completers from 2nd and 3rd most recent completer cohort (including alternate route completers) employed within two years of program completion, by gender and race-ethnicity—TPP, EPP. **PERSISTENCE**--Percent completers (traditional and alternate route) from the fourth most recent completer cohort who remain in teaching or other educational roles for one, two, and three years after initial entry. OR, percentage of completers attaining a second stage teaching license in states with multi-tiered licensure —TPP, EPP. Percentages for Employment and Persistence for each program to be compared to statewide mean average for each certification field and mean average for programs in all fields. EPP average to be compared to mean average for all EPPs statewide.
	Placement/ Persistence in High-Need Subjects/ Schools	**EMPLOYMENT**—Percent of completers from 2nd and 3rd most recent completer cohort (including alternate route completers) employed within two years of program completion in high needs schools and subjects, by gender and race-ethnicity—TPP., EPP. **PERSISTENCE**--Percent completers (traditional and alternate route) from the fourth most recent completer cohort who remain teaching in high-need subjects or in teaching or other educational roles in high-need schools for one, two, and three years after initial entry—TPP, EPP. Percentages for Employment and Persistence for each program to be compared to statewide mean average for each certification field and mean average for programs in all fields. EPP average to be compared to mean average for all EPPs statewide.

REFERENCES

Allen, M., Coble, C., & Crowe, E. (2014). *Building an evidence-based system for teacher preparation.* Council for the Accreditation of Educator Preparation. Retrieved from http://caepnet.org/~/media/Files/caep/accreditation-resources/tpa -report-full.pdf?la=en

Aragon, S. (2016, September 7). *Response to information request: Education Commission of the States.* Retrieved from https://www.ecs.org/wp-content/uploads/Use -of-Student-Test-Scores-in-Teacher-Evaluations.pdf

Associated Press. (2017, December 27). Nebraska eases scoring requirements for future teachers. *Lincoln Journal Star.* Retrieved from http://journalstar.com/ news/state-and-regional/nebraska/nebraska-eases-scoring-requirements-for- future-teachers/article_b64ab7fe-f94f-59cd-826a-0aa320a07d27.html

Ball, D. L., Thames, M. H., & Phelps, G. (2008). Content knowledge for teaching: What makes it special? *Journal of Teacher Education, 59*(5), 389–407.

Blazar, D., & Kraft, M. A. (2017). Teacher and teaching effects on students' attitudes and behaviors. *Education Evaluation and Policy Analysis, 39*(1), 146–170.

Council for the Accreditation of Educator Preparation. (2013). *CAEP Accreditation standards and evidence: Aspirations for educator preparation.* Retrieved from http://caepnet.org/~/media/Files/caep/standards/commrpt.pdf?la=en

Council of Chief State School Officers. (2012). *Our responsibility, our promise: Transforming educator preparation and entry into the profession.* Washington, DC: Author. Retrieved from https://www.ccsso.org/sites/default/files/2017-10/ Our%20Responsibility%20Our%20Promise_2012.pdf

Council of Chief State School Officers. (2016). *Accountability in teacher preparation: Policies and data in the 50 states & DC.* Washington, DC: Author. Retrieved from https://www.ccsso.org/sites/default/files/2017-10/50StateScan092216.pdf

Council of Chief State School Officers. (2017). *Transforming educator preparation: Lessons learned from leading states.* Washington, DC: Author. Retrieved from https:// www.ccsso.org/sites/default/files/2017-11/CCSSO%20Educator%20 Preparation%20Playbook.pdf

Council of Chief State School Officers. (2018). *Measuring what matters: Recommendations from states in in the Network for Transforming Educator Preparation (NTEP).* Washington, DC: Author. Retrieved from https://www.ccsso.org/resource -library/measuring-what-matters

Christensen, D. (1984). NCATE: The continuing quest for excellence. *Action in Teacher Education, 6*(4), 17–22.

Comb, M. (2018, January 17). *The Massachusetts preparation program accountability system.* Presentation, Illinois Partnership for Educator Preparation. Springfield, IL.

Crowe, E. (2010). *Measuring what matters: A stronger accountability model for teacher education.* Washington, DC: Center for American Progress. Retrieved from https:// www.americanprogress.org/issues/education-k-12/reports/2010/07/29/ 8066/measuring-what-matters/

Cubarrubia, A., & Perry, P. (2016). *Creating a thriving post-secondary education data ecosystem.* WestEd and Institute for Higher Education Policy. Retrieved from http:// www.ihep.org/sites/default/files/uploads/postsecdata/docs/resources/ postsecondary_education_data_ecosystem.pdf

Darling-Hammond, L. (2013, June 18). Why the NCTQ teacher prep ratings are nonsense. *The Washington Post.* Retrieved from https://www.washingtonpost .com/news/answer-sheet/wp/2013/06/18/why-the-nctq-teacher-prep -ratings-are-nonsense/?utm_term=.386ed28aaf35

Darling-Hammond, L., Burns, D., Campbell, C., Goodwin, A. L., Hammerness, K., Low, E. L., ... Zeichner, K. (2017). *Empowered educators: How leading nations design systems for teaching quality.* San Francisco, CA: Jossey-Bass.

Data Quality Campaign. (2017). *Using data to ensure that teachers are learner ready on day one.* Washington, DC: Author. Retrieved from https://2pido73em67o3eytaq 1cp8au-wpengine.netdna-ssl.com/wp-content/uploads/2017/08/DQC-EPP -primer-08032017-1.pdf

Deans for Impact. (2016.). *From chaos to coherence: A policy agenda for accessing and using outcomes data in educator preparation.* Austin, TX: Author. Retrieved from https://deansforimpact.org/wp-content/uploads/2016/11/From_Chaos_ to_Coherence.pdf

Delaware Department of Education. (2016a). *Educator preparation program guide.* Retrieved from https://www.doe.k12.de.us/cms/lib/DE01922744/Centricity/ domain/398/2016%20site%20files/EPP_The_Guide_2016.pdf

Delaware Department of Education. (2016b). *Delaware administrative code section 290. Approval of educator preparation programs.* Retrieved from http://regulations .delaware.gov/AdminCode/title14/200/290.shtml

Delaware Department of Education. (2016c). *Technical specifications for the 2016 Delaware educator preparation program reports.* Retrieved from https://www.doe. k12.de.us/cms/lib/DE01922744/Centricity/domain/398/2016%20site%20 files/ED_PREP_TECHNICAL_GUIDE_2016.pdf

Dobbie, W. (2011). *Teacher characteristics and student achievement: Evidence from Teach for America.* Unpublished manuscript. Harvard University, Cambridge, MA. Retrieved from http://blogs.edweek.org/edweek/teacherbeat/teachercharacteristicsjuly 2011.pdf

Doherty, K. M., & Jacobs, S. (2015). *State of the states 2015: Evaluating teaching, leading and learning.* Washington, DC: National Council on Teacher Quality. Retrieved from https://www.nctq.org/dmsView/StateofStates2015

Drake, G., Pomerance, L., Rickenbrode, R., & Walsh, K. (2018). *2018 Teacher prep review.* Washington, DC: National Council on Teacher Quality. Retrieved from https://www.nctq.org/publications/2018-Teacher-Prep-Review

Educational Testing Service. (2018). About the PPAT® Assessment. Website. Retrieved from https://www.ets.org/ppa/educator-programs/teachers/about

Ehlert, M., Koedel, C., Parsons, E., & Podgursky, M. (2014). The sensitivity of value-added estimates to specification adjustments: Evidence from school- and teacher-level models in Missouri. *Statistics and Public Policy, 1*(1), 19–27. Retrieved from https://www.tandfonline.com/doi/full/10.1080/2330443X .2013.856152

Feuer, M. J., Floden, R. E., Chudowsky, N., & Ahn, J. (2013). *Evaluation of teacher preparation programs: Purposes, methods, and policy options.* Washington, DC: National Academy of Education. Retrieved from https://eric.ed.gov/?id=ED565694

Fuller, E. J. (2013). Shaky methods, shaky motives: A critique of the National Council of Teacher Quality's review of teacher preparation programs. *Journal of Teacher Education, 65*(1), 63–77.

Gallup. (2014). *Teacher insight assessment: Frequently asked questions.* Retrieved from https://gx.gallup.com/teacherinsight.gx/DDmbCW9loRFGrEIU3bqoHRU

CBbMCJzUP_lxtwi_MM9oP3K2q7kP3o~wM7xG59Q~ZmjFplLtB64ZFx1KlZk
pa6RW2jmM7TqclyRkhIEa4Wac0/gprod3b.gallup.com

Gansle, K. A., Noell, G. H., & Burns, J. M. (2012). Do student achievement outcomes differ across teacher preparation programs? An analysis of teacher education in Louisiana. *Journal of Teacher Education, 63*(5), 304–317.

Goldhaber, D. (2007). Everyone's doing it, but what does teacher testing tell us about teacher effectiveness? *Journal of Human Resources, 42*(4), 765–94.

Goldhaber, D. (2013). *What do value-added measures of teacher preparation programs tell us?* Carnegie Knowledge Network. Retrieved from http://www.carnegie knowledgenetwork.org/briefs/teacher_prep

Goldhaber, D., Liddle, S., & Theobald, R. (2013). The gateway to the profession: Assessing teacher preparation programs based on student achievement. *Economics of Education Review, 34*(2), 29–44.

Hill-Jackson, V., Stafford, D., James, M. C., & Hartlep, N. D. (2018). *How to hire the best school leaders using Martin Haberman's protocols for selecting "star" teachers and principals.* Houston, TX: The Haberman Educational Foundation. Retrieved from https://habermanfoundation.org/wp-content/uploads/2018/01/Haberman -WP-Final-Jan18b.pdf

Henry, G. T., Campbell, S. L., Thompson, C. L., Patriarca, L. A., Luterbach, K. J., Lys, D. B., & Covington, V. (2013). The predictive validity of measures of teacher candidate programs and performance: Toward an evidence-based approach to teacher preparation. *Journal of Teacher Education, 64*(5), 439–453.

Herron, A., (2017, November 30). Teacher shortages, diplomas top Indiana's 2018 education priorities. *IndyStar.* Retrieved from https://www.indystar.com/story/ news/education/2017/11/30/teacher-shortage-diplomas-top-indianas -2018-education-priorities/902671001/

Hillman, N., & Weichman, T. (2016). *Education deserts: The continued significance of "place" in the twenty-first century.* Washington, DC: American Council on Education. Retrieved from http://www.acenet.edu/news-room/Documents/ Education-Deserts-The-Continued-Significance-of-Place-in-the-Twenty-First -Century.pdf

Holland, C. (2017, April 18). Assessing and resolving California's growing teacher shortage crisis. *Teachers College Record.* Retrieved from http://www.tcrecord .org/Content.asp?ContentID=21925

Iasevoli, B. (2017, March 28). Trump signs bill scrapping teacher-prep rules. *Education Week.*

Kennedy, M. M. (Ed.). (2010). *Teacher assessment and the quest for teacher quality: A handbook.* San Francisco, CA: Jossey-Bass.

Koedel, C., Parsons, E., Podgursky, M., & Ehlert, M. (2015). Teacher preparation programs and teacher quality: Are there real differences across programs? *Education Finance and Policy, 10*(4), 508–534.

Labaree, D. F. (2004). *The trouble with ed schools.* New Haven, CT: Yale University Press.

Levine, A. (2006). *Educating school teachers.* Washington, DC: The Education Schools Project. Retrieved from http://edschools.org/pdf/Educating_Teachers_ Report.pdf

Massachusetts Department of Elementary and Secondary Education. (2016). *Educator preparation early indicator system development bid. Attachment A.* Retrieved from https://www.commbuys.com/bso/external/bidDetail.sdo?bidId=BD-17 -1026-DOE02-DOE01-00000009319&parentUrl=activeBids

Mitchel, A. L., & Aldeman, C. (2016). *Peering around the corner: Analyzing state efforts to link teachers to the programs that prepared them.* Washington, DC: Bellwether Education Partners. Retrieved from https://bellwethereducation.org/sites/ default/files/Bellwether_TeacherPrep_Final.pdf

National Association of State Directors of Teacher Education and Certification. (n.d.). *Multistate Educator Lookup System.* Retrieved from http://www.nasdtec .net/?page=EducatorLookupSystem

National Commission on Teaching & America's Future. (1996). *What matters most: Teaching for America's future.* Washington, DC: Author. Retrieved from https:// eric.ed.gov/?id=ED395931

National Council for Accreditation of Teacher Education. (2010). *Transforming teacher education through clinical practice: A national strategy to prepare effective teachers.* Washington, DC: Author.

NCS Pearson. (2013). *Workplace personality inventory—II. Technical manual and user's guide.*

Noell, G. H., & Burns, J. L. (2006). Value-added assessment of teacher preparation: An illustration of emerging technology. *Journal of Teacher Education, 1*(57), 37–50.

Phelps, G., Weren, B., Croft, A., & Gitomer, D. (2014). *Developing content knowledge for teaching assessments for the Measures of Effective Teaching study.* ETS Research Report. Retrieved from https://onlinelibrary.wiley.com/doi/epdf/10.1002/ ets2.12031

Ronfeldt, M., & Campbell, S. L. (2016). Evaluating teacher preparation using graduates' observational ratings. *Educational Evaluation and Policy Analysis, 38*(4), 603–625. Retrieved from http://journals.sagepub.com/doi/full/10 .3102/0162373716649690

Ross, E. (2017). *2017 state teacher policy yearbook.* Washington, DC: National Council on Teacher Quality. Retrieved from https://www.nctq.org/publications/ 2017-State-Teacher-Policy-Yearbook

Sawchuk, S. (2014, January 7). AFT's Weingarten backtracks on using value-added measures for evaluations. *Education Week.* Retrieved from http://blogs.edweek .org/edweek/teacherbeat/2014/01/weingartens_retrenchment_on_va.html

Sawchuk, S. (2016, August 23). Teacher-prep accreditation group seeks to regain traction. *Education Week.* Retrieved from https://www.edweek.org/ew/articles/2016/08/24/teacher-prep-accreditation-group-seeks-to-regain-traction .html?qs=sawchuk+2016

Shuls, J. V. (2016). Can we simply raise the bar on teacher quality? *Educational Policy, 32*(7), 969–992. Retrieved from http://uca.edu/acre/files/2014/11/Shuls_ RaisingtheBar_05312016.pdf

Stanford Center for Assessment, Learning and Equity. (2018). *edTPA.* Retrieved from https://www.edtpa.com/

Sutcher, L., Darling-Hammond, L., & Carver-Thomas, D. (2016). *A coming crisis in teaching? Teacher supply, demand, and shortages in the U.S.* Palo Alto, CA: Learning Policy Institute.

Teacher Preparation Analytics. (2016). *A guide to the Key Effectiveness Indicators.* Retrieved from http://teacherpreparationanalytics.org/wp-content/uploads/2017/01/KEI-Guide-12-15-16.pdf

Tennessee Department of Education. (2017). *2016–17 Annual reports for Tennessee educator preparation providers.* Retrieved from https://www.tn.gov/content/dam/tn/education/reports/rpt_lic_annual_reports_guide_examples_epp.pdf

Tennessee State Board of Education. (2018). Tennessee educator preparation policy 5.504. Revised 01/06/2018. *Rules of the Tennessee department of education.* Retrieved from https://www.tn.gov/content/dam/tn/stateboardofeducation/documents/5.504_Educator_Preparation_Policy_7-28-17.pdf

Theobald, R., Conaway, C., Cowan, J., & Peske, H. (2020). *The teacher pipeline in Massachusetts: Connecting pre-service performance measures to in-service teacher outcomes.* Retrieved from https://ies.ed.gov/funding/grantsearch/details.asp?ID=2004 (manuscript in preparation)

Truong, D. (2017, December 11). Virginia's McAuliffe takes emergency steps to curtail teacher shortage. Washington, DC: *The Washington Post.* Retrieved from https://www.washingtonpost.com/local/education/virginias-mcauliffe-takes-emergency-steps-to-curtail-teacher-shortage/2017/12/11/121dbcaa-deb0-11e7-89e8-edec16379010_story.html?utm_term=.bd13dd244fd3

U.S. Department of Education. (2016a). *2016 Title II reports: National teacher preparation data.* Washington, DC: Author. Retrieved from https://title2.ed.gov

U.S. Department of Education. (2016b). *Preparing and credentialing the nation's teachers: The Secretary's 10th report on teacher quality.* Washington, DC: Author. Retrieved from https://title2.ed.gov/Public/TitleIIReport16.pdf

U.S. Department of Education Office of Postsecondary Education. (2017). *Higher Education Act Title II institutional and program report card system (IPRC) user manual.* Washington, DC: Author. Retrieved 3-14-18 at https://title2.ed.gov/public/ta/iprcmanual.pdf

Voorhees, R. A., Barnes, G. T., & Rothman, R. (2003). *Data systems to enhance teacher quality.* Boulder, CO: State Higher Education Officers. Retrieved from https://www.voorheesgroup.org/voorheesgroup-pubs/Data%20Systems%20to%20Enhance%20Teacher%20Quality.pdf

Walsh, K. (2001). *Teacher certification reconsidered: Stumbling for quality.* Baltimore, MD: The Abell Foundation. Retrieved from https://www.abell.org/reports/teacher-certification-reconsidered-stumbling-quality

Washington Professional Educator Standards Board. (2015). *Indicator-based program review/Phase #1 project summary / Fall 2015.* Retrieved from https://docs.google.com/document/d/1aLCMHiFXtp5fV0kVKbPsrRWYBnP9jrN2BVAqcdWMy6Q/edit#

Woods, J. R. (2016). *Mitigating teacher shortages: Alternative teacher certification.* Denver, CO: Education Commission of the States. Retrieved from http://www.ecs.org/wp-content/uploads/Mitigating-Teacher-Shortages-Alternative-Certification.pdf

CHAPTER 2

LEARNING TO TEACH

Optimizing Coursework and Fieldwork Requirements in Traditional Teacher Preparation

Courtney Preston
Florida State University

In an era of educational accountability, and largely in response to Race to the Top competitive grants launched by the United States Department of Education in 2009, more and more state agencies and researchers are evaluating teacher preparation programs (TPPs) based on graduates' contribution to raising student achievement (value-added) and finding differences among programs on this measure of teacher effectiveness (Goldhaber, Liddle, & Theobald, 2013; Henry, Patterson, Campbell, & Yi, 2013; Imig & Imig, 2008; Koedel, Parsons, Podgurksy, & Ehlert, 2015; Noell, Porter, Pratt, & Dahir, 2008; Tennessee Higher Education Commission, 2012), although reanalysis of these data suggest these differences may be negligible (von Hippel & Bellows, 2018). New requirements presented by the Council for Accreditation of Educator Preparation (CAEP) also include program impact on student learning as one of five standards for accreditation (CAEP,

Linking Teacher Preparation Program Design and Implementation to Outcomes for Teachers and Students, pages 33–61
Copyright © 2020 by Information Age Publishing
33

2013). There are several mechanisms through which TPPs could affect teacher quality and thereby affect student achievement, including through selection of teacher candidates, training of teacher candidates, or some combination of both (Ballou & Podgursky, 1998; Levine, 2006).

The value-added approach to evaluation of TPPs estimates the effectiveness of TPPs based on each TPP's graduates' contributions to student achievement gains. Studies using this approach may be meant to provide TPPs with data to facilitate continuous improvement and thereby, teacher quality, but are typically "black box" studies that do not separate the effects of the selection of teacher candidates into programs from the effects of program features, and do not investigate which mechanisms account for why one program's graduates may be more or less effective in raising student achievement. In spite of almost twenty years of policymakers and researchers recommending investigation of these questions, there is a paucity of research to help improve the quality of TPPs.

The field of teacher education lacks in-depth research to adequately describe and evaluate the content and quality of teacher preparation. TPPs have been criticized virtually since they were created: by education researchers (e.g., Labaree, 1996; Koerner, 1963), to teacher educators themselves (e.g., Holmes Group, 1986, 1995), to social critics (e.g., Kramer, 1991). One reason teacher education programs have been critiqued is their lack of rigor and relevance to the classroom (Levine, 2006; Labaree, 2004, 2008). Nearly twenty years ago, in a review of the extant literature on the relationship between teacher preparation and teacher effectiveness, Wilson, Floden, and Ferrini-Mundy (2001) recommended studying "the contribution of particular components of teacher education, by themselves or in interaction with one another, to prospective teachers' knowledge and competence" (p. 35). Similarly, Zeichner and Schulte (2001) recommended a focus on "gaining a better understanding of the components of good teacher education" (p. 279), with an emphasis on distinguishing between selection effects and program effects. While the field has begun to address these gaps in the research base with large scale studies encompassing multiple TPPs rather than single case studies (e.g., Boyd, Grossman, Lankford, Loeb, & Wyckoff, 2009; Harris & Sass, 2011; Ronfeldt, 2012; Ronfeldt, Reininger, & Kwok, 2013), there is much work to be done. Further, prior research has focused primarily on elementary TPPs (e.g., Boyd et al., 2009; Henry, Campbell, et. al., 2013), leaving a particular gap in the research on secondary TPPs.

Recent research provides some evidence that specific TPPs vary in the effectiveness of their graduates (Boyd et al., 2006, 2009; Harris & Sass, 2011; Henry, Bastian, & Smith, 2012; Henry, Thompson, Fortner, Zulli, & Kershaw, 2010, Henry, Patterson, et al., 2013; Noell et al., 2008; Plecki, Elfers, & Nakamura, 2012; Tennessee Higher Education Commission, 2012, 2011).

However, some studies show that there are greater differences in teacher effectiveness within TPPs than between TPPs (Goldhaber et al., 2013; Koedel et al., 2015), and newer evidence suggests that between-TPP differences are quite small (von Hippel & Bellows, 2018). As states focus more on the effectiveness of TPPs, TPPs face increasing pressure to demonstrate the effectiveness of their graduates. If programs are to improve the effectiveness of the teachers they produce, TPPs need to know which, if any, program features make graduates of some TPPs more effective than others in terms of increasing student achievement.

This chapter has two primary aims: (a) to describe the variation in program requirements of secondary English/language arts and mathematics TPPs in all 15 North Carolina public universities, comparing and contrasting across subjects and grade levels (middle grades versus high school); and, (b) to examine the relationships between the structural features (coursework and fieldwork requirements) of these preparation programs and beginning teacher effectiveness, as measured by student achievement gains (value-added) on North Carolina end-of-grade and end-of-course tests.

LITERATURE REVIEW

In this section, I review the literature that examines the role of typical components of TPPs in preparing teachers to teach. Throughout, I refer to the components of teacher education as *structural features*. The structural features of TPPs fall into two categories: coursework and field experiences. There are generally three domains of coursework included in TPPs: subject matter coursework, pedagogy coursework, and foundations coursework. Subject matter coursework is generally taught by faculty in the relevant discipline rather than by teacher education faculty. Taken together, pedagogy courses, foundations courses, and field experiences are often referred to as "professional education." Traditionally, field experiences fall into two domains: early field experiences and student teaching. Early field experiences are those that occur prior to student teaching and may include classroom observation, tutoring, or teaching for brief periods. Student teaching typically occurs at the end of a program and involves an extended period of time during which a teacher candidate holds full teaching responsibility. Other relevant aspects of student teaching include program supervision of student teaching, cooperating teacher characteristics, and whether programs require a student teaching seminar that links theory to practice. The amount of each structural feature required varies by TPP, but this variation has rarely been systematically documented, nor have the relationships between these features and teacher effectiveness been widely studied, in spite of researchers calling for such studies for almost two decades (Boyd et al., 2009; Wilson et al., 2001).

Coursework: What Teachers Need to Know to Teach

Teacher education coursework typically aims to develop seven types of knowledge in prospective teachers described in Shulman (1987): (a) content knowledge, (b) general pedagogical knowledge, (c) curriculum knowledge, (d) pedagogical content knowledge, (e) knowledge of learners and their characteristics, (f) knowledge of educational contexts, and (g) knowledge of educational ends, purposes, and values. This coursework generally falls into three categories: subject matter courses (a), pedagogy courses (b, c, d), and foundations courses (e, f, g), but in actuality, university coursework may not be well aligned with Shulman's categories. Curriculum knowledge may be included in pedagogy courses or in foundations courses, depending on the program. Programs may require foundations courses in some of the last three domains of knowledge, but not necessarily all.

Subject Matter Coursework

Shulman (1986) asserted that teachers should have content knowledge that is deeper than that of a "mere subject matter major" (p. 9) an idea that has been historically reflected in North Carolina guidelines for secondary teacher certification (Woellner, 1975). Shulman recommends specific sections of content area courses for teacher candidates that will promote these deeper understandings of content than generalist subject matter courses. In reality, teacher candidates primarily fulfill their subject matter coursework requirements outside of a school of education, in courses intended for a broad student audience, rather than in courses designed for teacher candidates to develop this deep content knowledge. A longitudinal comparative case study of two different pathways indicates that secondary preparation programs often have greater subject matter requirements than middle grades programs, which may be necessary as high school courses deal with more rigorous subject matter than those in elementary and middle school (Conklin, 2012). In an analysis of content knowledge prior to and at the end of teacher preparation, preservice high school teachers who receive more subject matter coursework have been shown to have greater increases in content knowledge over the course of their preparation programs (Kleickmann et al., 2013).

Much of the research on the importance of subject matter preparation for teaching effectiveness focuses on mathematics. There is some evidence to support the importance of subject matter knowledge. For example, 1987 NAEP data provides evidence of a positive relationship between the number of undergraduate mathematics courses a teacher took and students' 10th and 11th grade mathematics achievement, though with diminishing returns after five mathematics courses (Monk, 1994). Specifically, each additional mathematics course up to five courses is associated with a 1.2% increase in student achievement, while addition of a sixth course and beyond is only associated with a 0.2% increase. More recent work provides evidence that an increase in teachers' mathematics coursework is associated with increases in gains in their students' mathematics achievement, where a one mathematics course increase is associated with a 3% standard deviation increase in achievement (Henry, Campbell, et al., 2013).

However, the importance of subject area coursework for teaching effectiveness may differ by subject area. The same NAEP data provide inconsistent evidence for the importance of subject matter coursework in the sciences. Without controlling for any indicator of teacher academic ability, coursework in the life sciences has no relationship or a negative relationship with science achievement, while coursework in the physical sciences (chemistry, physics, and earth science) has a positive relationship with science achievement. Specifically, taking more than four physical science courses is associated with a 1.08 standard deviation increase in science achievement (Monk, 1994). Research examining the effect of English coursework on student achievement has yielded mixed findings (Boyd et al., 2009; Henry, Campbell, et al., 2013). One case study of an English major in a post-baccalaureate teacher training program suggests that those with strong subject matter expertise may have difficulty transferring their own expertise, or not understand the need to make explicit their own reading process as a part of secondary instruction in the absence of teacher education coursework (Holt-Reynolds, 1999).

Pedagogical Coursework

Pedagogy (or methods) courses are largely designed to increase preservice teachers' pedagogical knowledge, pedagogical content knowledge, and curricular knowledge. Mathematical knowledge for teaching is a subject-specific area of pedagogical content knowledge (Ball, Thames, & Phelps, 2008). Correlational analysis of a nationally representative dataset shows that there is some evidence to suggest that teachers with more methods coursework feel better prepared to teach (Ronfeldt, Schwartz, & Jacob, 2014), and coursework in mathematics pedagogy for preservice teachers at multiple grade levels has been linked to increased mathematical knowledge for teaching in certain domains and to student mathematics achievement (Monk, 1994; Youngs & Qian, 2013). However, other research contradicts these findings and provides evidence that there is a negative relationship between mathematics pedagogy coursework and teacher effectiveness as measured by student achievement (Allen, 2003; Henry, Campbell, et al., 2013).

Foundations Coursework

Foundations coursework is meant to address the three remaining areas of the Shulman (1987) knowledge base for teachers: (a) knowledge of learners and their characteristics; (b) knowledge of educational contexts; and (c) knowledge of educational ends, purposes, and values. Foundations coursework includes courses on the social foundations of education like history and philosophy of education, multicultural education, and education psychology. Such coursework may be important in preparing teachers to work with diverse student populations, to understand teaching as a profession, and "to see teaching as entailing reasoned and reasonable judgment about educational ends and preferred pedagogical means" (Liston, Whitcomb & Borko, 2009, p. 108). However, there is little research to support the importance of such courses for teacher effectiveness (Allen, 2003; Howey & Zimpher, 1989). Like most other structural features of teacher preparation, most of the research about these foundations courses is limited to descriptive case studies (e.g., Causey, Thomas, & Armento, 2000; Darling-Hammond & McDonald, 2000). Even so, case studies of programs considered exemplary by national reputation indicate that preparation programs have extensive course requirements for human development and foundations courses including urban education, education law, and social context (Koppich, 2000; Snyder, 2000). For middle grades programs in particular, theory suggests that foundations coursework should be the hallmark of a TPP, because such courses include adolescent development (Allen, 2003; Association for Middle Level Education, 2012; Howey & Zimpher, 1989; Jackson & Davis, 2000; Scales & McEwin, 1994).

Field Experiences: Putting What Teachers Need to Know Into Practice

The second primary element of traditional TPPs is field experience. National standards for TPPs specify that practice must be central to the teacher preparation experience (National Council for Accreditation of Teacher Education [NCATE], 2010), and such practice should come in the form of high-quality field experiences that are "early, ongoing, and take place in a variety of school- and community-based settings" (CAEP, 2013, p. 15). Preparation program alumni praise programs where they spend extensive amounts of time in schools, while a common alumni criticism is a desire for "more, longer, earlier, and better-integrated" field experiences (Levine, 2006, p. 41). Evidence from longitudinal case studies of individual programs suggests that field experiences may serve to socialize teachers to the secondary school environment, provide opportunities to try out various classroom management strategies, and offer opportunities to learn how to tailor teaching strategies to specific students (Beisenherz & Dantonio, 1991; Cheng, Tang, & Cheng, 2012).

Early Field Experiences

Early field experiences are those that occur before the student teaching internship. A decade ago, fewer than half of preservice teachers participated in early field experiences (Levine, 2006). More recently, the NCATE Blue Ribbon Panel on Clinical Preparation and Partnerships for Improved Student Learning (2010) recommended that fieldwork be integrated throughout TPPs. These early field experiences may be integrated into specific required coursework or stand-alone. Requirements vary from observation in both school and non-school settings, to more in-depth experiences where prospective teachers have the opportunity to plan and implement lessons or projects for brief periods (Daisey, 2012).

Student Teaching/Internship

Preservice teachers consistently report that student teaching experiences are the most beneficial aspect of preparation programs for their first year of teaching (Guyton & McIntyre, 1990; Van Zandt, 1998; NCATE, 2010), but research finds both positive and negative contributions of student teaching to teacher effectiveness (Ng, Nicholas, & Williams, 2010; Ronfeldt, 2015; Valencia, Martin, Place, & Grossman, 2009; Youngs & Qian, 2013). Student teaching frequently lasts 10 to 16 weeks, and often takes place during the spring semester (Levine, 2006; Ronfeldt et al., 2013). The American Association of Colleges for Teacher Education (2012) recommends a full year (30 weeks or 900 hours) of student teaching, with a semester (15 weeks or 450 hours) student teaching experience at a minimum.

An increasing body of literature links student teaching to various outcomes. There is evidence that the overall length of student teaching experience does not significantly increase elementary teachers' mathematical knowledge for teaching (Youngs & Qian, 2013). However, the amount of time that student teachers have full responsibility for teaching a class may serve to further develop their pedagogical content knowledge and to stretch their content knowledge (Brown, Friedrichsen, & Abell, 2013; Friedrichsen et al., 2009; Smith, 1999; Youngs & Qian, 2013). Ronfeldt and Reininger (2012) found that the duration of student teaching is unrelated to a variety of teacher candidate outcomes, including self-efficacy, feelings of preparedness, and their plans to remain in teaching; while Ronfeldt et al., (2014), examining teachers, found that teachers with more weeks of practice teaching felt better prepared to teach, where an additional week of student teaching was associated with a 3.5% of a standard deviation increase in feelings of preparedness. These seemingly contradictory findings may be due to different samples and measures. Ronfeldt and Reininger's (2012) sample consists of prospective teachers from only one urban district, surveyed prior to beginning teaching, where duration of student teaching was measured as a continuous variable in weeks. In contrast, Ronfeldt et al. (2014) used a nationally representative data set of teachers, include teachers with up to 5 years of experience, and measured duration of student teaching as a categorical variable. Teachers' feelings of preparedness are likely affected by whether or not they have classroom experience; that is, teacher candidates may feel better prepared to teach before they enter the classroom because they have not yet had to deal with the realities of classroom management on their own and do not fully understand whether their internship has prepared them to manage a class independently.

Clearly, there is growing evidence as to the importance of student teaching. Unfortunately, very little research exists examining how the amount of time that student teachers assume full responsibility for teaching in a classroom affects outcomes. Ronfeldt et al. (2013) examined the relationship between the amount of control over classroom and instructional decisions student teachers had by the end of student teaching and their feelings of instructional preparedness, self-efficacy, desire to teach under-served populations, and plans to remain in teaching. (While amount of control over the classroom and instructional decisions is not a direct correlate to full-time responsibility for teaching, they are similar concepts as pertains to gaining experience as a teacher.) They found that instructional autonomy, a measure of how much control and decision-making authority the cooperating teacher gave a student teacher over the classroom, was a significant positive predictor of each outcome except for the desire to work with underserved populations. This evidence suggests that this is both an important area for further study and a potentially important lever for increasing beginning teacher effectiveness.

Supervision of Fieldwork

University supervisors may play significant roles in field experiences through their observations and feedback (Feiman-Nemser & Buchmann, 1987; Griffin, 1989; McDiarmid, 1990). However, the actual influence university supervisors exert is unclear. Student teachers report dissatisfaction with university supervisors in that supervisors visit classrooms too infrequently and are unfamiliar with their teaching, thereby wielding little influence over student teachers (Borko & Mayfield, 1995; Griffin, 1989). However, when university supervisors are present, their advice and critical feedback can be crucial to student teacher improvement (Cheng et al., 2012) and they can play an important role in promoting critical reflection (Dinkelman, 2000). Evidence indicates that oversight of field experience is positively related to teacher effectiveness in both reading and mathematics (Boyd et al., 2009; Levine, 2006).

Field experiences may also be enhanced by a close connection between the school site experience and the university program. A persistent critique of university-based TPPs is the divide between the training TPPs provide and what beginning teachers experience in their classrooms (Boyd et al., 2009; Levine, 2006). One way some programs attempt to bridge this divide is through a student teaching seminar. Such courses often meet once a week or every other week and offer opportunities for students to work through issues that have arisen in their field experience, address aspects of curriculum and planning, or work on capstone portfolios (Borko, Michalec, Siddle, & Timmons, 1997; Whitford, Roscoe, & Fickel, 2000).

Considering Programmatic Features Together

Taken together, these structural features of TPPs—coursework and field experiences—are meant to provide prospective teachers with a broad knowledge of education and learners, content knowledge, pedagogical skills, and opportunities to put knowledge and skills into practice so that they are prepared to serve as effective beginning teachers. However, only a handful of quantitative research studies (e.g., Boyd et al., 2009; Harris & Sass, 2011) have begun to document these structural features and their relationship to teacher effectiveness.

For example, Boyd and colleagues (2009) examined 31 elementary TPPs in New York City. The study investigated both a wide range of program features and beginning teacher reports of their experiences in preparation programs. The program features examined were the amount of required content coursework in both mathematics and English language arts (ELA), whether a program required a capstone project, program oversight of field experiences, and percent of tenure-track faculty. Other features were not considered. Because of limited degrees of freedom owing to the small number of programs in their study, separate models for each program characteristic were estimated. Findings were mixed and varied between first- and second-year teachers and between mathematics and ELA. Program oversight of student teaching, the number of mathematics courses required, a required capstone project, and the percentage of tenure-line faculty were significant positive predictors of mathematics achievement gains for students of first-year teachers, but the required number of mathematics courses was the only feature that remained a significant predictor for second-year teachers. A required capstone project was the only significant predictor of gains in ELA for students of first year teachers. In the first-year sample, the required number of ELA courses had a negative relationship with achievement for these teachers, but in the second-year sample, although its coefficient was of a similar magnitude, its sign changed direction. It is unclear whether these changes were a result of an effect that only begins to manifest itself in the second year or due to sample attrition.

Harris and Sass (2011) examined the college transcripts of teachers trained in public institutions of higher education in Florida, focusing on the relationship between the credit hours that teachers actually take in their subject matter, three areas of pedagogy, classroom observation, and classroom practice and teacher effectiveness. Separate analyses were conducted at the elementary, middle, and high school levels for reading and mathematics scores. With one exception, findings suggested that college coursework was not related to teacher effectiveness at any level of K–12 education. The exception was coursework on classroom management at the high school level, where additional credits in classroom management had a positive relationship with teacher effectiveness as measured by student achievement gains.

The research detailed here has begun to answer questions of the mechanisms through which TPPs are more or less effective in producing graduates who raise student achievement. However, findings are inconsistent, studies tend to focus on elementary programs, and most address only one programmatic feature of teacher preparation at a time. Given the importance of programmatic features as the mechanisms through which TPPs influence their students' experiences, the field requires more evidence to provide programs with information on how to optimize requirements for each programmatic feature.

THE NORTH CAROLINA CONTEXT

Requirements for certification in North Carolina have changed in response to trends in teacher education and as part of efforts to professionalize teaching. Since the 1930s, for high school certification (Grades 7–12), North Carolina has required graduation from a 4-year college, between 15 and 30 hours of subject matter coursework in the specific subject, and 18 credit hours of foundations and pedagogy coursework, which include both observation and student teaching (Woellner & Wood, 1936). A certificate area specific to middle grades (4–9) was added in 1970. The professional education course requirements include 12 hours of foundations coursework, 6 hours of pedagogy, and a minimum of 18 subject matter coursework hours.

A significant shift in teacher certification in North Carolina occurred during the 1960s. Since the late 1960s, rather than certifying individual teachers, North Carolina has approved TPPs. These state-approved programs then recommend teacher candidates for certification who have successfully completed program requirements. Diverging from other states' certification requirements, North Carolina revised its certification requirements substantially in the early 1970s (Woellner, 1973, 1974). Rather than an exact prescription for preparation as in most states, these new requirements were a set of guidelines in the areas of general education, subject area specialization, and professional education. A practicum or student teaching experience was not specifically mentioned. Since 1983, graduation from an approved program became the only requirement for teacher certification (Woellner, 1984), making North Carolina a unique setting for examining the variation across programs and the relationships between structural features of these programs and student achievement outcomes.

Although North Carolina programs are bound by state accreditation standards, these standards do not spell out a prescriptive format for teacher preparation. This creates what Boyd and colleagues (2009) refer to as "constrained variation," where there are similarities among teacher education programs in that each requires some amount of coursework and fieldwork, but the amount varies. North Carolina maintains guidelines for TPP approval and grants separate, subject-specific certification for teachers in Grades 6–9 and 9–12, a shift from 1970 grade bands (Kaye, 2008). From 2005 to 2015, approved TPPs had to meet a set of requirements including a 70% pass rate on Praxis II exams, subject-specific exams that cover knowledge and teaching skills, and a 95% certification rate (95% of teacher candidates successfully meet the standards for candidate performance); develop a conceptual framework to guide the program; and meet six standards in the areas of candidate performance and program capacity: (a) candidate knowledge, skills and dispositions; (b) assessment and evaluation; (c) field experiences and clinical practice; (d) diversity; (e) faculty qualifications and performance; and (f) program governance (NCDPI, 2005). Additionally, each specialty area for licensure has its own set of more specific standards, relevant to the grade level and subject area.

North Carolina offers both baccalaureate and Master of Arts in Teaching (MAT) programs for initial teacher licensure. At the baccalaureate level for middle grades (6–9) and high school (9–12) certification, a preparation program is typically the last 2 years of undergraduate study. In their first 2 years of study, prior to formal admission to a preparation program, teacher candidates complete general university coursework required of all students, prerequisites for admission to teacher education, and some content area coursework. At the MAT level, teacher candidates typically have a bachelor's degree in their subject area or an equivalent number of subject matter credit hours. The MAT programs typically span only one school year, and may include summer coursework as well.

Research has identified differences in the effectiveness of teacher candidates prepared in the 15 University of North Carolina (UNC) system institutions, whose completers constitute 35% of the state's teacher workforce (Henry et al., 2014; Henry, Patterson, et al., 2013). While there are some institutions whose graduates consistently perform neither better nor worse than teachers prepared outside of UNC system institutions, the relative effectiveness of most institutions varies across years and subject area/grade level. For instance, teachers from one university outperformed teachers prepared outside of UNC system institutions in elementary reading in the 2010, 2011, and 2013 reports. Teachers from the same university outperformed others in high school social studies in the 2011 and 2013 report, but not in the 2010 report. In mathematics, teachers from this university outperformed other teachers in elementary mathematics in the 2010 report and in middle school Algebra I in the 2013 report, but not in the other two reports. In other grade levels/subject areas, teachers from this university performed no better or worse than other teachers across all three reports. Work has begun to identify effective evidence-based practices for teacher preparation, but questions explaining variations in TPP effectiveness remain unanswered.

As such, I ask two research questions:

1. What are the program features of initial teacher preparation programs for middle and secondary English/language arts and mathematics teachers in North Carolina public universities?
2. What are the relationships between the program features of these preparation programs and beginning teacher effectiveness, as measured by student achievement gains?

METHODS

To address my objectives, I created a longitudinal database combining three data sources in North Carolina. First, I obtained a teacher-level data set from the UNC General Administration, which included data on every teacher prepared in the UNC system, at both the undergraduate and graduate levels. The second data source was a longitudinal data set from the North Carolina Department of Public Instruction, which contained end-of-grade test scores, as well as teacher-, student-, and school-level demographic information. The final source was data collected from each of the 15 UNC institutions with TPPs detailing candidate requirements for participation in coursework and fieldwork. Using Classification of Instructional Program (CIP) codes and teachers' year of beginning a TPP, I linked each teacher to a specific program of study and characterized the nature of their coursework and field experiences. I used yearly end-of-grade tests in Grades 6 through 8 in mathematics and ELA and end-of-course tests in Algebra I and English I from 2007–2008 through 2010–2011 to estimate the relationships between structural features of TPPs and student achievement gains.

I assigned every required course in a TPP or subject matter major into one of four categories: foundations, pedagogy, subject matter, and fieldwork, and measured coursework in credit hours. Additionally, I determined whether a program's student teaching experience was accompanied by a seminar course, the hours of required early field experiences, the length of time student teachers assumed full responsibility of classrooms, and the minimum number of university supervisor observations of student teaching.

There were a number of structural features that do not vary across public university TPPs in North Carolina and therefore were excluded from my analysis. Across UNC institutions, requirements for cooperating teachers are the same: certification in the appropriate subject, at least 3 years of experience, and a principal's recommendation. Similarly, there was little variation in admissions requirements for entry into teacher education. Test score requirements, such as the Praxis I, a general knowledge test, are set by the state, and most programs required at least a 2.5 GPA for admission.

Sample

Because I expected the influence of TPPs to diminish over time, as teachers gain additional knowledge and skills through classroom experience (Clotfelter, Ladd, & Vigdor, 2007; Harris & Sass, 2011), I restricted my sample to teachers in their first 5 years of teaching. I included only teachers who completed a degree program for initial certification at the undergraduate or master's levels between 2007 and 2010, for a sample of 986 mathematics teachers and 822 English teachers that comprised all the mathematics and ELA teachers who were prepared by and recommended for certification by a UNC institution. My analytic sample consisted of every middle and secondary teacher who graduated from a UNC system TPP from 2006–2007 to 2010–2011, and who taught a tested grade or subject in a North Carolina public school during the years 2007–2008 to 2011–2012. This yielded an analytic sample of 248 middle school mathematics teachers, 258 high school Algebra I teachers, 175 middle school ELA teachers, and 209 high school English I teachers.

Analytic Methods

To examine the relationship between structural features and student achievement gains, I used a three-level hierarchical linear model (HLM) with students nested in classrooms, which are nested in schools. I controlled for prior achievement, as well as teacher, student, and school characteristics typically included in value-added models. North Carolina administers both end-of-grade and end-of-course tests. End of grade tests occur yearly in Grades 3 through 8 in mathematics and ELA. As this study focuses on middle and high school preparation programs only mathematics and ELA end-of-grade tests for Grades 6 through 8 are used, together with Algebra I and English I end-of-course tests administered at the high school level. Students were matched to the teachers who taught them in tested grades and subjects using class rosters. Scores from these student achievement tests served as the dependent variable for determining the relationship between structural features of TPPs and teacher effectiveness in value-added models that included prior achievement as a covariate. I used test scores from end-of-grade tests from 2007–2008 through 2011–2012 and end-of-course test scores in English I and Algebra I for the same years. Before restricting the sample to beginning teachers, scores for each grade and subject test were standardized at the state level, by year, to allow for the combination of multiple tests into one model. However, because of differences in the tests included as measures of prior achievement and to allow for the possibility of different relationships of features to achievement by subject area, I estimated separate models for each test.

Because students were nested within teachers and were therefore not independent observations from one another, I clustered standard errors at the teacher level (Koedel et al., 2015). I employed a three-level HLM model, with students nested in classrooms and classrooms nested within schools to provide estimates while accounting for clustering at the classroom and school levels, as student observations within a classroom were not independent from one another.

The level one (student) HLM model was

$$Y_{icjst} = \beta_0 + \beta_1 Y_{icjs(t-1)} + \pi_1 S_{icjst} + \varepsilon_{icjst} \tag{2.1}$$

where Y_{icjst} is student i's test score in classroom c,
taught by teacher j in school s at time t,
$Y_{icjs(t-1)}$ is student i's test score in the previous year,
S_{icjst} is a vector of student demographic characteristics for student i in classroom c taught by teacher j in school s at time t, and
ε_{icjst} is a student-specific error term.

The level two (classroom/teacher) model takes the form

$$\beta_0 = \pi_{00} + \pi_{01} \text{Program}_{jcst} + \pi_{02} C_{jsct} + \pi_{03} T_{jsct} + \mu_{jsct} \tag{2.2}$$

where Program_{jcst} represents the series of structural features of TPP that teacher j in classroom c of school s at time t attended,
C_{jsct} is a vector of classroom characteristics for classroom c taught by teacher j in school s at time t,

T_{jsct} is a set of teacher characteristics in classroom c of school s at time t, and

μ_{jsct} is a classroom-specific error term.

The level three (school) model takes the form

$$\pi_{00} = \gamma_{00} + \gamma_{01}SCH_{st} + r_{st} \tag{2.3}$$

where SCH_{st} is a vector of characteristics for school s at time t and rst is a school-specific error term.

Student-level covariates included prior achievement, a series of race/ethnicity dummy variables, gender, free/reduced price lunch (FRL) eligibility, English proficiency, attendance, and mobility. Teacher classroom-level covariates included the teacher's gender, a series of race/ethnicity dummy variables, and licensure (middle or secondary), as well as class size, classroom-average prior achievement, and binary indicators for advanced and remedial courses. Finally, school-level covariates included a series of school-level proportions of race/ethnicity, FRL-eligible students, and average per-pupil expenditures.

RESULTS

In this section, I first present descriptive results that address Research Question 1 and describe program features in coursework and fieldwork. This is followed by results for Research Question 2, relationships between program features and student achievement gains (value-added) for middle grades and high school mathematics and ELA.

Variation in Teacher Preparation Program Requirements

Table 2.1 provides descriptive statistics for the required structural features of all teachers from mathematics TPPs. Coursework is described in terms of credit hour requirements, but in considering what these structural features look like for a teacher candidate, it can be helpful to think in terms of numbers of required courses. Most courses are three credit hours. There are important differences in high school and middle-grade certified teachers, as well as between baccalaureate and master's level teachers. At the baccalaureate level, middle grade certified teachers are required to take fewer hours of mathematics subject matter coursework than those certified for high school. The average difference is almost 20 credit hours, with

TABLE 2.1 Structural Feature Requirements for all Certified Mathematics Teachers, 2006–2007 to 2010–2011

	MG Math (BA)		MG Math (MAT)		HS Math (BA)		HS Math (MAT)	
	Mean (SD)	Range	Mean (SD)	Range	Mean (SD)	Range	Mean (SD)	Range
Subject Matter (hours)	20.28*** (4.42)	15, 36	9.71*** (3.27)	6, 15	39.39*** (4.21)	27, 48	5.61*** (5.81)	3, 18
Pedagogy (hours)	14.59*** (4.96)	6, 24	19.41*** (1.87)	15, 21	11.57*** (3.01)	6, 15	9.87*** (4.49)	8, 21
Foundations (hours)	10.55*** (2.05)	6, 15	7.41** (1.87)	3, 9	7.60*** (1.60)	6, 12	9.61** (3.10)	3, 11
Early Field Hours	203.52*** (124.33)	20, 394	66*** (28.46)	0, 96	85.96*** (70.93)	20, 242	91.96*** (29.99)	0, 105
Full-Time Teaching (weeks)	5.59*** (2.97)	3, 15	3.71* (0.77)	3, 6	6.46*** (3.33)	3, 15	3.26* (0.69)	3, 6
Internship Length (weeks)	14.57*** (1.59)	10, 16	12.06 (2.54)	10, 15	13.64*** (2.15)	10, 16	11.65 (0.78)	10, 12
Minimum Observations	3.94*** (0.41)	3, 5	4 (0)	4	4.06 (0.65)	1, 6	4 (0)	4
Seminar	0.67*** (0.47)	0, 1	0.94 (0.24)	0, 1	0.50*** (0.50)	0, 1	0.96 (0.21)	0, 1
Course in Special Education	0.72*** (0.45)	0, 1	0.45 (0.51)	0, 1	0.61*** (0.49)	0, 1	0.04 (0.21)	0, 1
Course in Teaching ELLs	0 (0)	n/a	0 (0)	n/a	0 (0)	n/a	0 (0)	n/a
N	381		17		499		23	

Note: MG = middle grade. HS = high school.

*** $p < 0.01$, ** $p < 0.05$, * $p < 0.10$

Tests of significance between MG Math (BA) and HS Math (BA) and MG Math (MAT) and HS Math (MAT).

middle-grade requirements about half the average high school requirements. Conversely, middle-grade teachers are required to take, on average, about three credit hours more of foundations and pedagogy coursework than high school teachers. Middle grade teachers are also required to participate in twice as many early field hours as high school teachers, on average.

Masters of Arts in Teaching candidates are required to take far fewer subject matter credit hours during their programs, but are required to have a subject matter major or its equivalent for admission to a MAT program. At the middle grades level, MAT teachers are required to participate in far fewer early field experience hours than baccalaureate-prepared teachers. Of potential import, there are some MAT programs, at both middle grades and high school levels, that do not require *any* early field experience hours. Baccalaureate-prepared teachers also spend more weeks of student teaching with full-time teaching responsibility than MAT teachers. Baccalaureate-prepared teachers spend between 3 and 15 weeks with full-time responsibility, with an average of 5.6 weeks, compared to a range of between 3 and 6 weeks for MAT teachers, with an average of only 3.7 weeks. Almost all MAT teachers are required to take a seminar accompanying student teaching, while only 67% of middle grades baccalaureate and half of high school baccalaureate certified teachers are required to do so.

Table 2.2 provides the same descriptive statistics for mathematics teachers who are teaching tested grades—all middle grades teachers and high

TABLE 2.2 Structural Feature Requirements for Mathematics Teachers Teaching Tested Grades, 2006–2007 to 2010–2011					
	Middle School Mathematics			High School Algebra I	
	Mean (SD)		Range	Mean (SD)		Range
Subject Matter	23.77***	(8.69)	15, 58	38.58	(6.41)	15, 58
Pedagogy	13.90***	(4.97)	6, 24	11.95	(3.34)	6, 24
Foundations	9.93***	(2.50)	3, 15	7.55	(1.80)	3, 13
Early Field Hours	174.01***	(124.94)	0, 394	102.11	(79.31)	0, 394
Full-Time Teaching (weeks)	5.33***	(2.79)	3, 15	6.13	(3.20)	3, 15
Internship Length (weeks)	14.11***	(2.02)	10, 16	13.41	(2.29)	10, 16
Minimum Observations	3.93***	(0.40)	1, 5	1.41	(1.86)	0, 6
Seminar	0.65***	(0.48)	0, 1	0.45	(0.50)	0, 1
Course in Special Education	0.70	(0.46)	0, 1	0.65	(0.48)	0, 1
Course in Teaching ELLs	0	(0)	n/a	0	(0)	n/a
N	248			258		

Note: *** Significant differences between Middle school and High school, $p < 0.01$.

school Algebra I teachers. The only notable difference is that those actually teaching middle school mathematics take on average three credit hours more of mathematics subject matter courses than is required for all middle grades certified teachers.

Descriptive statistics of required structural features, and those for teachers of tested subjects, are found in Table 2.4. Similar to mathematics, there are key differences between middle grades and high school certified teachers and between baccalaureate and master's programs. Middle grades language arts certified teachers are required to take about 18 credit hours of subject matter coursework. High school English certified teachers are required to take almost twice as much subject matter coursework, just over 37 hours. At the MAT level, middle grades teachers are required to take about 7.5 credit hours of English coursework, and high school teachers are required to take just over nine hours. However, MAT teachers must have a subject matter major or its equivalent for admission to an MAT program. Middle grades MAT teachers are required to take about 19 credit hours of pedagogy coursework, while high school MAT teachers take only about 11 credit hours. The only ELA teachers who are required to take a course in teaching English language learners (ELLs) are high school English teachers (4%). About half are required to take a special education course, compared to two-thirds of mathematics teachers, but this varies from 40% to 68% across grade levels.

The average foundations coursework requirement is nine credit hours. Middle grades MAT, high school MAT, and high school baccalaureate programs all require, on average, just over seven credit hours of foundations coursework, while middle grades baccalaureate programs require almost 11 hours. Turning to requirements for fieldwork, teachers are required to participate in about 116 hours of early field experiences, on average. Very few MAT programs require any early field experiences, and at the baccalaureate level, middle grades programs require more hours of early field experiences than high school English programs. The average length of student teaching is 13.7 weeks. Most programs require a full semester of student teaching and much of the variation in this requirement comes from variation in the length of a semester. Of these 13.7 weeks, teachers are required to spend about 6.3 weeks with full-time teaching responsibility in the student teaching classroom. This requirement is longer for baccalaureate teacher candidates than for MAT candidates, and longer for high school certification than for middle grades. A minimum of about four observations by a university supervisor is required, and there is very little variation in this number. Finally, 63% of all sample teachers are required to take a seminar to accompany student teaching, with the vast majority (93%) of MAT teachers having this requirement.

In the zero-sum game of allotting coursework across subject area and professional education coursework, middle grades programs require far

TABLE 2.3 Structural Feature Requirements for all Certified ELA Teachers, 2006–2007 to 2010–2011

	MG Language Arts (BA)		MG Language Arts (MAT)		HS English (BA)		HS English (MAT)	
	Mean (SD)	Range	Mean (SD)	Range	Mean (SD)	Range	Mean (SD)	Range
Subject Matter (hours)	18.14*** (3.78)	15, 27	7.45 (5.76)	3, 18	37.39 (5.98)	27, 48	9.64 (3.37)	6, 15
Pedagogy (hours)	15.44*** (5.55)	6, 24	19.29*** (1.94)	15, 21	9.98 (2.59)	6, 14	10.95 (4.81)	6, 21
Foundations (hours)	10.91*** (1.86)	6, 15	7.29 (1.94)	3, 9	7.94 (2.71)	3, 12	7.45 (3.84)	3, 11
Early Field Hours	155.24*** (129.95)	20, 410	0***	0	93.06 (55.81)	20, 212	55.21 (52.70)	0, 105
Full-Time Teaching (weeks)	5.66*** (2.80)	3, 15	3.71 (0.83)	3, 6	7.45 (3.58)	3, 15	4.03 (2.76)	3, 15
Internship Length (weeks)	13.95 (2.05)	10, 16	12.14 (2.57)	10, 15	13.77 (1.85)	10, 16	12.77 (1.65)	10, 15
Minimum Observations	3.98** (0.42)	3, 5	4**	0	4.07 (0.69)	1, 6	3.88 (0.56)	1, 5
Seminar	0.52*** (0.50)	0, 1	0.93 (0.27)	0, 1	0.64 (0.48)	0, 1	0.93 (0.26)	0, 1
Course in Special Education	0.68*** (0.47)	0,1	0.50 (0.49)	0, 1	0.40 (0.49)	0, 1	0.40 (0.49)	0,1
Course in Teaching ELLs	0 (0)	n/a	0 (0)	0, 1	0.04*** (0.21)	0, 1	0 (0)	n/a
N	322		14		398		88	

Note: T Tests of significant difference between MG Language Arts (BA) and HS English (BA) and MG Language Arts (MAT) and HS English (MAT)

*** $p < 0.01$, ** $p < 0.05$

TABLE 2.4 Structural Feature Requirements for ELA Teachers Teaching Tested Grades, 2006–2007 to 2010–2011					
	Middle School ELA			High School English I	
	Mean (SD)		Range	Mean (SD)		Range
Subject Matter	23.78***	(10.01)	15, 56	32.90	(12.39)	3, 48
Foundations	10.01***	(2.41)	3, 15	8.23	(3.02)	3, 13
Pedagogy	14.49***	(5.63)	6, 22	10.11	(3.20)	6, 21
Early Field Hours	126.37***	(120.51)	0, 394	96.28	(69.62)	0, 394
Weeks Full-Time Teaching	5.94	(3.23)	3, 15	6.48	(3.51)	3, 15
Internship Length	13.46	(2.20)	10, 16	13.65	(1.90)	10, 16
Minimum Observations	3.93	(0.37)	3, 5	3.96	(0.60)	1, 6
Seminar	0.59*	(0.49)	0, 1	0.68	(0.47)	0, 1
Course in Special Education	0.66***	(0.47)	0, 1	0.43	(0.50)	0, 1
Course in Teaching ELLs	0.02	(0.13)	0, 1	0.02	(0.15)	0, 1
N	175			209		

Note: *** $p < 0.01$, * $p < 0.10$

more professional education coursework than high school programs, in the form of pedagogy and foundations coursework, while high school programs require more subject matter coursework. Both middle grades mathematics and ELA teacher candidates are required to take about 15 credit hours of pedagogy coursework and about 11 credit hours of foundations coursework. In contrast, high school teacher candidates are required to take six fewer pedagogy credit hours for ELA and three less for mathematics, and about three less foundations credit hours in both subjects. Requirements for student teaching are similar across grade levels and subjects, but there are large differences in requirements for early field experiences. One might expect that high school programs would compensate for less professional education coursework with more field experiences, but this is not the case. Middle grades programs require about 203 hours of early field experiences in mathematics or 155 hours in ELA, while high school programs require far fewer: about 86 hours in mathematics and 93 hours in ELA.

Relationships Between Structural Features and Student Achievement Gains

As to the relationships between structural features and student achievement gains, there are also differences across grade levels and subject areas. Table 2.5 displays results of HLM models estimating the relationship

TABLE 2.5	Structural Features and Student Achievement Gains			
	(1) Middle School Math	(2) High School Algebra I	(3) Middle School ELA	(4) High School English I
Subject Matter	−0.0066**	−0.0008	0.0026	0.0005
	(0.0021)	(0.0050)	(0.0016)	(0.0017)
Foundations	−0.0101	0.0070	−0.0022	−0.0063*
	(0.0057)	(0.0122)	(0.0031)	(0.0026)
Pedagogy	−0.0015	0.0072	0.0020*	−0.0056
	(0.0010)	(0.0053)	(0.0010)	(0.0032)
Other	0.1007**	0.0293	0.0331*	0.0069
	(0.0348)	(0.0604)	(0.0161)	(0.0249)
Early Field Hours	−0.0026***	0.0032	−0.0005	0.0030
	(0.0005)	(0.0029)	(0.0006)	(0.0019)
Weeks Full-Time Teaching	−0.0090***	0.0009	0.0009	0.0073*
	(0.0027)	(0.0066)	(0.0022)	(0.0029)
Minimum Observations	0.0025	0.0059	0.0235	−0.0208
	(0.0196)	(0.0176)	(0.0170)	(0.0127)
Seminar	0.0356**	0.0835	−0.0178	−0.0071
	(0.0123)	(0.0445)	(0.0093)	(0.0473)
N (students)	35,180	25,755	24,269	22,329

Note: *** $p < 0.01$, ** $p < 0.05$

between TPP structural features and student achievement gains for middle grades mathematics, high school Algebra I, middle school ELA, and high school English I. For middle grades mathematics (Column 1), subject area coursework, early field experience hours, and weeks of full-time student teaching all had negative relationships with student achievement gains, while requiring other courses and a seminar during student teaching had positive relationships with achievement gains. For middle grades ELA (Column 3), pedagogy coursework and requiring a course outside of subject matter, foundations, or pedagogy are positively related to student achievement gains. Foundations coursework, which middle grades scholars stress as being of particular importance for middle school teachers, does not appear to be related to student achievement in either subject in the aggregate. Additionally, I estimated the relationship between requiring two specific foundations courses, educational psychology and adolescent development, and achievement gains and found that neither was positively associated with mathematics achievement gains, but a required course in adolescent development was associated with a 0.05 standard deviation increase in middle school ELA achievement gains ($p = 0.03$).

At the high school level, no features of preparation appeared to be significantly related to achievement gains in Algebra I (Column 2), while in English I (Column 4), foundations coursework has a negative relationship to achievement gains and weeks of full-time student teaching is positively related to achievement gains. Across these models, results are consistent for a sample that excludes MAT teachers.

DISCUSSION

Similar to findings of Boyd and colleagues (2009), the relationships of features to student achievement vary across subject matters and grade levels, but overall this study provides few implications for TPPs as they consider how to most effectively prepare new teachers. Monk's (1994) study that found increased mathematics course taking was associated with increased student achievement ostensibly led to secondary TPPs increasing their requirements for subject area coursework. Unlike Monk, this study does not find that increased mathematics course taking is related to student achievement. One potential reason for this difference is that the high school mathematics teacher sample in Monk's study, using data from the Longitudinal Study of American Youth from the late 1980s, took an average of 7.7 mathematics courses (about 23 credit hours), while in this sample, the mean mathematics credit hours for high school mathematics teachers was 13 courses (almost 39 credit hours), and no high school mathematics teacher was required to take fewer than 27 credit hours. Middle grades mathematics teachers were required to take 21 credits on average. Monk found that increased subject area coursework in mathematics was associated with increased high school mathematics achievement, with diminishing returns to increased coursework setting in at five courses (15–20 credit hours). No program in the current study had requirements below 15 credit hours, which corresponds to Monk's point of diminishing returns. Indeed, results from high school English I models suggest that additional subject matter coursework is associated with decreased student achievement. Whether this indicates that programs should decrease subject matter coursework requirements is unclear. It may be the case, as Shulman (1987) suggested 30 years ago, that the broad content knowledge teacher candidates learn in general education subject area classes is not sufficient knowledge for teaching. Teacher preparation programs should consider working with schools and colleges across campus that teach these courses to provide courses more appropriate for education majors. One option may be for teacher education faculty to teach specific sections of required content courses, dedicated to education majors.

The strongest results point to the importance of field experiences for high school ELA teachers. While high school programs require fewer field experiences than middle grades programs, these field experiences may serve to compensate for fewer pedagogy courses at the high school level and be instrumental in linking theory and practice for high school teachers. That there was no relationship for middle grades teachers, who were required to participate in almost twice as many early field experience hours, suggests that there may be a point at which additional hours are of no benefit to teacher candidates.

LIMITATIONS AND IMPLICATIONS FOR FUTURE RESEARCH

Taken together these results suggest a few important directions for research on the components of TPPs as they relate to teacher effectiveness: first, the quality of the features of TPPs may be driving differences in effectiveness, rather than the quantity of coursework required. Indeed, a key limitation of this study is its high-level measures that only consider quantity rather than quality of the features of teacher education. Because program requirements are key policy levers that can be used to establish how much of various content and skills teacher candidates should receive, they are an important measure of TPPs. Yet, two programs that both require the same number of pedagogy credit hours may differ greatly in the content and quality of those credit hours. Beyond only relying on administrative data sets to gauge the effectiveness of program components, researchers must begin to collect data on the content and quality of teacher education coursework. This may involve analysis of syllabi, classroom observations, or faculty experience and qualifications. Such work is not easy: It is time consuming and often expensive, but necessary to further the field. Research questions and designs applied to K–12 classrooms should be applied to teacher education coursework. Much work has been done to develop observational protocols to assess quality of instruction in K–12 schools, but similar protocols have not been developed for or applied to TPPs.

Similarly, a growing body of quantitative, cross-program research focuses on the context of student teaching and the relationships between cooperating teachers and teacher candidates, rather than focusing on the duration of these experiences, as in the present study. Continuing to open the black box of teacher preparation and investigate the specific mechanisms by which programs influence teacher effectiveness is a key area for future research.

If TPPs are to understand what drives the effectiveness of their graduates with an eye toward program improvement, they must consider how they can determine these drivers as they undertake programmatic changes. Taking the previous example of a teacher education faculty teaching a section of a subject matter course, TPPs could systematically study the impact of instructor type by randomly assigning some students to subject matter professors and other students to teacher education faculty teaching the same course. Programmatic changes must be made in systematic ways that allow TPPs to study the effects of those changes in relationship to specific outcomes. If a program is considering increasing the number of required university supervisor observations of student teaching, student teachers should be randomly assigned to the old required number and the new required number within university supervisor, relevant proximal outcomes identified, and the relationship between them estimated. Such investigations would not be expensive or time-consuming compared to classroom observations of teacher education coursework, and could provide important information to programs seeking improvement.

Second, there may be other features of teacher preparation that impact teacher quality that this study has not captured, potentially related to faculty, cooperating teachers, selection, or peer effects among others. Peer effects and program selection effects in particular are two areas of teacher preparation that remain woefully understudied, in large part because it is complicated to tease out such effects. Just as teachers sort into classrooms, teacher candidates sort into universities and into specific grade level and subject area TPPs within those universities. While this study and others attempt to control for teacher background characteristics that may be related to teacher effectiveness, selection into TPPs has not been explicitly studied. Finally, student achievement gains may be too distal an outcome to the structural features of TPPs. One reason studies of TPPs often limit themselves to novice teachers is that school context plays a large role in teacher effectiveness, potentially overshadowing the influence of teacher preparation at some point. There is strong evidence that teachers sort across schools and it may be the case that teachers from specific preparation programs are hired to teach in schools with specific characteristics, which may be linked to student achievement. Other school context factors, such as mentoring and induction programs and school climate, also influence student achievement and may interact with the effects of teacher preparation in ways that mask the impact of TPPs. Future research on the effectiveness of teacher preparation should investigate both the quality of the various components of preparation as well as relating those features to more proximal outcomes, such as the quality of teacher's instruction, different types of teachers' knowledge, and teachers' ability to increase student engagement.

REFERENCES

Allen, M. (2003). *Eight questions on teacher preparation: What does the research say? A summary of findings.* Denver, CO: Education Commission of the States.

American Association of Colleges of Teacher Education. (2012). *Where we stand: Clinical preparation.* Washington, DC: Author.

Association for Middle Level Education. (2012). *Middle level teacher preparation standards.* Westerville, OH: Author.

Ball, D., Thames, M., & Phelps, G. (2008). Content knowledge for teaching: What makes it special? *Journal of Teacher Education, 59*(5), 389–407.

Ballou, D., & Podgursky, M. (1998). The case against teacher certification. *The Public Interest, 132,* 17–29.

Beisenherz, P., & Dantonio, M. (1991). Preparing secondary teachers to student science teaching. *Journal of Science Teacher Education, 2*(2), 40–44.

Borko, H., & Mayfield, V. (1995). The roles of the cooperating teacher and university supervisor in learning to teach. *Teaching and Teacher Education, 11*(5), 501–518.

Borko, H., Michalec, P., Siddle, J., & Timmons, M. (1997). Student teaching portfolios: A tool for promoting reflective practice. *Journal of Teacher Education, 48*(5), 345–357.

Boyd, D., Grossman, P., Lankford, H., Loeb, S., & Wyckoff, J. (2006). How changes in entry requirements alter the teacher workforce and affect student achievement. *Education, 1*(2), 176–216.

Boyd, D., Grossman, P., Lankford, H., Loeb, S., & Wyckoff, J. (2009). Teacher preparation and student achievement. *Educational Evaluation and Policy Analysis, 31*(4), 416–440.

Brown, P., Friedrichsen, P., & Abell, S. (2013). The development of prospective secondary biology teachers PCK. *Journal of Science Teacher Education, 24*(1), 133–155.

Causey, V., Thomas, C., & Armento, B. (2000). Cultural diversity is basically a foreign term to me: The challenges of diversity for preservice teacher education. *Teaching and Teacher Education, 16*(1), 33–45.

Cheng, M., Tang, S., & Cheng, A. (2012). Practicalising theoretical knowledge in student teachers' professional learning in initial teacher education. *Teaching and Teacher Education, 28,* 781–790.

Clotfelter, C. T., Ladd, H. F., & Vigdor, J. L. (2007). Teacher credentials and student achievement: Longitudinal analysis with student fixed effects. *Economics of Education Review, 26*(6), 673–682.

Conklin, H. G. (2012). Company men: Tracing learning from divergent teacher education pathways into practice in middle grades classrooms. *Journal of Teacher Education, 63*(3), 171–184.

Council for the Accreditation of Educator Preparation. (2013). *CAEP accreditation standards and evidence: Aspirations for educator preparation.* Washington, DC: Author.

Daisey, P. (2012). The promise of secondary content area literacy field experiences. *Literacy Research and Instruction, 51*(3), 214–232.

Darling-Hammond, L., & MacDonald, M. (2000). Where there is learning there is hope: The preparation of teachers at the Bank Street College of Education.

In L. Darling-Hammond (Ed.), *Studies of excellence in teacher education: Preparation at the graduate level* (pp. 1–95). Washington, DC: American Association of Colleges for Teacher Education.

Dinkelman, T. (2000). An inquiry into the development of critical reflection in secondary student teachers. *Teaching and Teacher Education, 16,* 195–222.

Feiman-Nemser, S., & Buchmann, M. (1987). When is student teaching teacher education? *Teaching and Teacher Education, 3*(4), 255–273.

Friedrichsen, P. J., Abell, S. K., Pareja, E. M., Brown, P. L., Lankford, D. M., & Volkmann, M. J. (2009). Does teaching experience matter? Examining biology teachers' prior knowledge for teaching in an alternative certification program. *Journal of Research in Science Teaching, 46,* 357–383.

Goldhaber, D., Liddle, S., & Theobald, R. (2013). The gateway to the profession: Assessing teacher preparation programs based on student achievement. *Economics of Education Review, 34,* 29–44.

Griffin, G. (1989). A descriptive study of student teaching. *Elementary School Journal, 89*(3), 343–364.

Guyton, E., & McIntyre, D. J. (1990). Student teaching and school experiences. In W. Robert Houston (Ed.), *Handbook of research on teacher education* (Vol. 1; pp. 514–534). New York, NY: Macmillan.

Harris, D. N., & Sass, T. R. (2011). Teacher training, teacher quality and student achievement. *Journal of Public Economics, 95*(7), 798–812.

Henry, G. T., Bastian, K. C., & Smith, A. A. (2012). Scholarships to recruit the "Best and Brightest" into teaching who is recruited, where do they teach, how effective are they, and how long do they stay? *Educational Researcher, 41*(3), 83–92.

Henry, G. T., Campbell, S. L., Thompson, C. L., Patriarca, L. A., Luterbach, K. J., Lys, D. B., & Covington, V. M. (2013). The predictive validity of measures of teacher candidate programs and performance toward an evidence-based approach to teacher preparation. *Journal of Teacher Education, 64*(5), 439–453.

Henry, G. T, Patterson, K., Campbell, S., & Yi, P. (2013). *UNC teacher quality report: 2013 teacher preparation program effectiveness report.* Chapel Hill, NC: Education Policy Initiative at Carolina.

Henry, G. T., Purtell, K. M., Bastian, K. C., Fortner, C. K., Thompson, C. L., Campbell, S. L., & Patterson, K. M. (2014). The effects of teacher entry portals on student achievement. *Journal of Teacher Education, 65*(1), 7–23.

Henry, G. T., Thompson, C. L., Fortner, C. K., Zulli, R. A., & Kershaw, D. C. (2010). *The impact of teacher preparation on student learning in North Carolina public schools.* UNC Chapel Hill, Carolina Institute for Public Policy.

Holmes Group. (1986). *Tomorrow's teachers: A report of the Holmes Group.* East Lansing, MI: Author.

Holmes Group. (1995). *Tomorrow's schools of education: A report of the Holmes Group.* East Lansing, MI: Author.

Holt-Reynolds, D. (1999). Good readers, good teachers? Subject matter expertise as a challenge in learning to teach. *Harvard Educational Review, 69*(1), 29–50.

Howey, K., & Zimpher, N. (1989). *Profiles of preservice teacher education.* Albany: State University of New York Press.

Imig, D., & Imig, S. (2008). From traditional certification to competitive certification: A twenty-five year retrospective. In M. Cochran-Smith, S. Feiman

Nemser, & D. McIntyre (Eds.), *Handbook of research on teacher education: Enduring issues in changing contexts* (3rd ed.; pp. 806–907). New York, NY: Routledge.

Jackson, A., & Davis, G. (2000). *Turning points: Educating adolescents in the 21st century.* New York, NY: Teachers College Press.

Kaye, E. A. (Ed.). (2008). *Requirements for certification of teachers, counselors, librarians, administrators for elementary and secondary schools, 2008–2009.* Chicago, IL: University of Chicago Press.

Kleickmann, T., Richter, D., Kunter, M., Elsner, J., Besser, M., Krauss, S., & Baumert, J. (2013). Teachers' content knowledge and pedagogical content knowledge: The role of structural differences in teacher education. *Journal of Teacher Education, 64*(1), 90–106.

Koedel, C., Parsons, E., Podgursky, M., & Ehlert, M. (2015). Teacher preparation programs and teacher quality: Are there real differences across programs? *Education Finance and Policy, 10*(4), 508–534.

Koerner, J. D. (1963). *The miseducation of American teachers.* Boston, MA: Houghton Mifflin.

Koppich, J. (2000). Trinity University: Preparing teachers for tomorrow's schools. In L. Darling-Hammond (Ed.), *Studies of excellence in teacher education: Preparation in a five-year program* (pp. 1–48). Washington, DC: American Association of Colleges for Teacher Education.

Kramer, R. (1991). *Ed school follies: The miseducation of America's teachers.* Lincoln, NE: iUniverse.

Labaree, D. F. (1996). The trouble with ed schools. *The Journal of Educational Foundations, 10*(3), 27–45.

Labaree, D. F. (2004). *The trouble with ed schools.* New Haven, CT: Yale University Press.

Labaree, D. (2008). An uneasy relationship: The history of teacher education in the university. In M. Cochran-Smith, et. al. (Eds.), *Handbook of research on teacher education: Enduring questions in changing contexts* (3rd ed.; pp. 290–306). New York, NY: Routledge.

Levine, A. (2006). *Educating school teachers.* Washington, DC: The Education Schools Project.

Liston, D., Whitcomb, J., & Borko, H. (2009). The end of education in teacher education: Thoughts on reclaiming the role of social foundations in teacher education. *Journal of Teacher Education, 60*(2), 107–111.

McDiarmid, G. W. (1990). *What to do about differences? A study of multicultural education for teacher trainees in the Los Angeles Unified School District.* East Lansing, MI: National Center for Research on Teacher Education.

Monk, D. (1994). Subject matter preparation of secondary mathematics and science teachers and student achievement. *Economics of Education Review, 13*(2), 125–145.

Ng, W., Nicholas, H., & Williams, A. (2010). School experience influences on preservice teachers' evolving beliefs about effective teaching. *Teaching and Teacher Education, 26*(2), 278–289.

National Council for the Accreditation of Teacher Education. (2010). *Transforming teacher education through clinical practice: A national strategy to prepare effective* teachers. *A report of the Blue Ribbon Panel on Clinical Preparation and Partnership for Improved Student Learning.* Washington, DC: Author.

Noell, G., Porter, B., Pratt, R. M., & Dahir, A. (2008). *Value-added assessment of teacher preparation in Louisiana: 2004–2005 to 2006–2007.* Baton Rouge, LA: Louisiana State University.

North Carolina Department of Public Instruction. (2005). *North Carolina program approval standards.* Raleigh, NC: State Board of Education.

Plecki, M. L., Elfers, A. M., & Nakamura, Y. (2012). Using evidence for teacher education program improvement and accountability: An illustrative case of the role of value-added measures. *Journal of Teacher Education, 63*(5), 318–334.

Ronfeldt, M. (2012). Where should student teachers learn to teach? Effects of field placement school characteristics on teacher retention and effectiveness. *Educational Evaluation and Policy Analysis, 34*(1), 3–26.

Ronfeldt, M. (2015). Field placement schools and instructional effectiveness. *Journal of Teacher Education, 66*(4), 304–320.

Ronfeldt, M., & Reininger, M. (2012). More or better student teaching? *Teaching and Teacher Education, 28*(8), 1091–1106.

Ronfeldt, M., Reininger, M., & Kwok, A. (2013). Recruitment or preparation? Investigating the effects of teacher characteristics and student teaching. *Journal of Teacher Education, 64*(4), 319–337.

Ronfeldt, M., Schwartz, N., & Jacob, B. (2014). Does pre-service preparation matter? Examining an old question in new ways. *Teachers College Record, 116*(10), 1–46.

Scales, P., & McEwin, K. (1994). *Growing pains: The making of America's middle school teachers.* Columbus, OH: National Middle School Association.

Shulman, L. S. (1986). Those who understand: Knowledge growth in teaching. *Educational Research, 15*(2), 4–14.

Shulman, L. S. (1987). Knowledge and teaching: Foundations of the new reform. *Harvard Educational Review, 57*(1), 1–23.

Smith, R. (1999). Piecing it together: Student teachers building their repertoires in primary science. *Teaching and Teacher Education, 15,* 301–314.

Snyder, J. (2000). Knowing children-understanding teaching: The developmental teacher education program at the University of California-Berkeley. In L. Darling-Hammond (Ed.), *Studies of excellence in teacher education: Preparation at the graduate level* (pp. 1–95). Washington, DC: American Association of Colleges for Teacher Education.

Tennessee Higher Education Commission. (2011). *2011 report card on the effectiveness of teacher training programs.* Nashville, TN: State Board of Education.

Tennessee Higher Education Commission. (2012). *2012 report card on the effectiveness of teacher training programs.* Nashville, TN: State Board of Education.

Valencia, S. W., Martin, S. D., Place, N. A., & Grossman, P. (2009). Complex interactions in student teaching lost opportunities for learning. *Journal of Teacher Education, 60*(3), 304–322.

Van Zandt, L. (1998). Assessing the effects of reform in teacher education: An evaluation of the 5-year MAT program at Trinity University. *Journal of Teacher Education, 49*(2), 120–131.

von Hippel, P., & Bellows, L. (2018). How much does teacher quality vary across teacher preparation programs? Reanalyses from six states. *Economics of Education Review, 64*, 298–312.

Whitford, B. L., Ruscoe, G., & Fickel, L. (2000). Knitting it all together: Collaborative teacher education in Southern Maine. In L. Darling-Hammond (Ed.), *Studies of excellence in teacher education: Preparation at the graduate level* (pp. 1–95). Washington, DC: American Association of Colleges for Teacher Education.

Wilson, S. M., Floden, R. E., & Ferrini-Mundy, J. (2001). *Teacher preparation research: Current knowledge, gaps, and recommendations: A research report prepared for the US Department of Education and the Office for Educational Research and Improvement, February 2001.* Seattle, WA: Center for the Study of Teaching and Policy.

Woellner, E. (1973). *Requirements for certification.* (38th edition). Chicago, IL: University of Chicago Press.

Woellner, E. (1974). *Requirements for certification.* (39th ed.). Chicago, IL: University of Chicago Press.

Woellner, E. (1975). *Requirements for certification.* (40th ed.). Chicago, IL: University of Chicago Press.

Woellner, E. (1984). *Requirements for certification.* (49th ed.). Chicago, IL: University of Chicago Press.

Woellner, R. C., & Wood, M. A. (1936). *Requirements for teaching certificates.* Chicago, IL: University of Chicago Press.

Youngs, P., & Qian, H. (2013). The influence of university courses and field experiences on Chinese elementary candidates' mathematical knowledge for teaching. *Journal of Teacher Education, 64*(3), 244–261.

Zeichner, K. M., & Schulte, A. K. (2001). What we know and don't know from peer-reviewed research about alternative teacher certification programs. *Journal of Teacher Education, 52*(4), 266–282.

CHAPTER 3

USING CASE STUDY DATA OF COMPLETERS AS EVIDENCE IN A CONTINUOUS IMPROVEMENT MODEL

Bruce Weitzel
University of Portland

Hillary Merk
University of Portland

Jacqueline Waggoner
University of Portland

James Carroll
University of Portland

Randy Hetherington
University of Portland

Linking Teacher Preparation Program Design and Implementation to Outcomes for Teachers and Students, pages 63–85
Copyright © 2020 by Information Age Publishing

This chapter discusses the development and implementation of a case study approach for tracking the effectiveness of new teachers in P–12 classrooms. Using national and state standards as a framework of best practices, we initiated a study of our program completers that was grounded in the literature of program evaluation (Darling-Hammond 2000, 2006, 2009, 2010; Ginsberg & Kingston, 2014; Lasley, Siedentop, & Yenger, 2006). We collected data using teacher assessments from a unit of instruction, observations of teachers in their classrooms, surveys of teachers' principals, interviews of teachers' principals, and data from teachers' performance evaluations in their clinical experiences. Because this approach follows the Council for the Accreditation of Educator Preparation (CAEP, 2013) Standard 4 (Program Impact) guidelines, we believe it will be useful to other teacher preparation programs interested in national accreditation and those interested in strategies to improve programs based on early career program completers' performance and feedback.

The intent of this case study approach is to help us understand if teachers we prepared are positively impacting P–12 student learning, if teachers we prepared are continuing to employ practices they developed as part of their initial preparation program, and if principals can confirm our own observations of performance of teachers we prepared. We seek these data to communicate to accreditors and others the impact our graduates are having on P–12 student learning.

We are faculty members at a small liberal arts university in Oregon of approximately 3,500 undergraduate students and 1,000 graduate students, and we graduate about 100 initial-licensure teacher candidates each year. The faculty consists of 14 tenure-track members who provide instruction in a variety of advanced programs in addition to initial-licensure preparation. The context of faculty size and diversity of assignments, and the impact on resources will also be discussed.

Our School of Education has been accredited over four iterations of National Council for the Accreditation of Teacher Education (NCATE) review. The NCATE was the national accreditation organization prior to CAEP. In addition, individual programs are reviewed on a 7-year cycle by a state teacher standards board. Of the 19 university-based initial teacher preparation programs in Oregon, six are accredited through NCATE, and one was accredited through CAEP in 2017. The remaining preparation programs are approved by the state teacher standards board and are pursuing national accreditation per a new state mandate.

LITERATURE REVIEW

An extensive literature review on the history of reform policies in the United States provides insight into the call for greater accountability for teacher preparation (Cohen & Mehta, 2017; Li, 2017). Following this call, there are numerous teacher preparation program reforms currently in place or proposed in many states across the nation (Darling-Hammond, 2017; Russell, Meredith, Childs, Stein, & Prine, 2015). These reforms are framed by high standards for teacher performance and "by the assumption that improving teacher quality is a central strategy for improving a nation's ability to compete in the global knowledge economy, ensure the quality of its workforce, and meet rising social expectations related to diversity and equality" (Cochran-Smith, Piazza, & Power, 2013, p. 7).

Teacher education programs seeking national accreditation have been charged with producing and using multiple measures to assess the success of their completers in bridging the gap between teacher candidate preparation and P–12 learning gains of completers' students (Darling-Hammond, 2006; Reusser, Butler, Symonds, Vetter, & Wall, 2007). However, the identification and use of accessible and consistent measures that span the two developmental phases of an educator's preparation and practice have proven to be difficult (Hamel & Mertz, 2005).

The CAEP (2013) requires valid and reliable measures capable of demonstrating teachers' impact on P–12 student learning, and has identified a number of possible measures that can be used to connect teacher preparation and P–12 student learning growth. Specifically, CAEP suggests the use of value-added measures, student-growth percentiles, and student learning and development objectives to assess P–12 student learning and argues that "the paramount goal of [teacher preparation] providers is to prepare teacher candidates who will have a positive impact on P–12 students" (CAEP, 2013, p. 13).

Increasingly, teacher preparation programs are critiqued on the degree to which they contribute to the effectiveness of teacher candidates and practicing teachers (e.g., Kagan, 1992). Although state and national organizations with oversight for teacher preparation program performance have asked for program impact accountability data for many years (Darling-Hammond, 2006; Harris, Salzman, Frantz, Newsome, & Martin, 2000), teacher preparation programs have had difficulty tracking their teachers after graduation and collecting data on the learning of P–12 students in program completer classrooms. Solutions are possible, albeit labor intensive, requiring a committed and coordinated effort by states, school districts, and schools of education. Nevertheless, national and state accreditation agencies are asking to see complex data systems in place to track teachers' impact on P–12 student learning and for aggregated data to be used to inform teacher preparation program improvement processes.

In addition to logistical issues surrounding many of the suggested measures of teacher performance, questions have been raised about the ability of the measures to provide quality information about teacher performance.

For instance, there is considerable debate about the recent attempts to construct value-added models (VAM) that accurately gauge teachers' contributions to the growth of students. Professional concerns and questions of appropriateness of VAM (Amrein-Beardsley, 2008; Guarino, Reckase, & Wooldridge, 2014) have been added to more general concerns about the validity and stability of these measures of teacher effectiveness (Darling-Hammond, 2015). More recently, von Hippel and Bellows (2018) suggest that even when VAM strategies are implemented appropriately, results are unable to demonstrate meaningful differences among teacher preparation programs. Additionally, VAM data are not available in all states and typically only available for a relatively small proportion of teachers who teach in grades and subjects in which students are annually tested.

Another data gathering challenge is developing and collecting valid and reliable survey measures of completer and employer satisfaction with preparation programs. These activities are often beyond the reach of smaller preparation programs due to a lack of resources, chiefly time. Once measures are available, it is challenging to track and attain completer contact information, to identify completers who are employed as P–12 teachers, and to ensure an acceptable rate of survey return, given the mobility of completers. More specifically, many state agencies and teacher preparation programs struggle with their surveys of graduates and their P–12 employers due to the difficulty locating both the graduates and the employers. Even when they are successful in doing so, some states have been faced with response rates as low as 7% or 12% (Oregon Association of Colleges for Teacher Education, 2014; Wineburg, 2006). As a result, survey data may suffer from response bias or be of limited generalizability.

Other states have been more successful in surveying teachers and principals. Indiana uses a principal survey targeted specifically on teacher preparation program efficacy (Indiana Department of Education, 2018), and Texas requires principals to complete a similar survey (Texas Education Agency, 2018a). In addition, Texas uses a required program evaluation exit survey for all teacher candidates (Texas Education Agency, 2018b). These approaches require state-level support including embedding survey requirements in administrative rule. That level of support is not always available even in states that have been innovative in evaluating preparation programs (Coggshall, Bivona, & Reschly, 2012).

Even if VAM or survey measures of program completers and their employers could produce accurate, stable, and sufficient data for use in determining the strength of a completer's preparation program, individually these data still would not meet CAEP accreditation requirements for multiple measures of completer success. Hence, as teacher preparation programs search for meaningful and attainable measures to assess their teachers' ability to impact the students in P–12 classrooms, teacher preparation programs are in need of methods and instruments that can be used in combination to provide program feedback and to demonstrate to a wider audience their ability to bridge the gap between preservice preparation and in-service practice (Popham, 2013). Darling-Hammond (2006) describes the difficulty of relying on single measures and suggests use of multiple measures during both teacher preparation and in teachers' initial years of teaching.

A case study approach is an example of a method to investigate program impact that necessitates a multiple measures approach (Creswell, 2017). Wideen, Mayer-Smith, and Moon (1998) discuss the effective use of case-studies in evaluating teacher preparation programs and include cautions around generalizing too widely from limited data. This point of view is reiterated by CAEP (2015), which describes case studies as a means to an end for developing and evaluating new measures. The Council for the Accreditation of Educator Preparation includes an example of using case studies in providing evidence for Standard 4—Program Impact. They list guidelines for case studies including: identifying the topic to be studied, generating ideas for change, defining measurements, and testing promising solutions.

What follows is a description of our case study approach guided by CAEP's typology of research design. We highlight successes in using a case study approach in informing our practice and comment on tensions that have arisen that require further study. Our hope is that this work contributes to the body of literature around program evaluation for teacher preparation programs and will be useful for other institutions embarking on the evaluation process to determine whether their programs are preparing teachers to have a positive outcome on P–12 students' learning.

METHODS

This section addresses the sample, instrumentation, data collection, and analysis processes used during the case study. The study is ongoing to meet the needs of the continuous improvement model adopted by our institution.

The Sample

Our teacher candidates were placed in clinical experiences within a 30-mile radius of our campus in public and private schools, and approximately 15% of our placements were made in an adjoining state. Approximately 50% of our graduates become teachers in our state public schools. Approximately 5% never enter teaching, and the remainder teach in private schools or out of state.

Teachers and principals participated in this study on a voluntary basis. The associate dean contacted first or second year teachers who were within a 30- to 40-mile radius of the campus. This represented approximately half of those program graduates who became employed in our state. The initial contact was used to explain why we needed the graduate's assistance, why this would be of benefit to both the graduate and us, what data we sought to gather, and how data would be collected. This system generated responses from an average of 15 teachers per year representing 30% of the in-state teachers who have graduated from our programs. Teachers who chose to participate were offered a $50 gratuity (the maximum allowed by state law) for their time and effort. Volunteers were contacted a second time by faculty members to arrange the logistics of the process.

Instrumentation

The methods for data collection in this study were developed over a 13-year period and continue to undergo development. Following CAEP guidance, each mode of data collection is developed, tested, and revised. New modes are added as the previously gathered data suggest additional areas for study. What follows is a chronological listing of the development of each data collection process which is now included in our comprehensive case study approach.

Principal Survey
In 2004, the primary set of standards within which the School of Education functioned was our locally developed conceptual framework—what CAEP now calls Shared Values. Our interest at the time was to gather employer perceptions to address questions based on the conceptual framework, such as: Were our teachers still exhibiting the knowledge, skills, and professional dispositions that had been the foundation of our preparation program? We designed a 20-question survey targeting the elements of our conceptual framework. The associate dean visited volunteer principals who were supervising teachers from our program. The survey was administered in person and the associate dean provided an opportunity for principals to discuss their responses. After the first iteration, the survey was expanded to 23 questions to include questions about teacher use of technology.

In 2013, based on the acceptance at the national level of Interstate New Teacher Assessment and Support Consortium (InTASC) standards as the primary standards by which programs would be evaluated, the assessment committee of our School of Education worked to align the existing instrument with InTASC standards (Council of Chief State School Officers, 2011). Since that revision, the instrument has remained the same. Beginning in

2004, the instrument was used as part of principal interviews every 2 years. Now the instrument is used each time we interview a principal who is supervising a teacher who is participating in our case study assessment. Because of small sample sizes, these data are analyzed descriptively.

Principal Interview

Designed at the same time as the principal survey, we assembled an interview protocol to assess principal perceptions of teacher performance and impact on student learning. Questions were guided not only by our own interest in program improvement but also by accreditation reporting requirements. During the arranged interview time, the survey was completed first, followed by the principal interview with the associate dean using a protocol to guide discussion. The protocol questions included:

1. Do/Did you have any concerns about the graduate's performance (areas that graduates needed help) during their early years of teaching?
2. Based on their efforts thus far, are graduates impacting student learning?
3. If yes, how are they impacting student learning? Do you have any suggestions as to how impact on student learning could be improved through better preservice preparation?
4. Does the graduate respect and value student differences/diversity, and have the necessary skills and dispositions to help all students increase their learning? If yes, what evidence have they shown to indicate this?

Interviews were designed to be completed in about 20 minutes. However, they averaged considerably longer because administrators frequently provided detailed answers to the prompts and expanded their responses to include suggestions for the improvement of the teacher preparation program. Interview responses were analyzed using a constant comparative methodology (Glaser & Strauss, 1967).

State-Administered Principal Satisfaction Survey and Teacher Satisfaction Survey

In 2009, under pressure from all of the state teacher preparation programs that were pursuing national accreditation, a state association of colleges of teacher education funded a vendor to prepare and administer matched employer satisfaction and teacher satisfaction surveys addressing the quality of preparation programs. The surveys were initially distributed in 2011 to first- and second-year teachers and their principals in public schools statewide. The vendor for these surveys compiled results and provided summary data to each teacher preparation program which included statewide averages and scores for only those respondents who had completed the preparation program to which the report had been sent. Survey responses were anonymous.

After the adoption of the InTASC standards nationally in 2013, the survey was revised by the vendor to reflect both InTASC standards specifically and the CAEP reporting requirements around CAEP Standard I—Content and Pedagogical Knowledge, in addition to the reporting requirements for CAEP Standard 4—Program Impact. This revised second iteration of the survey appeared in 2014. Because response rates had been unacceptably low on the 2011 iteration of the surveys, the vendor worked with the state to improve contact information for early career teachers and their principals. Currently, the funding source for administration of the survey is the 19 schools of education in the state. In the 2016 version of the instrument, the response scale for satisfaction was revised to an 8-point scale instead of the previous 4-point scale. While the entire survey consisted of 53 items, only the 23 items that directly addressed candidate preparation around the inTASC standards were analyzed for this study and reported on in the results.

Teacher Unit of Instruction Assessment Data

Teacher candidates were required to complete a pre-assessment and post-assessment of student learning in their clinical experiences as part of a work sample for a unit of instruction. During clinical experiences, candidates were mentored by university supervisors and cooperating teachers in all areas of preparation including the development of appropriate assessments within the unit of instruction. The quality of all assessments, including the unit pre/post assessment, was evaluated and discussed as part of formative and summative clinical experience assessment.

Candidates provided disaggregated student data by gender, ethnicity, and learning needs (special education, talented and gifted, English language learners, and students on 504 Plans) and analyzed learning gains for all learners. Results of the assessments were submitted to the School of Education in a pre-formatted Excel spreadsheet. Assessment scores were converted to percent correct scores, and learning gains were computed for each student (Waggoner, Carroll, Merk, & Weitzel, 2015). Practicing teachers in our case study were asked to follow a similar methodology based on the work they had experienced as teacher candidates. Teachers were asked to select a unit of study from their grade-level subject matter curriculum, identify student demographic data, conduct matching pre-assessments and post-assessments of their students, record the student scores for both assessments, and submit the scores to us.

Teacher pre-assessment and post-assessment results, completed during clinical placements as teacher candidates, were compared to the data gathered from the unit of instruction in the teacher case study. None of the controls on the quality or use of the pre/post assessment that were in place during clinical experiences were present in the early-career teachers' unit of instruction. Because all of the teachers in the case study had successfully implemented this assessment practice in their clinical experiences within the previous 2 years, the comparison of scores was seen as a potentially valuable data-informed heuristic.

Teacher Observation Assessment

In 2014, we decided that we needed another data source to improve the trustworthiness of the data gathered for principal interactions, statewide assessment, and the unit of instruction assessment data. One of our faculty members had been working with early career teachers in a new teacher support group. Those teachers indicated an interest in having the faculty member observe in their classrooms. This inspired the development of a strategy to visit teacher classrooms as part of our case study of program impact.

We developed an observation instrument based on the four InTASC learning standards and progressions: (a) The learner and learning, (b) content knowledge, (c) instructional practice, and (d) professional responsibility. The instrument was tested, and faculty and university supervisors were trained in its use. In addition to using the instrument with teacher candidates, we tested the use of the observation instrument in teacher classrooms. Two changes had to be made to the existing instrument. First, it was difficult to observe teachers relative to InTASC Standards 9 and 10, which address professional responsibilities that often occur outside of the school timetable. Those items were removed from the instrument. In addition, the original instrument was built on four-level rubrics which included descriptors of each level for each assessment item. Teachers and their principals were uncomfortable that this might be perceived as an external evaluation of practicing teachers. Our solution was to keep each of the assessment items (12 in total) but to write narrative descriptions of the observed performances. In this manner, the teachers felt that the observation instrument functioned as a discussion tool rather than an evaluation instrument. These data were then analyzed using descriptive coding to identify themes.

Data Collection

For state surveys of principal and early-career teacher satisfaction, the vendor who administered the survey worked with the state teacher licensing agency to develop a contact list for those who were in the respondent pool. Emails requesting participation were sent to the contact list by the vendor early in the spring semester. Summary reports of the survey results were distributed to the schools of education in May of the year in which the survey was administered.

Case study data collection began early in the fall semester each year with an email contact of all graduates from our programs who were first- and second-year teachers at schools within a 30- to 40-mile radius of campus. The request included a description of the procedures we were asking them to complete. Teachers who agreed to participate were given instructions for selecting a unit of instruction in their classrooms, creating a matched pre-assessment and post-assessment of the unit, and reporting the results of the assessments to the School of Education. Fifty-three teachers representing 1,204 students volunteered to participate in the present study from 2014 through 2016.

Added to the case study in 2014 were teacher observations. The same request to participate was used except that a request for classroom observation was added. Teachers who agreed to participate were assigned faculty members who were the teachers' observers. The assigned faculty member communicated with the teacher to arrange a time for the teacher to be observed. The faculty member completed the observation and reported the results of the observation to the School of Education. After the observations were completed for the year (usually in early spring) a faculty member completed data analysis of all of the observation reports.

On a 2-year cycle, the associate dean made email contact with principals of first- or second-year teachers who completed our program, requesting an interview. That contact included a description of the purpose of the visit and the nature of data that would be collected. After principals agreed to participate, the associate dean arranged a time to meet with the principal. During the visit, the associate dean administered the School of Education principal survey and completed the principal interview. Data from the interviews were given to a faculty member for analysis. The number of principals agreeing to participate averaged about 27 principals per year.

Data Analysis

Analysis of principal and first- and second-year teacher satisfaction surveys were done descriptively. The response rates were insufficient to warrant more in-depth analysis. Mean scores were reported for each of the four InTASC categories based on CAEP Standard 1 reporting requirements. Descriptive tables allow for visual comparison across sections of the surveys.

Assessment data from units of instruction were converted to percent correct scores and differences between pre-assessment and post-assessment scores were computed. Scores from all the assessments were accumulated into a single data set and analysis of variance (ANOVA) comparisons based on gender, ethnicity, and learning needs were completed. In addition, the pre/post assessment data from the teachers that was submitted as part of the clinical experience while they were enrolled in our teacher preparation program was compared with the data collected from teacher's unit of instruction assessment. Differences between the preservice program assessment and the new teacher assessment in the areas of overall learning gains or the degree to which the teacher appeared to be meeting the needs of all students were recorded.

Narratives based on the observation protocol were completed immediately after the observation. Teachers reviewed the narratives and discussed the observations with the faculty member who had completed the observation. The faculty member expanded the narrative after the discussion to capture the teacher's comments. Final narratives were emailed to the teachers to confirm the accuracy of the observation and post-conversation discussion. Descriptive coding was used with the narratives to identify themes. Initially, coding was done individually by the faculty member who conducted the observation. Then, the research team met to discuss and adjust coding categories as needed. Emergent themes and exemplars were then agreed upon by the researchers in consultation. In addition, during this consultation data that potentially indicated program strengths or challenges were noted. As observation narratives were added to the data set, constant comparative coding was used to identify themes across observations and themes which were unique to a single observation.

Data from the in-person principal surveys were accumulated into a single data set. The data were analyzed descriptively looking at counts within categories for each of the survey questions. We had 14 years of data from this survey; however, data from the other instruments used in this study did not date back as far. Therefore, only principal survey data for the period of this study were reviewed in this work.

Principal interviews were analyzed similarly to the teacher observation data. Data from each interview were analyzed using descriptive codes. As interview data were added to the data set, constant comparative strategies were applied to confirm themes from previous interviews and to identify themes unique to the interview being reviewed.

RESULTS

State Administered Principal Satisfaction Survey and Teacher Satisfaction Survey

Over a 2-year period, responses from 15 principals and 33 teachers to the state Preparation Program Satisfaction Survey were provided to the School of Education by the vendor responsible for administering the survey. Table 3.1 shows response rates for the 2015 version of the survey. Although the questions remained the same, the response scale for the instruments was changed in 2016 (Table 3.2). Response rates from both iterations of the survey were about 7% of the possible sample. The tables include 23 of the 53 items in the survey that pertain to candidate preparation around InTASC standards. Responses were combined into 4 reporting categories (InTASC 1 & 2: learner and learning; InTASC 3, 4, & 5: content knowledge; InTASC 6, 7, & 8: instructional practice; and InTASC 9 & 10: professional responsibilities). In general, responses from both teachers and principals moved toward the lower end of the response scales from 2015 to 2016.

In the earlier version of the instrument teachers and principals responded to a question rating overall preparation. In the 2016 version the question was changed to rating satisfaction with preparation making these two questions not comparable. Responses to the 2016 satisfaction question are shown in Table 3.3.

TABLE 3.1 2015 Satisfaction Survey Percent Within Response Categories for Teachers (*n* = 20) and Principals (*n* = 3) by InTASC Categories

	Completely Unprepared	2	3	Very Well Prepared
Learner and Learning (5 questions)				
Teacher	2	15	39	44
Principal	0	0	40	60
Content Knowledge (5 questions)				
Teacher	0	13	37	50
Principal	0	13	27	60
Instructional Practice (6 questions)				
Teacher	1	8	38	53
Principal	0	13	47	40
Professional Responsibilities (6 questions)				
Teacher	0	7	34	59
Principal	0	0	20	80
Overall Preparation (1 question)				
Teacher	0	3	38	57
Principal	0	0	0	100

TABLE 3.2   2016 Satisfaction Survey Percent Within Response Categories for Teachers (_n_ = 13) and Principals (_n_ = 12) by InTASC Categories

	Completely Unprepared	2	3	4	5	6	7	Very Well Prepared	Don't Know
Learner and Learning (5 questions)									
Teacher	0	6	5	9	20	23	32	5	
Principal		0	5	23	20	23	15	13	
Content Knowledge (5 questions)									
Teacher	2	3	6	15	20	34	11	9	3
Principal	0	2	10	22	17	27	12	8	
Instructional Practice (6 questions)									
Teacher	0	5	6	15	10	9	45	9	2
Principal	0	2	5	22	20	30	13	7	
Professional Responsibilities (6 questions)									
Teacher	0	4	4	10	17	22	36	8	
Principal	3	5	8	17	15	20	28	13	

TABLE 3.3   2016 Satisfaction Survey Percent Within Response Categories for Teachers (_n_ = 13) and Principals (_n_ = 12) for Overall Program Approval

	Very Dissatisfied	Somewhat Dissatisfied	Somewhat Satisfied	Very Satisfied
Teacher	1	2	26	70
Principal	0	21	25	54

Teacher Unit of Instruction Assessment Data

Teachers reported matched pre-assessment and post-assessment scores for students in a unit of instruction. Those scores were converted to percent correct scores and learning gains were reported as percent growth (Table 3.4). Teacher pre/post assessment data showed learning gains of about 40% from pretest to posttest for P–12 students in teachers' classrooms. Average learning gains were compared by gender, ethnicity, and learning needs of students. No statistically significant differences were found in ANOVA comparisons of disaggregated groups except that talented and gifted students showed significantly higher learning gains than English language learners ($p < 0.001$), 504 Plan students ($p = 0.005$), and students with no identified learning needs ($p < 0.001$). These binary comparisons were done post hoc.

TABLE 3.4   Percent Learning Gains by Gender, Ethnicity, and Identified Learning Needs (2014–2016)

	n	Mean	Std. Dev.
Gender			
Girls	578	40.34	27.39
Boys	605	37.93	27.50
Ethnicity			
African American	47	43.74	27.08
Caucasian	689	39.95	26.64
Hispanic/Latino	213	38.04	29.80
Asian	124	34.21	25.39
Am Indian/Pacific Islander	33	40.94	29.79
Mixed	75	39.89	30.45
Other	23	35.92	28.31
Learning Needs			
English Language Learner	129	36.23	27.37
Talented and Gifted	105	49.87[a]	25.77
Special Education	83	43.48	28.40
504 Plan	47	37.02	25.43
No Identified Need	840	37.91	27.45

Note: Data on 1,204 students in classrooms of 53 teachers graduating from 2014 through 2016.

[a] Talented and gifted students had significantly higher learning gains than English language learners, 504 Plan students, and students with no identified learning need.

Comparison of Clinical Experience Assessment Data With Teacher Unit of Instruction Assessment Data

Student learning gains from the unit of instruction that teachers had completed during their teacher preparation program were compared to the learning gains from the unit of instruction completed as part of the case study (Table 3.5). Although a larger negative difference appeared in 2014, overall differences and annual differences for the remaining years of the study were small.

Principal Survey

Results from the in-person principal survey showed principals were satisfied with new teacher performance in all areas addressed by the survey (Table 3.6). Ratings for teacher knowledge of learners tended to be lowest.

TABLE 3.5   Differences Between Clinical Experience Assessment Gains and Teacher Unit of Instruction Assessment Gains

	n	Mean	Std. Dev.
2014	10	−17.49	33.87
2015	12	−0.48	25.85
2016	8	4.49	11.67
2017	9	−4.26	17.33
Overall	39	−4.70	24.90

TABLE 3.6   In-Person Principal Survey of Completer Qualities

	Total			Elementary School			High School		
Year	2012	2014	2016	2012	2014	2016	2012	2014	2016
n	25	23	32	19	17	15	6	6	17
Lifelong learner	4.9	4.9	4.8	4.9	4.9	4.8	4.8	4.9	4.8
Empathy and respect	4.8	4.7	4.7	4.9	4.8	4.7	4.7	4.6	4.6
Communication	4.8	4.7	4.7	4.8	4.7	4.8	4.8	4.6	4.6
Knowledge of diversity	4.8	4.8	4.7	4.8	4.9	4.7	4.7	4.7	4.7
Content knowledge	4.6	4.5	4.6	4.6	4.5	4.7	4.8	4.5	4.5
Knowledge of learners	4.4	4.4	4.5	4.5	4.4	4.6	4.1	4.4	4.4
Pedagogical knowledge	4.6	4.5	4.5	4.5	4.5	4.7	4.3	4.5	4.4
Theory into practice	4.5	4.4	4.6	4.6	4.3	4.6	4.2	4.7	4.6

Note: Survey contained 23 items rated from *strongly agree* = 5 to *strongly disagree* = 1.

No statistically significant differences between the scores at the elementary versus the high school level or statistically significant differences among response years appeared.

Teacher Observation Assessment

Data from teacher observations were sorted by InTASC standards, which allowed for the identification of themes and informed program improvement efforts. Descriptive theme analysis of the data indicated completers generally were well organized, had relationship-building activities for each class taught, constructed friendly and respectful learning environments, used a wide variety of formative assessment strategies, and delivered accurate curriculum content using strategies appropriate for the instructional task at hand. The observational data indicated that one area for improvement was completers' efficiency in the use of instructional time. Use of higher-order questioning during the lesson and formative assessment strategies during guided practice were also identified as areas for improvement.

While formative assessment data were generated using multiple and varied strategies, it was unclear from the observations and discussions with the teachers following the observations how such data were being managed and considered to inform pedagogy or future assessment.

Principal Interview

Interview responses were positive overall. Three major themes emerged from among principal suggestions for improvement: The new teachers could improve in classroom management, differentiation of instruction, and collaboration with colleagues. Regarding management, administrators considered managing behaviors as separate from creating a warm and caring classroom community. Specifically, they saw a need for improvement in completers' skills in addressing noncompliant behaviors. Administrators' responses to questions about completers' impact on student learning praised completers' ability to increase student learning, use technology effectively, and address the needs of diverse learners. They articulated a need for improving completer skills with differentiation of instruction as a general best practice in classrooms. Principals appeared to consider teacher use of technology both as a tool for pedagogical work with students and as a professional tool for preparing materials, collaborating with colleagues, and managing student data. This may account in part for the discrepancy with teachers' own perceptions about their abilities with technology and observed use of technology by faculty observers. The final question asked the administrators about completers' skills and their professional dispositions. The theme that emerged from the administrators' responses to this question indicated the completers were able to build safe and respectful learning environments. Administrators appeared to distinguish between a teacher's ability to build a safe and respectful environment, for which our completers were praised, and their skills in addressing behavioral issues in the classroom, which was identified as a possible area of continued growth.

DISCUSSION

From the 2015 state satisfaction survey over 80% of teachers reported that they were well prepared in all four InTASC areas. Principals agreed. Data from the 2016 survey suggested that both teachers and principals were less satisfied with program preparation. Response scales with more intermediate points may have tempered more positive responses (Kieruj & Moors, 2010).

The teacher pre/post assessment learning gains of about 40% were typical of other studies of learning gains. Waggoner et al. (2015), using learning gain results from 19,000 students in teacher candidate classrooms, showed an overall learning gain percent during the final program semester clinical experience of 40.26. In this study, when compared by subcategory, no statistically significant differences appeared by gender or ethnicity. Talented and gifted students showed statistically significant gains over English language learners, students with 504 Plans, and students who had no identified learning needs. In general, evidence showed that teachers were meeting the needs of all students. Larger gains for talented and gifted students had not appeared in parallel studies done on teacher candidates using similar analysis strategies (Waggoner et al., 2015). A possible explanation for this is that teachers' assessments were better designed than those they used during clinical experiences avoiding ceiling effects that may have constrained growth in scores among talented and gifted students.

Comparison of the learning gains in classrooms for teachers when they were teacher candidates to learning gains that were computed from their units of instruction as teachers were similar from year to year except for teachers in 2014 whose scores were lower than those during their student teaching experience. Although assessment strategies early-career teachers used were not verifiable, in most years the overall differences were small suggesting that instructional strategies learned as teacher candidates may have carried over into their work as teachers.

From the survey that each teacher's principal completed during the interview visit, principals gave teachers high scores in all areas. Principals observed that teachers were demonstrating characteristics that defined our programs. There were no observable differences between elementary and secondary principal responses or overall by year. Scores were somewhat lower in the area of knowledge of learners, which were reinforced by some principals suggesting differentiation of instruction as an area for improvement.

The qualitative analysis of notes from teacher observations demonstrated the use of instructional time as a concern. More specifically, what was frequently coded in this category were inefficiencies in transitions between instructional activities. Observations also revealed that teachers' use of higher order questions during instruction was limited; opportunities to probe basic student responses and access higher order thinking were often missed. Problems related to teacher questioning strategies have been reviewed repeatedly. Gayle, Preiss, and Allen (2009) summarize 50 years of literature related to this issue, emphasizing the positive impact of effective questioning.

Observed strengths included forming positive learning environments, diversity in formative assessment strategies, and curriculum content that was appropriately aligned with instruction. Technology use for instruction was observed both as a strength and an area for improvement; while teachers were consistently using technology both as a teaching and administrative tool, the need to refine those skills was noted by observers in several observations. Qualitative analysis of principal interviews reinforced that teachers were building respectful learning environments but pointed to classroom management, specifically addressing behavioral issues, as an area for continued growth.

Using the Data for Program Improvement

In order to ensure that our teacher preparation program continues to graduate excellent teachers, faculty members used data from the multiple measures of completer efficacy when setting goals for next steps for the teacher preparation program's continuous improvement efforts. Data were reviewed by a school of education assessment committee to identify areas for improvement. From the case studies the committee identified a need to focus on transition times and the use of higher-order questioning from the classroom observation data, differentiation of instruction from the principal data, and review of instruction around developing unit summative assessments based on the pretest/posttest data.

The committee suggested to the full faculty that discussion around transition times be reinforced in methods classes. University supervisors were told of transition time as a potential weakness and they focused on the sections of the formative clinical experience evaluation that attended to this issue. The committee also suggested that a follow-up question around managing transitions be added to the principal interview protocol for future iterations of the interviews. Methods classes were also targeted for enhancing instruction around probing initial student responses to encourage and develop higher order critical thinking skills. Supervisors were already evaluating this skill on a formal lesson observation instrument, and they were tasked with highlighting opportunities for its use with preservice candidates. In terms of differentiation of instruction, the committee reviewed program instruction around formative assessments and suggested that instructors show more examples of linking pedagogical choices to pre-assessment of students including adapting and modifying objectives as needed to meet the needs of all students. We added a differentiation module to the curriculum for our master's level initial licensure candidates. University supervisors began to look more closely at unit-of-instruction plans to help teacher candidates identify opportunities to apply effective formative assessment strategies and then guide them in interpreting the results to inform their teaching.

The committee added a focused review of clinical experience evaluations to target evidence that teacher candidates were effective in identifying

individual learning needs. As a result of this review, a new clinical observation (Kaplan, Brownstein, & Graham-Day, 2017) and reporting instrument piloted in the fall of 2017 and implemented for all teacher candidates
in 2018 provides specific "look-fors" around the identification of student
learning needs to enhance the quality of feedback to the preservice candidate. As a third effort, the committee that included one of the instructors
of assessment classes discussed ways teacher candidates could improve summative assessments of units of instruction. These were communicated to
university supervisors for use during planning sessions with teacher candidates and will be reinforced during assessment methodology courses. The
committee also added to the plan a more focused review of learning gain
data to assess improvement in this area. In the State of Oregon, student
testing data are not shared with preparation programs. In fact, teacher collective bargaining contracts assure that testing data associated with a particular teacher will not be made publicly available. These restrictions limit
our ability to understand student achievement within our graduates' classrooms. This requires a continuous attention to innovation around measuring student learning.

Based on faculty discussion of improvement strategies, the faculty saw a
need for better communication with university supervisors and cooperating teachers, in general. The two faculty who work most closely with these
groups added discussion of observed teacher weakness to the twice-yearly
group meetings of clinical experience supervisors.

The second use of the case study data is to provide evidence to external
audiences that teachers from our programs are helping P–12 learners suc-
ceed. Of equal importance to the data that we gather from the case studies
is that we have systematized working with teachers and their supervisors
after the teachers have graduated from our programs. Results from satisfaction surveys administered by the state, assessment of student learning in
teacher classrooms, and data from discussions with teachers and supervisors are used to represent our teacher graduates' success when data from
standardized assessment of P–12 student learning are not available. This
is a reporting function, and the data available make a positive case for our
teachers as they move into early careers.

Limitations

Continuous improvement applies not only to our curriculum but also to
our processes for monitoring our impact. We do not contend that what we
did fits the classic definitions of *valid* and *reliable*. What we did was attempt
to improve the quality of data that we gathered on our graduates' impact
on learners. There is no one method to understand the success of new

teachers. Nor can we expect whatever method is used to be perfect the first time it is implemented.

Our graduates work in diverse educational settings across public, private, and charter schools. School districts, schools, and even programs within schools can mandate pedagogies or practices to be used, and graduates must adhere to these. Results from surveys, observations, and interviews must therefore be considered within the context of individual graduates and the expectations put upon them in their teaching positions.

CONCLUSION

The implications of this ongoing case study analysis on the effectiveness of our preparation program, on the impact of our graduates on P–12 students, and on our program's continuous improvement initiative are many; however, three stand out.

Beyond the demands of accreditation, data collected in this study, upon consideration by faculty, has instigated immediate changes to existing courses to address perceived and observed areas of weakness among our graduates. These changes included, but are not limited to, additional or revised course content and an increased focus by university supervisors on identified areas of weakness during clinical support and supervision.

Second, degree program requirements must be reassessed to ensure that students have access to instruction directly related to areas of weakness and that such instruction can occur across program offerings where needed. This reassessment applies to all courses associated with clinical practice.

Third, we need to continue to work diligently at identifying valid and reliable sources of data that can account for the incredible academic, social, and emotional complexity that exist in P–12 classrooms. Our decisions need to be data-informed, so it is critical that the data upon which decisions are made are valid, reliable, and confirmed through multiple measures.

This case study model was designed to be improved continually. The individual elements of the model were reviewed each time they were used. We have implemented strategies to try to improve response rates to satisfaction surveys. We reviewed the observation protocols and have implemented a new protocol for both teacher candidates and teachers that has been externally validated. We are revising the questions on the principal survey to reflect changes in our curriculum. We are beginning to explore electronic tools for gathering interview data. We are experimenting with strategies to reduce the resource load on the School of Education for gathering these teacher data.

Faculty members in schools of education often find assessment of programs as something peripheral to the primary work of preparing quality teachers. Adopting existing approaches can reduce the initial work necessary to develop program assessment. Whatever strategies are adopted, teacher preparation programs will be well served to find effective ways to help accreditors and the public understand the impact of the work we do. The approach that we described matches the suggestions most recently from CAEP and from NCATE before it. What makes the set of strategies unique is that we have designed a process for improving the model into the work from the beginning.

REFERENCES

Amrein-Beardsley, A. (2008). Methodological concerns about the education value-added assessment system. *Educational Researcher, 37*(2), 65–75.

Cochran-Smith, M., Piazza, P., & Power, C. (2013). The politics of accountability: Assessing teacher education in the united states. *Educational Forum, 77*(1), 6–27.

Coggshall, J. G., Bivona, L., & Reschly, D. J. (2012). *Evaluating the effectiveness of teacher preparation programs for support and accountability.* Washington, DC: National Comprehensive Center for Teacher Quality.

Cohen, D. K., & Mehta, J. D. (2017). Why reform sometimes succeeds: Understanding the conditions that produce reforms that last. *American Educational Research Journal, 54*(4), 644–690.

Council for the Accreditation of Educator Preparation. (2013). *CAEP 2013 standards for accreditation of educator preparation.* Retrieved from http://www.caepnet.org

Council for the Accreditation of Educator Preparation. (2015). *CAEP evidence guide.* Retrieved from http://www.caepnet.org

Council of Chief State School Officers. (2011). *Interstate Teacher Assessment and Support Consortium (InTASC) Model core teaching standards: A resource for state dialogue.* Washington, DC: Author.

Creswell, J. W. (2017). *Qualitative inquiry and research design: Choosing among five approaches* (4th ed.). Thousand Oaks, CA: SAGE.

Darling-Hammond, L. (2000). Reforming teacher preparation and licensing: Debating the evidence. *Teachers College Record, 102*(1), 28–56.

Darling-Hammond, L. (2006). Assessing teacher education: The usefulness of multiple measures for assessing program outcomes. *Journal of Teacher Education, 57*(2), 120–138.

Darling-Hammond, L. (2009). Recognizing and enhancing teacher effectiveness. *The International Journal of Educational and Psychological Assessment, 3*(1), 1–24.

Darling-Hammond, L. (2010). Evaluating teacher effectiveness: How teacher performance assessments can measure and improve teaching. Washington, DC: Center for American Progress.

Darling-Hammond, L. (2015). Can value added add value to teacher evaluation? *Educational Researcher, 44*(2), 132–137.

Darling-Hammond, L. (2017). Education policy moving forward: Power and progress at the state level. *Voices in Urban Education, 45.* Retrieved from ERIC database. (EJ1137645)

Gayle, B. M., Preiss, R. W., & Allen, M. (2009). How effective are teacher-initiated classroom questions in enhancing student learning? In B. M. Gayle, R. W. Preiss, & M. Allen (Eds.), *Communication and instructional processes: Advances through meta-analysis* (pp. 279–293). Mahwah, NJ: Erlbaum.

Ginsberg, R., & Kingston, N. (2014). Caught in a vice: Facing teacher preparation in an era of accountability. *Teachers College Record, 116,* 1–48.

Glaser, B. G., & Strauss, A. L. (1967). *The discovery of grounded theory: Strategies for qualitative research.* Chicago, IL: Aldine.

Guarino, C. M., Reckase, M. D., & Wooldridge, J. M. (2014). *Can value-added measures of teacher performance be trusted?* Education Finance and Policy, 10(1), 117–156.

Hamel, F. L., & Mertz, C. (2005). Reframing accountability: A preservice program wrestles with mandated reform. *Journal of Teacher Education, 56*(2), 157–167.

Harris, L. B., Salzman, S., Frantz, A., Newsome, J., & Martin, M. (2000, February). *Using accountability measures in the preparation of preservice teachers to make a difference in the learning of all students.* Paper presented at the Annual Meeting of the American Association of Colleges for Teacher Education, Chicago, IL. Retrieved from ERIC database. (ED440926)

Indiana Department of Education. (2018). *Principal survey.* Retrieved from https://www.doe.in.gov/licensing/principal-survey

Kagan, D. M. (1992). Professional growth among preservice and beginning teachers. *Review of Educational Research, 62*(2), 129–169.

Kaplan, C. S., Brownstein, E. M., & Graham-Day, K. J. (2017). One for all and all for one: Multi-university collaboration to meet accreditation requirements. *SAGE Open: Issues in educator accreditation: Just in time topics for educator preparation programs in the United States, 7*(1), 2158244016687610.

Kieruj, N. D., & Moors, G. (2010). Variations in response style behavior by response scale format in attitude research. *International Journal of Public Opinion Research, 22*(3), 320–342.

Lasley, T. J., II, Siedentop, D., & Yinger, R. (2006). A systematic approach to enhancing teacher quality: The Ohio model. *Journal of Teacher Education, 57*(1), 13–21.

Li, Y. Y. (2017). Processes and dynamics behind whole-school reform. *American Educational Research Journal, 54*(2), 279–324.

Oregon Association of Colleges for Teacher Education. (2014). *Survey of PK–12 school administrators.* Retrieved from https://education.oregonstate.edu/sites/education.oregonstate.edu/files/m3_state_employer_report_2014.pdf

Popham, W. J. (2013). *Evaluating America's teachers: Mission impossible?* Thousand Oaks, CA: Corwin.

Reusser, J., Butler, L., Symonds, M., Vetter, R., & Wall, T. J. (2007). An assessment system for teacher education program quality improvement. *The International Journal of Educational Management, 21*(2), 105–113.

Russell, J. L., Meredith, J., Childs, J., Stein, M. K., & Prine, D. W. (2015). Designing inter-organizational networks to implement education reform: An analysis of state Race to the Top applications. *Educational Evaluation and Policy Analysis, 37*(1), 92–112.

Texas Education Agency. (2018a). *Important changes to principal surveys to evaluate Texas educator preparation programs.* Retrieved from https://tea.texas.gov/About_

TEA/News_and_Multimedia/Correspondence/TAA_Letters/Important _Changes_to_Principal_Surveys_to_Evaluate_Texas_Educator_Preparation_ Programs

Texas Education Agency. (2018b). *Educator program candidate exit survey.* Retrieved from http://www.pvamu.edu/wp-content/uploads/sites/29/2013/08/Educator_Preparation_Program_Candidate_Exit_Survey_2012_21.pdf

von Hippel, P. T., & Bellows, L. (2018). How much does teacher quality vary across teacher preparation programs?: Reanalysis from six states. *Economics in Education Review, 64,* 298–312.

Waggoner, J., Carroll, J. B., Merk, H., & Weitzel, B. N. (2015). Critics and critical analysis: Lessons from 19,000 P–12 students in teacher candidate classrooms. *Teacher Education Quarterly, 42*(1), 97–108.

Wideen, M., Mayer-Smith, J., & Moon, B. (1998). A critical analysis of the research on learning to teach: Making the case for an ecological perspective on inquiry. *Review of Educational Research, 68*(2), 130–178.

Wineburg, M. S. (2006). Evidence in teacher preparation: Establishing a framework for accountability. *Journal of Teacher Education, 57*(1), 51–64.

CHAPTER 4

EDUCATING EFFECTIVE SCIENCE TEACHERS

Preparing and Following Teachers Into the Field

Elizabeth B. Lewis
University of Nebraska-Lincoln

Ana M. Rivero
Seattle University

Aaron A. Musson
Omaha Public Schools

Lyrica L. Lucas
University of Nebraska-Lincoln

Amy Tankersley
University of Nebraska-Lincoln

Brandon Helding
Boulder Learning, Inc.

Linking Teacher Preparation Program Design and Implementation to Outcomes for Teachers and Students, pages 87–129
Copyright © 2020 by Information Age Publishing
All rights of reproduction in any form reserved.

The landscape of teacher preparation is complex and from a research perspective presents itself as a multilevel, multivariable puzzle. For decades, federal and state policymakers, teacher education institutions, educational researchers, school districts, administrators, and other stakeholders have tried to determine and measure the key, malleable factors that result in effective teaching. In a still-referenced vision of teacher preparation, Bransford, Darling-Hammond, and LePage (2007) highlighted three areas of skills, knowledge, and dispositions important for teaching effectiveness:

> (a) knowledge of learners and how they learn and develop within social contexts; (b) conceptions of curriculum content and goals: an understanding of the subject matter and skills to be taught in light of the social purpose of education; and (c) an understanding of teaching given the content and learners to be taught, as informed by assessment and supported by classroom environments. (p. 10)

In the United States, due to a lack of standardization, a large variety of approaches to teacher education have been developed and are overseen by a similarly wide range of state certification policies that affect over 2,100 teacher preparation programs (TPPs; National Commission on Teaching and America's Future, 2016). Through all the research that has been conducted on teacher preparation, no one factor can independently account for observed variability in teacher effectiveness; however, rarely has research been conducted systematically to better inform optimal TPP designs. To address the knowledge gap, Cochran-Smith and Villegas (2016) encourage educational researchers to produce studies that examine "the impact and implications of particular mixes of teacher characteristics, school contexts, and program features" (p. 458). Such studies are especially needed in science education, specifically of TPPs that focus on practicing teaching and learning science using scientific practices (i.e., collecting and analyzing data, carrying out investigations), collaborative work, or a project-based approach to understand science content (van Driel, Berry, & Meirink, 2014; Windschitl & Stroupe, 2017). Due to space constraints we also refer readers to chapters on science teacher preparation (Loughran, 2014) and teacher knowledge (van Driel et al., 2014) for more comprehensive reviews.

The goal of the *Next Generation Science Standards* (NGSS; NGSS Lead States, 2013) is to educate K–12 students to be scientifically literate citizens, as well as encourage more students to pursue science, technology, engineering, and mathematics (STEM) careers to meet the national call for a more highly qualified workforce. This national vision has been outlined in such reports as *Before It's Too Late* (National Commission on Mathematics and Science Teaching for the 21st Century, 2000) in which there was an urgent call for better prepared science and math teachers and systematic professional development to reform K–12 mathematics and science education.

In a review chapter, Bianchini (2012) summarized what researchers have learned about the views, experiences, and classroom practices of beginning science teachers. She found that little was known about the science teaching induction period and recommended that more studies follow beginning science teachers from preservice teacher education into classroom practice, and trace connections, or lack thereof, across induction training, beginning teachers' classroom practices, and student learning. Our research contributes to designing science TPPs to prepare teachers who can provide engaging, reform-based, learning opportunities for diverse students.

This chapter focuses on: (a) our development of a research-based, graduate-level science TPP for teachers with a degree in science; (b) an analysis of teachers' subject matter knowledge (SMK) as it relates to their subsequent use of inquiry-based instruction; and (c) results of a longitudinal study of beginning science teachers who graduated from a master's level TPP in comparison with the instructional practices of science teachers prepared through a traditional undergraduate program. We offer what we consider to be a typical case of an undergraduate and less typical case of a graduate science teacher preparation program that occur at a large, land-grant, 4-year state university in a Great Plains state in the United States. The undergraduate and graduate programs have some overlapping coursework and clinical experiences, but provided different entry points, depth of coursework, culminating degrees, and rates of completion.

CONCEPTUAL FRAMEWORK AND BACKGROUND LITERATURE

Rationale for Study

There are few comprehensive studies of beginning science teachers that correlate aspects of teacher preparation programs with enacted teaching practices (NRC, 2010). Our work begins to address this research gap. The two TPPs in the study focused on developing preservice teachers' inquiry-based science instruction, classroom discourse, knowledge of student diversity, and curriculum development in accordance with reform-based science education standards and practices. We compare the undergraduate program to the graduate program, which is more rigorous in terms of requiring more science and more education coursework. We explore how program factors, including subject matter knowledge and pedagogical knowledge, affected beginning science teachers' instruction. By studying how individual aspects of teacher qualifications and teaching interact, we can better understand how to prepare teacher candidates during the induction period to reduce attrition and accelerate professional growth.

Conceptual Framework

We present our study's conceptual framework in Figure 4.1. The key aspects of the TPPs are grouped by SMK, pedagogical knowledge, and knowledge of learners. We consider SMK to be a mediating variable along with teachers' internal factors that include, but are not limited to, teacher self-efficacy, beliefs, and attitudes. The learning in the TPPs is then mediated by these factors, resulting in more or less reformed-based instruction. We make a distinction between the broader classification of *reform-based teaching* and *inquiry-based instructional practices*, which are a particular set of desired scientific practices that science teachers should strive to include in science lessons. We measured teachers' SMK, self-efficacy, and beliefs about reform-based teaching; in this chapter we report mainly on the relationship between SMK, the effect of having completed an undergraduate or graduate science TPP, and beginning science teachers' implementation of inquiry-based science lessons. We organize our literature review in the same way in the sections that follow.

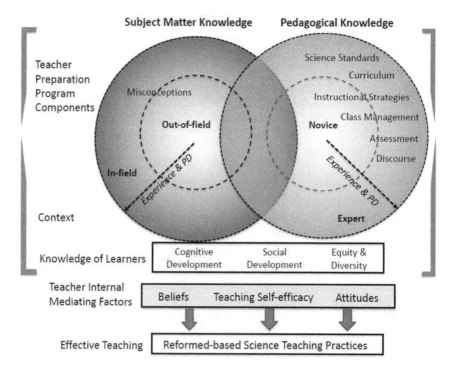

Figure 4.1   Conceptual framework of teacher preparation program and reformed-based science teaching practices.

Teachers' Subject Matter Knowledge and Misconceptions in Science

With insufficient SMK, teachers may have a weak foundation for teaching science (Yip, 1998). Moreover, weak SMK might prevent teachers, especially novice teachers, from using inquiry-based teaching methods (Roehrig & Luft, 2004). This is a critical issue for teachers who are assigned to teach out-of-field in a subject area in which they are not certified (e.g., teaching chemistry when only certified for biology). Strong SMK may help teachers to take more risks in their instructional strategies (Nehm & Ridgeway, 2011; Treagust, 2010) and trust themselves to facilitate students' learning using scientific practices and to elicit students' thinking.

A critical role of science teachers in the development of their students' scientific literacy is to address students' common misconceptions. Insufficient SMK and teachers' failure to understand scientific theories and concepts may result in the spread of misconceptions. Misconceptions are "scientifically incorrect ideas that are persistent and commonly held" (Leonard, Kalinowski, & Andrews, 2014, p. 180). They are considered obstacles to new learning, difficult to change, and persist over time (Hamza & Wickman, 2008). To address students' misconceptions, teachers must identify those misconceptions and create proper remediation that confronts and corrects them (Tekkaya, 2002). While there are few studies about teachers' misconceptions and minimum SMK to teach science, science education researchers agree that misconceptions do reflect insufficient SMK for teaching (Sadler & Sonnert, 2016).

Therefore, TPPs should foster strong conceptual understanding by requiring a set of subject matter courses that strongly align with the teaching competencies that future teachers will be required to teach. Otherwise, teacher educators risk endorsing teachers with subject-specific misconceptions that could be transferred to students through overgeneralizations, inadvertent poor planning and execution of lessons that affects students' long-term learning (Hashweh, 2002; Kikas, 2004; Murphy, 2005; Özmen, 2010). Since teachers play a crucial role in addressing misconceptions, the quality of science teacher preparation could characterize the effectiveness of future science instruction (McDermott, 1990). In summary, these few studies suggest that strong SMK is likely to facilitate science teachers' use of inquiry-based teaching practices and reduce teachers' and students' misconceptions.

Science Teachers' Pedagogical Knowledge and Curricular Choices

Science is considered an indispensable part of K–12 curriculum, especially with the introduction of the *National Science Education Standards* in the mid-1990s (NRC, 1996). Science education supports the development of the next generation of scientists, engineers, and innovators, and is also important for educating informed citizens in a world influenced by technology, scientific values, and ideas (Osborne, 2007). Scientifically literate citizens should be able to:

- understand, use, and interpret scientific explanations of the natural world;
- generate and evaluate scientific evidence and explanations;
- understand the nature and development of scientific knowledge; and
- participate productively in scientific practices and discourse (NRC, 2012, p. 251).

Reform-based science educators strive to construct inquiry-based curricula that promote these principles to develop students' scientific literacy and higher-order thinking skills. Teachers' curricular choices control students' opportunities to learn science. While the depth of science content in lessons varies, it should be sufficiently rigorous to challenge all students.

Teaching science through inquiry-based instruction. Based upon social constructivist theories of learning, the science education community has concluded that *teaching science as inquiry* or inquiry-based instruction is the most effective method for teaching science (Crawford, 2014; Osborne, 2014). In the *Next Generation Science Standards* (NGSS), inquiry is broken into *scientific practices* (e.g., planning and carrying out investigations, analyzing and interpreting data, and arguing from evidence; NGSS Lead States, 2013). Inquiry-based instruction is important for 21st century learning and contributes to developing students' skills such as argumentation, creativity, critical thinking, and decision-making. Unfortunately, the *2012 National Survey of Science and Mathematics Education* (Banilower, Trygstad, & Smith, 2015) revealed low use of inquiry-based practices among science teachers.

Inquiry-aligned assessment practices. Effective teaching starts with planning (Wiggins, 1998) and determining what students already know about a topic by assessing prior knowledge (Bell & Cowie, 2001). Assessment of prior knowledge exposes misconceptions that teachers should address during instruction. Bell and Cowie (2001) identifed teacher noticing and action in response to assessment data as critical elements of formative assessment. Specifically, formative assessment requires teachers to adapt instruction to students' needs based on the evidence collected. Therefore, strong SMK and a rich pedagogical tool box supports adaptive instruction by enabling teachers to find alternative ways to accomplish learning objectives.

Greater teaching experience can yield stronger understanding of how students learn and what is challenging for students to learn. A lack of teaching experience can be balanced with strong SMK and exemplary internship mentoring during the TPP. Therefore, as we certify new teachers, we need to ensure that they have sufficient SMK and pedagogical knowledge to develop high self-efficacy with using assessment during inquiry-based science instruction.

Knowledge of Students: Equity and Diversity Issues

Inquiry-based instruction can also be an instrument of social justice in teaching diverse students; inquiry-based curricula has been shown to support students with special needs as well as English language learners (Lee & Luykx, 2007; McGinnis & Stefanich, 2007). By employing scientific practices within experiential learning-focused curricular activities, teachers can encourage all students to engage in scientific explanations, reasoning, and construction of new knowledge, through understanding of different social meanings and using multiple realities (Calabrese-Barton, 1998; Windschitl, Thompson, Braaten, & Stroupe, 2012). Science teachers should facilitate and model a scientific classroom discourse community in which all perspectives and experiences are valued in the process of scientific meaning making (Lewis, Baker, Bueno Watts, & van der Hoeven Kraft, 2016).

Mediating Factors That Support or Inhibit Reform-Based Science Teaching

Several internal factors have been shown to be mediating factors in either supporting or inhibiting change in teachers' instructional practices. Some of these include self-efficacy, attitudes, and beliefs about reform-based practices in science education that have been included in national standards documents (i.e., NGSS).

Teacher self-efficacy.   Teachers' self-efficacy and inquiry-based instruction seem to have a strong relationship. For example, high levels of teacher self-efficacy have long been shown to be an indicator of more innovative teaching (Guskey, 1988) and to be related to higher student achievement (Evans, 2011). Lakshmanan, Heath, Perlmutter, and Elder (2011) found a positive correlation between the amount of growth in self-efficacy and the extent to which inquiry-based instruction was implemented by elementary and middle-school science teachers. Therefore, teachers who have high self-efficacy are more likely to try new teaching strategies, provide opportunities for students to engage in scientific practices, and address students' misconceptions. However, it is important to note that sometimes teachers have conflicting, or competing belief sets (Crawford, 2007), or experience school culture and external pressures (McGinnis, Parker, & Graeber, 2004) that can disrupt the positive relationship between self-efficacy and inquiry-based science instruction. Therefore, it is even more important in such cases that teachers have strong SMK so that they can be sufficiently self-efficacious to be critical of curricular and instructional mandates.

Attitudes and beliefs about science teaching and learning.   Problematically, inquiry-based instruction that supports authentic learning is not common in secondary science classrooms. Science teachers often rely on direct instruction, teacher-centered methods, and verification lab activities over inquiry-based instruction (Crawford, 2014). Many new teachers have had little experience with learning through inquiry-based instructional approaches during their own secondary school experiences but were still successful in science

(Windschitl & Stroupe, 2017). Thus, TPPs are challenged to prepare science teachers to think beyond their own experiences to embrace using inquiry-based pedagogical strategies by changing their preconceived attitudes and beliefs about teaching and learning science. While many programs use constructivist strategies and theories in teaching methods courses, these may be insufficient to induce conceptual change in preservice science teachers with strong beliefs about a teacher-centered classroom (Feldman, 2000). An excellent review of science teachers' attitudes and beliefs (Jones & Leagon, 2014) can be found in the most recent volume of the *Handbook of Research on Science Education* (Lederman & Abell, 2014).

Beginning Science Teachers' Instructional Practices

Upon graduation from a TPP, science teachers should have sufficient SMK, pedagogical knowledge, and knowledge of students to implement a wide range of science curriculum (NRC, 2010). As Hill, Rowan, and Ball (2005) indicated, teachers highly proficient in a subject will help others learn that subject "only if they are able to use their own knowledge to perform the tasks they must enact as teachers" (p. 376). That is, science teachers' strong SMK facilitates understanding content and choosing effective strategies to support student learning. TPPs should prepare science teachers to use their SMK to develop inquiry-based instruction to connect students' prior knowledge and everyday experiences with science content.

However, despite completing reform-based TPPs, beginning secondary science teachers often tend to revert to more traditional educational practices during their first years as teachers (Russell & Martin, 2014). For example, beginning teachers often lack the ability to demonstrate the connection between science and everyday life (Bianchini, 2012) or identify big ideas or substantive relationships between scientific concepts to help students to understand natural phenomena (Windschitl et al., 2012). Inquiry-based instruction requires beginning science teachers to reflect on instructional practices, strategies, and routines in order to mature and transform into effective professionals (Duffy, Miller, Parsons, & Meloth, 2009). Reflection and metacognition help novice teachers to plan, monitor, and assess their science teaching experiences, improve inquiry-based teaching practices, and increase their self-efficacy. Moreover, science teachers should learn adaptability, social skills, non-routine problem-solving skills, self-development, and systems thinking (Treagust & Tsui, 2014) to develop, for example, formative assessment strategies. Therefore, both preparation and induction phases should include opportunities for teachers to reflect upon their development as teachers and learn from their experience. Experience should support novice teachers to develop a greater capacity for implementing lesson plans effectively, design better student-centered strategies, enact inquiry-based instruction, and be more responsive to student needs (Bianchini, 2012). Nonetheless, how teachers learn from experience remains poorly understood in science education (Russell & Martin, 2014) and more work should be done to understand the interaction between beginning teachers' knowledge, reflection, practices, and professional growth.

TEACHER PREPARATION PROGRAM STUDY CONTEXT

Our longitudinal study focused on two secondary science teacher programs, one at the undergraduate level and one at the graduate level, at the University of Nebraska-Lincoln (UNL), a large Midwestern, land-grant, 4-year state university. For the graduate-level TPP, we recruited teacher candidates who had earned at least a bachelor's degree in a scientific field, thus meeting a key element of the federal definition of a "highly-qualified" teacher. This Master of Arts in teaching (MAT) program is a 14-month, 42-credit hour program that provides a pathway for recent science graduates and practicing scientists to become science teachers. MAT students begin as a cohort in May and are expected to graduate in August of the following year. Table 4.1 summarizes program coursework and how it differs from the traditional undergraduate program that did not require an undergraduate

TABLE 4.1 Comparison of Undergraduate and MAT Teacher Education Programs

Program	Undergraduate	Master of Arts
Science Coursework	**Prior and concurrent to acceptance:** Sufficient science coursework for Nebraska secondary science teaching endorsement (~24 credit hours on one area with another 12 hours among other three areas).	**Prior to Acceptance:** Undergraduate major in one area of science; some MA students have graduate-level science coursework or advanced degree.
Education Coursework	**Pre-professional education coursework** (including the common coursework with *): Foundations of Education; Adolescent Development & Practicum (13 credit hours)	**MAT coursework:** History and Nature of Science (Cohorts 1–2 only); Reading in the Content Areas (Cohort 3 and onward); Teaching ELLs in the Content Area; Intro to Educational Research; Curriculum Theory; Teacher Action Research Project
Common Coursework	Accommodating Exceptional Learners Adolescent Development* Science Teaching Methods (two classes, each with a practicum experience) Multicultural Education* or Pluralistic Society	
Resulting Degree	BA Secondary Science Education	MA with emphasis in science teaching

degree in science (Lewis, Musson, & Lu, 2014). The MAT program has coursework required for teacher certification, graduate-level courses that include a capstone action research project, and extensive (650 hours or more) clinical experiences.

Student Diversity and Science Achievement

On an annual basis, through both programs, UNL educates 35–40% of Nebraska's newly certified secondary science teachers. Like other largely rural states, Nebraska has many small school districts in small population centers classified as rural (79.5%) and small towns (15.6%) with high levels of local control. Most teachers in our MAT program were supported by National Science Foundation Noyce stipends that required them to teach in a high-need school district for 2 years and most of them took teaching positions in high-need schools.

While Nebraska K–12 teachers are overwhelmingly White, female, and middle class, their students are more ethnically diverse with higher rates of poverty. A recent National Assessment of Educational Progress (NAEP) report (U.S. Department of Education [ED], Institute of Education Sciences [IES], 2015)[1] indicated that 43% of Nebraska youth qualify for free or reduced lunch (FRL), which is similar to the national average; nationwide, about half of all children qualify for FRL. In 2015, on the NAEP science test, Nebraska eighth-grade students performed slightly above average with a score of 160, as compared to the national average score of 153. There were score gaps between White students and Black (–29 points) and Hispanic students (–23 points), as well as a gap between students who qualified for FRL (–21 points) and those who did not (ED, IES, 2015).

Science Content Knowledge

The UNL's TPP candidates can be grouped into three categories: (a) undergraduates seeking a BS degree in secondary science education, (b) recent content-area BS graduates who start the MAT program upon completion of a BS in an area of science, and (c) science professionals who are changing careers to become teachers and enroll in the MAT program. Both undergraduate and graduate programs meet the state's minimum endorsement requirements (Table 4.2).

The undergraduate program results in a major in secondary science education with 24 credit hours in one area of science. In addition to the courses in the chosen main science area, each endorsement area requires

TABLE 4.2 Teaching Qualifications
Nebraska State Secondary Science Teacher Endorsements
• A single-subject endorsement requires 24 credit hours as a minimum in 1 of 4 core science areas (biology, chemistry, physics, or earth and space science) • Many Nebraska science teachers apply for a "broad field science endorsement," which allows science teachers to teach any area of science, but only requires a minimum of 12[a] credit hours in each of the 4 areas to do so.
NSF/Federal Definition of "Highly qualified" Teacher
• NSF Noyce/Federal guidelines define "highly qualified" science teachers as having an undergraduate major in the content area that they teach. This could be a hybrid of science and education coursework (i.e., a secondary science education major with teaching credential) instead of an undergraduate science degree.

[a] Effective 2012

coursework in supporting sciences. For example, teacher candidates seeking a biology endorsement are also required to take chemistry, Earth and space science, and physics courses, totaling a minimum of 12 credit hours.

Beyond Mandated Teacher Certification Coursework: MAT Program

In response to the need for more highly qualified teachers prepared to teach diverse learners, we designed a rigorous MAT program that recruited individuals with at least an undergraduate degree in science. This 42 credit-hour program could then focus on education coursework and pedagogy, including courses in teaching English language learners and the nature of science. At the third cohort, we replaced the nature of science course with a course in reading in the content areas. MAT teacher candidates were also required to complete a teacher action research project and coursework in curriculum theory and educational research. Conversely, undergraduate teacher candidates only needed to take the minimum coursework required by the state (Table 4.2).

Common Requirements of the Teacher Preparation Programs

In preparing teachers through both programs, we were mindful of the Interstate Teacher Assessment and Support Consortium (InTASC) standards (CCSSO, 2011), as well as the National Council for the Accreditation of Teacher Education (NCATE) standards (NCATE, 2008).[2] We also followed the National Science Teacher Association (NSTA) science teacher preparation standards (Veal & Allen, 2014).

Science Teaching Standards and Teaching Methods Coursework

The UNL's two science teaching methods classes have aligned curriculum development and lesson planning with the national framework for K–12 science education (NRC, 2012) and resulting *Next Generation Science Standards* (NRC, 2013), which Nebraska adapted as its state science standards in September 2017. Both TPP programs were designed to emphasize constructivist teaching principles, such as inquiry and active learning approaches. The MAT program was aligned with the priorities of two National Science Foundation (NSF) Robert Noyce Teacher Scholarship program grants that provided stipends for preservice science teachers with strong content knowledge (i.e., had an undergraduate degree in science). The NSF required teacher candidates with Noyce stipends to complete a 2-year service requirement by teaching in high-need schools following graduation.

Science-specific pedagogy is emphasized in two semester-long teaching methods courses, and preservice teachers design lesson plans, unit plans, and a year-long plan throughout the three-semester internship and student teaching seminar. Specific science teacher preparation standards are addressed with assignments to build a conceptual bridge between the theoretical basis and instructional strategies taught in the methods course and practical experiences gained in the internship. During the first methods course, teacher interns: (a) question and analyze specific components of their teaching with a lesson study (Lewis, 1995); (b) begin lesson- and unit-level planning and investigate curricular construction within their discipline; (c) develop and teach inquiry-based lessons; (d) interview secondary students about common misconceptions; and (e) complete a science safety course. The second methods course emphasizes scientific discourse practices, educative assessment, and long-term planning. The concurrent internship provides opportunities to experience and explore curricular and instructional decisions by planning and enacting lessons with an experienced teacher. Together, teaching methods courses, internships, and the student teaching seminar form a "central spine" for the science teacher education program.

Clinical Teaching Experiences

Teacher interns complete a three-phase, 650-hour internship in which they assume greater responsibility for teaching from phase to phase. In Phase 1, undergraduate students complete an internship during the spring semester in junior year, and MAT students are in summer school and science camp settings (Table 4.3). Interns co-teach, explore student misconceptions, and interview students about specific science topics. In Phase 2 teacher interns in both programs spend 10 hours per week in formal classroom

TABLE 4.3 Science Teaching Methods, Internship, and Student Teaching Sequence With Additional MAT Focus on Teacher Action Research Project

Phase 1	Phase 2	Phase 3
BS: Spring semester during normal school year. MAT: Summer school, science camp sessions.	BS and MAT placements in fall semester during normal school year and in the same course section.	BS and MAT student teaching placements in spring semester.
5-week, 50 hours	15-week, 150 hours	15-week, 450 hours
Focus: Science safety, students' ideas about science interviews, lesson planning, lesson study, and sketch broad ideas of one curricular unit.	*Focus:* Planning and enacting curriculum and instruction, lesson and unit planning with greater emphasis on formative assessment practices and supporting science discourse. *Teacher Action Research Coursework* (MAT only): MAT teacher candidates learn about different educational research approaches, including teacher action research. Course culminates in writing a teacher action research proposal to do during the student teaching.	*Focus:* Student teachers have an 80% full-time teaching load for the semester: four classes if short periods, and two classes if longer periods in a block schedule is used. *Teacher Action Research Coursework* (MAT only): As student teaching starts the MAT teacher candidates make minor adjustments as necessary to their research plan. They collect data to address their research questions and preliminary analysis.

settings, plan and teach science lessons, conduct a lesson study, and design unit-level curriculum. In Phase 3, interns become student teachers. Student teachers teach two courses, a total of four sections, and have two preparation periods.

Interns are rotated to new cooperating teachers from phase to phase to provide experience with different teaching approaches in settings with diverse student populations, middle and high schools in urban, suburban, and sometimes rural districts, and different endorsement subjects. Teaching interns experience working with students of different abilities, planning and teaching science lessons that include accommodations for students with special needs, developing classroom management skills, generating assessment plans and instruments, and working in professional learning communities. Each teaching internship is unique due to varying settings, cooperating teachers, grade level and science content; however, basic components of the coursework are consistent (Table 4.3).

METHODOLOGY

We used a longitudinal, exploratory, multi-method approach to investigate beginning science teachers' subject matter knowledge, science misconceptions, self-efficacy, and instructional practices in two TPPs. We provide research questions, specific data sources, and methods for each part of the study as follows.

Research Questions

The main research questions we investigated were:

1. What are the common discipline-specific misconceptions of teacher candidates and other undergraduates who take science courses with a range of SMK?
2. What is the minimum amount of SMK needed to avert common science misconceptions in chemistry, physics, and middle-school life science?
3. What is the self-efficacy of beginning science teachers who completed a graduate level preparation program and how does it change during their first 3 years of teaching?
4. To what degree are the instructional practices of science teachers with a range of SMK inquiry-based? How does inquiry-based instruction compare over time among science teachers who completed undergraduate and graduate level preparation programs?

Methods

In the following subsections, we provide descriptions of the data sets and analytic methods used to address the research questions. Sample sizes are presented along with findings for some analyses. We refer readers to other reports (Lewis, Rivero, Lucas, Musson, & Helding, under review; Lewis, Rivero, Lucas, Tankersley, & Helding, 2018) for greater in-depth presentation and discussion of our research projects due to a lack of space here to provide full analytic details.

Subject Matter Knowledge and Misconceptions Methods

Subject matter knowledge was examined through an analysis of Misconceptions-Oriented Standards-Based Assessment Resources for Teachers (MOSART) test scores and transcript analysis. MOSART scores are based on multiple-choice tests that assess students' understanding of science concepts. We used the MOSART chemistry (9–12), physics (9–12), and life science (5–8)[3] tests (Sadler et al., 2010). The preservice teachers in the undergraduate and MAT programs took the tests at the end of their program after student teaching. We obtained participant transcripts and analyzed courses taken,[4] number of credit hours, and GPA earned in the categories of life science, chemistry, physics, and Earth science. We report descriptive statistics with each content area analysis. Using an approach outlined by Miles, Huberman, and Saldaña (2014), for each of the subject area analyses, we divided participants into four categorical groups based on the amount of credit hours taken in each subject (i.e., chemistry, life science, physics): (a) Group 1 = 0–8; (b) Group 2 = 9–16; (c) Group 3 = 17–24; and (d) Group 4 = 25 or more. We determined each group's average test score and compared these with the recommended passing score and tallied items for persistent misconceptions. Finally, we analyzed course transcripts to identify courses commonly taken by participants in each of the four groups.

To identify possible SMK predictors, we regressed participants' GPA and science credit hours on the corresponding MOSART test scores. When examining participants' SMK, we used two primary outcome measures for each content area: (a) MOSART test scores and (b) that same MOSART test score transformed into a pass/fail or binary outcome. The MOSART test developers' recommended cutoff for a passing score is 80%. Thus, we recorded scores equal to or above 80% as passing scores and below as failing scores. We also coded sex to investigate if there were any differences between male and female test takers' performances on the tests.

Teacher Self-Efficacy Methods

We evaluated MAT program graduates at the end of their student teaching (ST, $n = 41$) and each year thereafter (Y1, $n = 24$; Y2, $n = 20$; Y3, $n = 8$). We used the *Teacher Sense of Efficacy Scale* (TSES), a 24-item survey instrument with a 5-point scale developed by Tschannen-Moran and Hoy (2001), to investigate teachers' self-efficacy in three areas: (a) student engagement, (b) classroom management, and (c) instructional strategies. We examined teacher self-efficacy using a multivariate analysis of variance (MANOVA). Our outcome variables were the instrument's three subscales. We used number of years of teaching experience to predict change across the multiple outcome measures.

Longitudinal Study Methods

We conducted a 4-year longitudinal study of five cohorts of master's level science teacher education program graduates (Lewis, Rivero, Musson, Lu, & Lucas, 2016). We coded and analyzed science lessons from student teaching to fifth year post-program to describe teachers' enacted practices, and administered annual surveys of teacher self-efficacy and beliefs about

TABLE 4.4 Number of Lessons by Years of Teaching Experience (2015–2016 and 2016–2017 Data)

Program	Student Teaching	1	2	3	4	5	Total
MAT	28	68	74	81	53	24	328
Undergraduate	32	41	45	23	12	6	159
Total	60	109	119	104	65	30	487

TABLE 4.5 Number of Teachers by Years of Teaching Experience (2015–2016 and 2016–2017 Data)

Program	Student Teaching	1	2	3	4	5	Total
MAT	10	13	11	14	10	4	62
Undergraduate	16	8	9	9	2	1	45
Total	26	21	20	23	12	5	107

reform-based science teaching (Lucas & Lewis, 2017). For the study's second 2 years (academic years 2015–2016 and 2016–2017), we also coded science lessons of a comparison group of teachers from our undergraduate secondary science TPP (Table 4.4). For these 487 lessons (Table 4.5), we coded the lessons using two instruments, the Electronic Quality of Inquiry Protocol (EQUIP) instrument (Marshall, Horton, Smart, & Llewellyn, 2009) and the Discourse in Inquiry Science Classrooms (DiISC; Baker, et al., 2008) to measure the quality of inquiry-based instruction.

RESULTS

Subject Matter Knowledge and Misconceptions by Discipline

In our analysis of inquiry-based practices, we tried to determine how much SMK was necessary for beginning teachers to teach reform-based science lessons. First, we needed to determine teachers' SMK with a range of science coursework and any persistent misconceptions (Research Question #1). Therefore, we analyzed participants' transcript information for common undergraduate science coursework to compare with their scores on the domain-specific science misconceptions tests (MOSART). Based on a conceptual change model, we considered participants' misconceptions as an outcome of the SMK domain. Our premise was that the fewer misconceptions a secondary science teacher held, the better prepared the teacher should be to teach inquiry-based science. We present the results in three sections, one for each of the three disciplines.[5]

Chemistry

To analyze chemistry knowledge, we used a sample of 97 participants, from three groups: (a) preservice MAT teachers ($n = 44$) with at least an undergraduate degree in science, (b) preservice undergraduate secondary science teachers ($n = 31$), and (c) undergraduate students ($n = 22$) pursuing minors and majors in chemistry. We divided all participants into four groups based upon the amount of chemistry coursework taken at the time of the test. We calculated the average and standard deviation for both chemistry hours and chemistry GPA, tallied the common chemistry coursework for each group, and compared these three variables with the MOSART test scores (Table 4.6). Using the MOSART chemistry (9–12) test scores for each group, we identified items with less than an average of 50% correct responses as persistent misconceptions and concluded that there were few or no misconceptions for those items with an average of 90% or more correct responses.

Qualitative Analysis of Chemistry SMK

As shown in Table 4.6, we observed that with increasing chemistry coursework, participants had fewer misconceptions. For example, Group 4 with more than 25 credit hours had 10 correct concepts, while Group 1 only had three correct concepts. Moreover, we could only identify one misconception in Group 4, while we identified seven misconceptions in Group 1.

The two topics with the most persistent misconceptions, appearing in all four groups, were chemical bonding and nuclear processes. When considering participants' chemistry coursework, we found that advanced chemistry coursework, such as physical chemistry or organic chemistry, still did not seem to help test takers to overcome misconceptions about metallic bonding. In a review of a general chemistry college textbook (Brown, LeMay, Bursten, & Murphy, 2008), only two paragraphs were devoted to metallic bonding in the chapter on chemical bonding. Metallic bonding would probably only be addressed in any depth in an inorganic chemistry course. Only those with more than 25 credit hours of chemistry had a higher percentage of correct responses. Easier items on the chemistry test concerned periodicity and questions about atomic particles. These had the highest percentages of correct answers overall. Most participants had taken *General Chemistry I* and *II* courses (93% and 88%, respectively). The content covered in those courses appeared to facilitate a basic understanding of atomic particles, content, and arrangement of the periodic table. Groups with introductory levels of chemistry SMK showed an average score for Group 1 at 65% compared with an average passing score of 88% for high levels of chemistry SMK (Group 4). Teachers with 9–16 credit hours of chemistry coursework (e.g., including organic chemistry) had, on average, better results ($M = 74\%$) and held fewer misconceptions than those with

TABLE 4.6 Science Teachers' Chemistry Credit Hours, GPA, Coursework Commonly Taken, and MOSART Test Results

Group	Commonly Taken Coursework	Credit Hours M (SD)	GPA M (SD)	MOSART Test Score (%) M (SD)	Number of Items With Misconceptions[a]	Number of Items With Few Misconceptions[b]
Group 1 (n = 10)	General Chemistry I	8 (1)	2.8 (0.6)	65 (15)	7	3
	General Chemistry II					
Group 2 (n = 65)	General Chemistry I	13 (2)	3.3 (0.6)	74 (15)	3	2
	General Chemistry II					
	Organic Chemistry I					
Group 3 (n = 11)	General Chemistry I	21 (2)	3.3 (0.4)	77 (11)	3	5
	General Chemistry II					
	Organic Chemistry I					
	Organic Chemistry II					
	Organic Chemistry Lab					
Group 4 (n = 11)	General Chemistry I	41 (17)	3.2 (0.4)	88 (10)	1	10
	General Chemistry II					
	Organic Chemistry I					
	Organic Chemistry II					
	Organic Chemistry Lab					
	Inorganic Chemistry					
	Physical Chemistry					
All (n = 97)	General Chemistry I	16 (11)	3.2 (0.6)	75 (15)	2	2
	General Chemistry II					
	Organic Chemistry I					

[a] Less than 50% of group gave correct responses.
[b] More than 90% of group gave correct responses.

just two general chemistry courses. However, only Group 4 reliably passed the test (Lewis et al., 2018).

Quantitative Analysis of Chemistry Subject Matter Knowledge

We also conducted an analysis to identify variables that contributed significantly to the SMK outcome measure (Table 4.7). Considering the variability associated with MOSART chemistry test scores, chemistry coursework GPA uniquely accounted for 27% of that variance ($\beta = 0.32$, $t = 2.99$, $p < 0.01$), number of chemistry credit hours uniquely accounted for 28% of that variance ($\beta = 0.29$, $t = 3.16$, $p < 0.01$), and physics coursework GPA uniquely accounted for 24% of that variance ($\beta = 0.28$, $t = 2.66$, $p = 0.01$). For each 0.10 increase in chemistry GPA, participants were 1.22 times more likely to pass the test ($e^\beta = 7.47$). Empirically, the regression model suggests that a minimum of 30 chemistry credit hours and an average chemistry GPA of 3.21 were associated with an average score on the MOSART chemistry test of 80% or better (i.e., passing).

Physics and Physical Science

We recruited preservice science teachers ($n = 70$) and undergraduate physics students ($n = 21$) to take the MOSART physics (9–12) test (Sadler et al., 2010), examined course transcripts of all physics test takers, and created four groups based upon physics credit hours. The analytic approach was identical to the approach with the chemistry test data.

TABLE 4.7 Descriptive Statistics for the MOSART Chemistry (9–12) Test			
Predictor	Mean (or Mode where indicated)	σ	n
MOSART chemistry score	75.41	15.11	105
Pass/Fail (1/0) MOSART score	0 (mode)	n/a	105
Pass			47 (44.3%)
Fail			58 (55.2%)
Sex of participant	1 (mode)	n/a	101
Male			37 (36.6%)
Female			64 (63.4%)
Delay between last coursework and test (years)	2.63	5.38	105
Total number of credit hours of chemistry coursework	16.65	11.42	105
Chemistry coursework GPA	3.21	0.56	104
Total number of credit hours of physics coursework	9.22	8.68	104
Physics coursework GPA	3.11	0.56	85

Qualitative Analysis of Physics Subject Matter Knowledge

We found that the number of physics credit hours was positively correlated with MOSART scores (Table 4.8). For instance, 23 out of 25 items (92%) on the physics test appeared to be easier for Group 4 as compared to Group 1, who performed well on only six of 25 items (24%). Similarly, test takers with at least 17 physics credit hours exhibited few or no misconceptions on topics with which their counterparts with less than 17 credit hours struggled (i.e., items on which at least 50% of participants answered incorrectly). On average, Groups 1 and 2 participants with less than 17 credit hours did not meet the 80% passing score for the physics test. In our analyses of physics courses taken, we also observed that participants with less than 9 credit hours usually took algebra-based or descriptive introductory physics courses, which are less mathematically rigorous as compared to calculus-based introductory physics courses taken by participants with at least 17 credit hours. While participants with at least 17 credit hours were more likely to pass the physics test, the type of introductory physics courses taken by participants may have influenced their test performance.

Courses taken by the participants provide insight into their physics misconceptions. For instance, Group 1 participants mainly took one general physics course (i.e., *General Physics I*) that only includes topics in mechanics, heat, waves, and sound. Concepts in electricity, magnetism, optics, relativity, atomic and nuclear physics are commonly included in *General Physics II*. Analysis of items correctly answered by each group showed that Group 1 participants had persistent misconceptions on electromagnetic waves, electromagnetism, and quantization of energy, which are topics addressed in the *General Physics II* course. The test also surprisingly revealed that Group 1 participants still held persistent misconceptions on Newton's laws of motion and wave properties, even though these topics are taught in *General Physics I*.

Similar to Group 1, Group 2 participants with a range of 9–16 credit hours also appeared to struggle with electromagnetism and modern physics concepts. Misconceptions with Newton's laws of motion and wave properties persisted among Group 2 participants despite having a greater range of introductory physics courses than Group 1. These results suggest that taking fewer than 17 credit hours of physics courses is insufficient for preservice teachers to develop the content knowledge needed to teach a high school physics course.

Quantitative analysis of physics SMK. We used multiple variable regression using each of the six predictors listed in Table 4.9 to predict the MOSART physics (9–12), and a logistic regression for the pass/fail scores, using the same predictors.

Physics and chemistry coursework, specifically credit hours and GPA, and (unlike the other subject areas we investigated) teachers' sex had a

TABLE 4.8 Science Teachers' Physics Credit Hours, GPA, Commonly Taken Coursework, and MOSART Test Results

Group	Commonly Taken Coursework	Credit Hours M (SD)	GPA M (SD)	MOSART Test Score (%) M (SD)	Number of Items With Misconceptions[a]	Number of Items With Few Misconceptions[b]
Group 1 (n = 25)	General Physics I	5 (2)	2.77 (0.70)	67 (17)	7	6
	General Physics I Lab					
Group 2 (n = 48)	General Physics I	11 (2)	3.25 (0.50)	70 (13)	8	8
	General Physics I Lab					
	General Physics II					
	General Physics Lab II					
	General Physics III					
	Elements of Electrical Engineering					
Group 3 (n = 8)	General Physics I	23 (3)	3.17 (0.40)	85 (10)	0	8
	General Physics Lab I					
	General Physics II					
	General Physics Lab II					
	General Physics III					
	General Physics Lab III					
	Physics and Astronomy					
	Mathematics					
	Lasers and Optics					
	Concepts in Modern Physics					

(continued)

TABLE 4.8 Science Teachers' Physics Credit Hours, GPA, Commonly Taken Coursework, and MOSART Test Results (continued)

Group	Commonly Taken Coursework	Credit Hours M (SD)	GPA M (SD)	MOSART Test Score (%) M (SD)	Number of Items With Misconceptions[a]	Number of Items With few Misconceptions[b]
Group 4 (n = 10)	General Physics I	48 (15)	3.39 (0.36)	90 (6)	2	23
	General Physics II					
	General Physics II					
	General Physics Lab I					
	General Physics Lab					
	II General Physics					
	Lab III					
	Physics and Astronomy					
	Electrical and Electronic Circuits					
	Mechanics					
	Thermal Physics					
	Experimental Physics I					
	Electromagnetic Theory					
	Quantum Mechanics					
	Optics and Electromagnetic Waves					
Total (n = 91)	General Physics I	12 (9)	3.12 (0.58)	73 (15)	4	8
	General Physics I Lab					
	General Physics II					

[a] Less than 50% of group gave correct responses.
[b] More than 90% of group gave correct responses.

TABLE 4.9 Descriptive Statistics for the MOSART Physics (9–12) Test

Predictor	Mean (or Mode where indicated)	σ	n
MOSART physics score	72.75	15.44	97
Pass/Fail (1/0) MOSART score	0 (mode)	n/a	97
Pass			42 (43.3%)
Fail			55 (56.7%)
Sex of participant	1 (mode)	n/a	97
Male			49 (50.5%)
Female			48 (49.5%)
Delay between last coursework and test (years)	2.52	5.46	97
Total number of credit hours of chemistry coursework	13.35	11.65	97
Chemistry coursework GPA	3.13	0.64	86
Total number of credit hours of physics coursework	13.13	11.11	97
Physics coursework GPA	3.15	0.58	94

Note: A number of undergraduate physics students had not taken any chemistry coursework, which was correctly coded as 0 total credit hours, but then resulted in no GPA. Thus in the category of GPA it appears as if there is missing data, but in these cases GPA does not exist.

statistically predicted MOSART scores. Because the content in this case was physics, we chose physics coursework GPA, number of physics credit hours, and sex as the predictors in the final model. Specifically, physics coursework GPA uniquely accounted for 34% of the variance in MOSART physics test scores ($\beta = 0.35$, $t = 4.10$, $p < 0.01$) and number of physics credit hours uniquely accounted for 31% of that variance ($\beta = 0.33$, $t = 3.64$, $p < 0.01$); the relationship between both physics GPA and hours of coursework and MOSART physics test scores was positive. Sex uniquely accounted for 19% of that variance ($\beta = -0.20$, $t = 2.28$, $p = 0.03$). The relationship between sex and MOSART physics test scores, however, was negative. That is, female participants tended to score lower than male participants, although we suspect that this was an artifact of having few women with more credit hours in physics in the sample. Because our sample of participants did not have enough women with high numbers of physics credit hours, we were not able to run an analysis that included both sex and the minimum credit hours to predict a passing score on the test.[6] In our final analysis, each additional credit hour of physics coursework significantly increased the likelihood of an individual passing the MOSART physics test by 19% ($e^{\beta} = 1.19$).

Life Science

For the middle-school life science SMK analysis, we examined participants ($n = 72$) from the two TPPs. Unlike the other subject areas we were sufficiently powered with the preservice teacher test takers and did not recruit any life science majors to take the test. The analytic approach was identical to the approach with the chemistry test data.

Qualitative analysis of preservice teachers' life science SMK.   In grouping the preservice teachers' SMK into four categories, all four groups had average scores over the 80% passing score. Group 1 not only had the lowest average score at 83%, but 50% of this group ($n = 8$) also scored under the 80% cutoff score (Table 4.10). The easiest items for all four groups concerned energy movement in an ecosystem. Participants in Groups 1 and 2 exhibited misconceptions about cell specialization and population growth and carrying capacity. Groups 1 and 3 scored less than 80% on items related to population dynamics as well. Group 2 had an average of 86% on the standard associated with population dynamics. Group 2 did not have any individuals that missed all three questions for this standard, but Groups 1 and 3 did. Even Group 3 showed misconceptions in four critical standards: (a) cell specialization, (b) population dynamics, (c) population growth and carrying capacity, and (d) disease. The confusion with these ecological concepts is not surprising due to the lack of an ecology course in the list of common courses taken by Group 3. While Group 4 participants on average did not have a much higher MOSART score than Groups 2 or 3, Group 4 did not show any persistent misconceptions. Group 4 had the greatest number of different courses and life science electives beyond general biology; the variety of classes taken by Group 4 may have been what led to the lack of persistent misconceptions identified by the test despite the average for Group 4 (90%) only being slightly above the average for Group 2 (89%).

Quantitative Analysis of Preservice Teachers' Life Science SMK.   We used multiple regression with four predictors of the middle school MOSART (5–8) life science test score and a logistic regression using the same possible prediction of the probability of a teacher pass/fail test score. Descriptive statistics are presented in Table 4.11. Biology coursework accounted for 12.4% of the variance in MOSART test scores ($R^2 = 0.12$), with a positive relationship of 0.35 ($\beta = 0.35$). Thus, as preservice science teachers took more college-level biology credit hours, their MOSART test scores, on average, increased. Additionally, for each credit hour of biology a teacher

TABLE 4.10 Science Teachers' Biology Credit Hours, GPA, Coursework Commonly Taken, and MOSART Test Results

Group	Coursework Commonly Taken	Credit Hours M (SD)	GPA M (SD)	MOSART Test Score (%) M (SD)	Number of Items With Misconceptions[a]	Number of Items With few Misconceptions[b]
Group 1 (n = 8)	General Biology Principles of Ecology Elements of Biochemistry and Lab	4.5 (2.6)	3.9 (0.5)	83 (6)	8	3
Group 2 (n = 12)	General Biology General Biology Lab Principles of Ecology Ecology Lab Elements of Biochemistry and Lab	12.25 (2.3)	3.2 (0.5)	89 (7)	2	6
Group 3 (n = 21)	General Biology General Biology Lab General Botany Human Physiology Human Physiology Lab Microbiology Microbiology Lab Introduction to Zoology and Lab	23.4 (1.5)	3.45 (0.3)	86 (7)	4	1
Group 4 (n = 31)	Cell Structure and Function Organismic Biology General Genetics Principles of Ecology Microbiology Microbiology Lab	36.4 (10.8)	3.3 (0.5)	90 (7)	0	3
Total (n = 72)		24.6 (12.6)	3.4 (0.5)	88 (7)	3.5	3.4

[a] Less than 80% of group gave correct responses.
[b] More than 98% of group gave correct responses.

TABLE 4.11 Predictors and Descriptive Statistics for MOSART Life Science (6–8) Test

Predictor	Mean (or Mode where noted)	σ	n
MOSART Life Science score	88.96	7.01	83
Pass/Fail MOSART test score	1 (mode)	n/a	83
Pass		n/a	76 (91.6%)
Fail		n/a	7 (8.4%)
Sex of Participant	1 (mode)	n/a	83
Male		n/a	37 (44.5%)
Female		n/a	46 (55.4%)
Delay between last coursework and test (years)	3.34	5.92	83
Total number of credit hours of biology coursework	28.44	15.63	83
Biology coursework GPA	3.40	0.45	83

earned, the odds of passing the life science MOSART test increased by 9.8% ($e^{\beta} = 1.098$).

Teacher Self-Efficacy

In response to Research Question #3, we examined MAT teachers' self-efficacy using a multivariate analysis of variance (MANOVA). Our three outcome variables were the three subscales on the self-efficacy instrument, regarding: (a) student engagement, (b) instructional strategies, and (c) classroom management (Table 4.12). We used number of years of teaching experience to predict change across the multiple outcome measures. Time

TABLE 4.12 Average Teacher Self-Efficacy of MAT Graduates

	Post-Student Teaching	Post-Year 1	Post-Year 2	Post-Year 3
Number of teachers	41	24	20	8
Student Engagement Mean*	3.84	3.54	3.49	3.56
SD	0.46	0.36	0.35	0.39
Classroom Management Mean	4.05	3.76	3.84	3.97
SD	0.42	0.37	0.34	0.39
Instructional Strategies Mean*	4.15	3.94	4.01	3.92
SD	0.49	0.47	0.51	0.50

* statistically significant difference when $p < 0.05$ level.

spent teaching accounted for average differences across the three measures, Wilk's Lambda $(9, 211) = 2.02$, $p = 0.04$. In follow-up tests using a Bonferonni adjustment, we found statistically significant changes over all available time points on self-efficacy related to student engagement $(F(3, 89) = 4.54$, $p < 0.01)$ and instructional strategies $(F(3, 89) = 3.17$, $p = 0.03)$, but not classroom management $(F(3, 89) = 1.18$, $p = 0.32)$ subscales.

Pairwise comparisons indicated statistically significant changes between Years 1 and 2 of teaching for self-efficacy related to student engagement, and between student teaching and Year 1 of teaching for self-efficacy related to instructional strategies. This indicated a complex relationship between the subscale scores and teaching experience. This was complicated by potential measurement issues and underpowered tests. We resolved this matter by concluding that the relationship between scales, subscales, and time points within scales and subscales needs to be further analyzed and otherwise becomes too complex to be practical. To summarize, the number of years a teacher taught mattered when predicting overall self-efficacy and specifically for self-efficacy associated with student engagement and instructional strategies. It is important to note that longitudinal comparisons were only meaningful when we used the teachers as their own controls (i.e., we treated the data from the first time they took the survey after they finished the TPP as a baseline measure). This suggested that either self-efficacy had stabilized or the measurement instrument was not sensitive to changes in self-efficacy after two or more years of having exited the MAT program. Over time, MAT teachers who persisted through the induction period maintained a generally positive outlook on their own agency (i.e., they perceived they could do "some" to "quite a bit" to affect positive change) in these three teaching areas.

Beginning Science Teachers' Enacted Practices Using Inquiry-Based Instruction

A major goal of our longitudinal study was to investigate the impact of observation-level variables (i.e., time, level of observed lesson [high school vs. middle school], length of observed lesson, and mode of observation [video vs. real-time] and teacher-level characteristics [i.e., teacher's sex and education program]) on the likelihood of an observed science lesson being at or below a certain level of inquiry (i.e., pre-inquiry, developing, proficient, or exemplary) on the EQUIP instrument, our measure of inquiry-based instruction. In response to Research Question 4, we used 455 classroom observations from four academic years of data (2012–2013 to 2015–2016) of 51 science teachers' lessons from both programs. Hierarchical generalized linear models were built to investigate the relationship between level of inquiry-based instruction and the predictor variables at both levels. For more meaningful interpretation, we calculated the corresponding predicted probabilities for observed lessons taught by teachers in the two different preparation programs and controlled for other observation- and teacher-level characteristics. This allowed us to plot the probability of a lesson employing a particular level of inquiry-based instruction across years of teaching. Figure 4.2 shows the change in probability for science lessons taught by teacher graduates of the two TPPs (Lucas & Lewis, 2017).

Among teacher-level characteristics, only the teacher preparation program was found to be statistically significant. Compared to teachers from

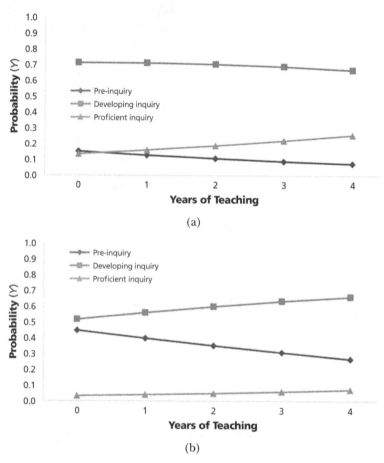

Figure 4.2 Change in probability of an observed science lesson being at or below a proficiency level of inquiry-based instruction across years of teaching: (a) teacher has a master's degree in science teaching; and (b) teacher has a bachelor's degree in secondary science education (from Lucas & Lewis, 2017).

the undergraduate TPP, MAT teachers appeared to show more rapid growth in their use of inquiry-based teaching practices. Using a ratio of –2LL statistics, we determined that the likelihood of an observed lesson having no use of inquiry-based instruction (e.g., lecture-based) was significantly lower for MAT teachers than the undergraduate TPP. These findings imply that program differences affect the development of inquiry practices. For example, a beginning MAT teacher with 1 year of teaching experience had about a 13% chance of teaching through more traditional methods, while an undergraduate TPP teacher had a likelihood of 40% of doing so. Additionally, over the induction period MAT teachers taught lessons at the proficient inquiry level at twice the rate of undergraduate teachers.

Changes in Teachers' Use of Inquiry-Based Science Instruction

Along with our model building of teachers' use of inquiry-based instruction, when we reviewed our MAT program data set on the four specific areas of inquiry-based teaching on the EQUIP instrument (i.e., instructional, discourse, assessment, and curriculum factors) we found particular patterns of growth and areas of challenge. Growth, or lack thereof, in these areas can be considered to be a result of teachers acquiring teaching experience without much professional development, as teachers reported that they were mainly in survival mode and had little time to do anything but teach. We identified four areas of growth as teachers gained experience: (a) teaching for knowledge acquisition, (b) questioning level they employed (i.e., asking more questions that required critical thinking), (c) conceptual development of science concepts, and (d) content depth. Encouragingly, all four of these aspects of teaching science were strongly addressed during the teacher education program and appeared to support teachers' growth during the induction period without much additional formal professional development. Alternatively, some areas of little or no discernable growth included teachers: (a) using an inquiry-based order of instruction, specifically with student exploration preceding explaining; (b) promoting classroom interactions through discourse; (c) accessing students' prior knowledge for use in revising instruction; and (d) positioning learner centrality in the enacted curriculum.

Subject Matter Knowledge Relationship With Inquiry-Based Instruction

Chemistry Lessons

We examined the variability associated with observations of high-school chemistry lessons, using the DiISC and EQUIP observation instruments to assess 13 teachers with 63 lessons. The mean chemistry credit hours was

24.95 ($SD = 2.16$); the mean physics credit hours was 9.62 ($SD = 0.45$). We only used six items on the DiISC that focused on inquiry-based teaching practices as a single factor, but used all EQUIP items grouped into two factors. Using a multivariate analyses (i.e., MANOVA), we found that teachers' total number of chemistry credit hours predicted inquiry-based instruction ($F(3, 59) = 4.60$, $p < 0.01$). Thus, the more chemistry credit hours a teacher had, the more inquiry-based the lesson tended to be. In predicting inquiry-based teaching practices, total number of chemistry credit hours accounted for 19% of the variance (*partial* $\eta^2 = 0.190$). We also noted that total number of physics credit hours was statistically significant as a predictor alone ($F(2, 59) = 4.60$, $p < 0.01$), but not in the same model with chemistry credit hours ($F(3, 58) = 2.06$, $p = 0.12$).

Physical Science Lessons

We examined the variability associated with middle- and high-school physical science lessons using observations of 88 lessons taught by 28 teachers (Table 4.13). Using the factor scores from the EQUIP and DiISC, we used multivariate analyses (MANOVA) with three independent variables (TPP, teaching experience, total science GPA), and three dependent variables (EQUIP Factor 1 score on discourse and assessment, EQUIP Factor 2 score on instructional strategies and curricular choices, and DiISC inquiry scale).[7] Total science GPA had a statistically significant relationship with the combined dependent variables, $F(3, 82) = 3.589$, $p < .05$, Wilk's Lambda $= 0.884$, *partial* $\eta^2 = 0.116$. Thus, a teacher's average weighted GPA in all science courses was associated with inquiry-based instruction in physical science lessons; the higher the total science GPA, the more inquiry-based the lesson tended to be.

We performed follow-up univariate ANOVAs with a Bonferroni adjustment to examine the main effect of total science GPA. Total science GPA had a significant relationship with EQUIP Factor 1 score (i.e., discourse and assessment; $F(1, 84) = 8.936$, $p < 0.0167$, *partial* $\eta^2 = 0.096$), but not with EQUIP Factor 2 score (i.e., instructional strategies and curricular

TABLE 4.13 Descriptive Data Associated With Physical Science Teachers' Inquiry-Based Instruction			
Variable	N (%)	Mean	SD
Number of teachers	28		
Number of lessons	88		
BA	14 (16%)		
MA	74 (84%)		
Total science GPA		3.43	0.33
Teaching experience (in days)		364.80	187.04

choices; $F(1, 84) = 2.215$, $p = 0.140$, *partial* $\eta^2 = 0.026$) or the DiISC inquiry score ($F(1, 84) = 0.327$, $p = 0.569$, *partial* $\eta^2 = 0.004$). Thus, averaging across TPPs and teaching experience, the higher the total science GPA of a physical science teacher, the more inquiry-based the discourse and assessment practices tended to be in a lesson.

Life Science Lessons

Using the same analytic approach as we adopted for the chemistry and physical science lessons, we examined the variability associated with 178 middle-school life science and high-school biology lessons taught by 51 teachers (Table 4.14). Of the 178 lessons, the most common lessons taught were on: (a) genetics and heredity (17%), (b) disease and the human body (16%), (c) organisms (14%), and (c) evolution and biodiversity (10%). Using MANOVA, we found a significant relationship between three predictors and the level of inquiry-based science lessons by these teachers: (a) total number of science credit hours, $F(3, 157) = 3.87$, $p = 0.01$; (b) Earth and space science GPA, $F(3, 157) = 3.10$, $p = 0.01$; and (c) middle- or high-school classroom, $F(3, 157) = 4.15$, $p < 0.01$ with high school teachers outperforming middle school teachers.

Using teachers' SMK variables and teaching level to predict their inquiry-based teaching practices in life science and biology lessons, we found the following effect sizes: (a) total number of science credit hours uniquely accounted for 6.9% of the variance (*partial* $\eta^2 = 0.069$); (b) Earth and space science GPA uniquely accounted for 5.6% of the variance (*partial* $\eta^2 = 0.056$); and (c) middle or high school uniquely accounted for 7.4% of the variance (*partial* $\eta^2 = 0.074$), that is, high school biology teachers used more inquiry-based approaches than middle school teachers.

TABLE 4.14   Descriptive Data Associated With Life Science Teachers' Inquiry-Based Instruction

Factor	N (%)	Mean	SD
Number of teachers	51		
Number of lessons	178		
BA	39 (22%)		
MA	139 (78%)		
Total science credit hours		68.55	1.05
Earth and space credit hours		75.22	1.45
Number of middle school lessons	49 (28%)		
Number of high school lessons	164 (72%)		

DISCUSSION

Subject Matter Knowledge, Misconceptions, and Connections to Teaching

The MOSART chemistry (9–12) and physics (9–12) tests were originally designed as diagnostic tools for teachers to use with high school chemistry and physics students at the beginning of those courses, while the MOSART life science (5–8) test was designed to address common misconceptions at the middle-school level. We used these tests as measures of teachers' SMK to correlate with coursework completed in each discipline to determine the minimum amount of coursework and mastery level (i.e., GPA) that teachers would need to have to demonstrate competency within a discipline.

High School Chemistry

Interestingly, even though the curriculum of a standard high school chemistry course would be very similar to introductory coursework in chemistry, it took much more than two introductory college-level chemistry courses for participants to overcome common chemistry misconceptions. Study participants on average did not pass the MOSART chemistry (9–12) test, but there was great variability around a passing score of 80%. The analysis also revealed that the participants' chemistry GPA was a significant predictor of the likelihood of obtaining a passing score on the chemistry test. Thus, GPA in chemistry coursework is indicative of whether a teacher is likely to hold common chemistry misconceptions. When we showed the results to our two chemistry experts, they were not surprised to see the participants' common misconception in nuclear processes and explained that this topic was not commonly taught in undergraduate chemistry courses.

In terms of program design, we balanced the required minimum amount of science coursework in the state's teacher certification rules with the university guidelines for undergraduate degrees not to exceed a total of 120 credit hours. Therefore, students in our undergraduate TPP had, at most, only the minimum required number of 24 credit hours in one area of science. Because our analysis indicated that common misconceptions in chemistry could only reliably be overcome with 30 or more credit hours in chemistry, the undergraduate program (with the state-mandated minimum of 24 credit hours in chemistry) appears not to be rigorous enough to ensure that its teacher candidates' SMK was sufficient to avoid misconceptions about the content they must teach. Finally, when we investigated the relationship of teachers' SMK to the degree of inquiry used in their chemistry lessons, the total number of chemistry credit hours accounted for 19% of the variance in inquiry-based instruction. Thus SMK appears to make a real difference in the degree of teacher's use of inquiry-based teaching.

High School Physics and Physical Science

Study participants on average did not pass the MOSART physics (9–12) test. However, on average our test takers had taken only 13 credit hours in physics. The analysis also revealed that the participants' physics GPA was a significant predictor of a passing score on the MOSART physics test. Thus, both a greater number of physics credit hours and a higher physics GPA can be used to predict whether a teacher candidate is likely to avoid common physics misconceptions.[8] Most of the few physics-endorsed teachers in our sample came from our MAT program, who were all male and had at least an undergraduate degree in physics. These individuals had strong SMK and were well-prepared to teach both upper level high school physics and middle school or ninth-grade physical science courses. But most teachers who were teaching middle school and ninth-grade physical science lessons did so with few credit hours in physics (i.e., 4 to 12 credit hours). Thus, the majority of the lessons we observed were taught by teachers who had not achieved a passing score on the physics test. Previous studies (Hashweh, 2002; Murphy, 2005) have shown that teachers' SMK influences their planning for content instruction and use of explanatory representations. This also likely explained why teachers' physical science lessons tended to lack an inquiry-based approach to teaching science.

Middle School Life Science

Unlike our high school level physics and chemistry SMK results, study participants on average passed the MOSART life science (5–8) test. This is likely due to the much higher average number of life science credit hours (M = 28 credit hours) taken by the test takers as well as the fact that the middle school level test content was easier than that of the the MOSART physics and chemistry high school exams. However, despite easier middle school life science content, some misconceptions still persisted among teachers who had less than 25 life science credit hours. Although misconceptions persisted, most teachers with more than eight hours of life science credit hours passed the middle school MOSART life science (5–8) test, which suggests that they are qualified to teach these concepts. However, a biology teacher with more than 24 hours of life science credit hours would teach middle-school life science with fewer misconceptions.

Teacher preparation program designers should look at specific course requirements and gaps in undergraduate preservice teachers' life science knowledge. In our study, MAT teachers with an undergraduate degree in biological sciences had fewer middle-school life science misconceptions; without having administered the MOSART biology (9–12) test to enough participants we cannot comment at this time on the comparable minimum amount and mastery of SMK that would be necessary to teach high school biology.[9]

Teacher Self-Efficacy

As MAT teachers gained experience, their self-efficacy in the areas of student engagement and instructional strategies increased (Lewis et al., 2016). We suspect that the positive nature and stability of the MAT science teachers' self-efficacy during the induction period is related to strong SMK and a rigorous TPP that results in progressively more inquiry-based instruction in their classrooms. The more that teachers use reform-based curriculum and instruction that involves students using scientific practices that require active learning, the more engaged students are likely to be (Minner, Levy, & Century, 2010). The literature we reviewed in this chapter also claims that teachers with stronger SMK are potentially more capable of designing and adapting curriculum to reflect the nature of science within that particular discipline and teach using an inquiry-based stance.

Strengths and Challenges of Different Program Designs

As described in this chapter, our research has been situated within two programmatic designs for science teacher education, an undergraduate and a master's level program. There were limitations and benefits to each design in terms of developing teachers' SMK and education coursework and resulting pedagogical knowledge for teaching physical science. MAT teachers with a master's degree in science teaching showed higher initial use and faster growth in using inquiry-based teaching practices as compared to undergraduate teachers. However, when we tested undergraduate preservice teachers we found that on average, when they had about the same average amount of coursework and GPA, they tended to test slightly higher on the MOSART tests. This is likely because (a) they had taken their science courses more recently than the MAT teachers who may have been out of school for a period of time, and (b) that we had been able to control which science courses the undergraduate teachers had to take for certification because we had vetted the courses in advance. The latter was done to ensure that the science courses taken were the most aligned with what these future teachers were going to have to teach, whereas when MAT teachers applied to the program we reviewed their coursework and made accommodations for courses that were within the guidelines, but perhaps were not optimal for teaching aligned with secondary science education standards. While there were differences in the amount of science and education coursework between both programs, all teachers in the study took the same two science teaching methods courses. By treating these two courses as a static variable we chose to focus on identifying which science coursework specifically accounted for the amount of variance in those teachers who used more inquiry-based instruction.

RECOMMENDATIONS

Based upon our and other researchers' work in science teacher preparation (Loughran, 2014), we make recommendations in three critical areas of teacher preparation concerning: (a) TPP designers, (b) education researchers, and (c) policymakers and stakeholders.

Recommendations for Teacher Preparation Program Designers

In designing an effective TPP that went beyond minimal requirements for state certification, we not only ensured that the science teaching methods courses reflected the reform-based priorities for teaching science in the NGSS, but also attended to research on teaching diverse students to ensure that our MAT program design was aligned with best practices. Due to the maximum program credit hour restriction for undergraduate majors set by the university, we were unable to add a course in teaching ELLs without taking out another course, which was not feasible since all of their education coursework was necessary for certification. With the MAT program we had the freedom to include such a course because the MAT candidates were not taking science courses concurrently with teacher education certification courses. Teacher candidates who were career-changers tended to prefer shorter certification programs so that they could start working as soon as possible. Thus, we restricted admission to the program to those who had completed their science coursework as there were practical limits as to how much coursework could be completed within 14 months without sacrificing quality of learning. In summary, by optimizing both SMK and pedagogical knowledge development we have seen not only stronger beginning teaching practices by MAT graduates, but also higher rates of growth over time throughout the induction period, relative to teachers from the undergraduate program.

We found some disciplines more straightforward than others to determine which courses, and at what level, yielded the most aligned SMK for teaching science. We found that chemistry and physics had a more linear order to its scope and sequence than did the biological sciences and thus it is easier to recommend specific course work in chemistry and physics since there are fewer options. Additionally, those test takers who took a calculus-based physics course were generally stronger test takers, but these individuals also had greater than 17 credit hours in physics, thus were more squarely in-field than those who did not pass the MOSART physics test. The difference in algebra and calculus-based introductory physics courses may not matter as long as an individual persists in taking more physics courses, but it could also be a proxy for weaker math skills that are needed to perform well in physics.

Recommendations for Education Researchers

There is a need for more research in order to reliably determine how teachers' SMK relates to credit hours, associated GPA, and scores on discipline-specific comprehensive exams such as the Praxis II biology, chemistry, Earth science, and physics tests. However, there is also an equally strong argument to be made for more research to determine which education courses and types and hours of clinical placements contribute significantly to the variance seen among new science teachers in terms of reform-based classroom instruction with diverse students. In our research we found that while beginning teachers' science SMK was a significant contributor to inquiry-based teaching, it was clearly only part of the whole teacher preparation picture. More studies of beginning teachers are needed to identify the challenges of translating teacher learning in TPPs to classrooms, in particular in diverse classrooms (Cochran-Smith & Villegas, 2016; Carter & Darling-Hammond, 2016). In future analyses, we plan to examine the roles of in-service teacher professional development and teachers' beliefs about reform-based science teaching as well as science teaching in more and less diverse classrooms.

A second recommendation emerging from our study is in relation to research instruments and validation. The availability and use of validated instruments has been a perennial issue in studying teacher preparation and effective teaching. There is a need for research instruments that can bridge preservice and in-service teaching to facilitate longitudinal research. Some reliable instruments that have been developed are inappropriate for use with preservice teachers (e.g., Tschannen-Moran & Hoy, 2001) and thus make it difficult, for example, to track how teacher self-efficacy changes over time from TPP to experienced teacher. Additionally, some instruments take much calibration to use reliably (e.g., Reformed Teaching Observation Protocol; Piburn & Sawada, 2000; and EQUIP), which can be costly unless one has a well-funded research project, or were developed with particular projects in mind and thus adapting them for other purposes can potentially undermine instruments' consequential validity.

Implications for Policymakers and Stakeholders

Bybee (2011) argued that what science education needs now is a consistent system of coordinated purposes, policies, programs, and practice that can reduce the need for continually addressing inconsistencies. Part of that system must be a research-based set of standards for teacher certification. Our work has provided evidence that factors such as science content area credit hours, science GPA, and test scores are indicative of teachers' subject matter knowledge and possible misconceptions. Policymakers can leverage these and other findings to refine state guidelines for teacher certification to ensure that teachers are strongly prepared. For secondary science teachers, state departments of education that set teacher certification policy should consider making a careful distinction among specific science disciplines, as all sciences are not the same in their learning progressions, degree of linear accumulation of knowledge, and diversity of topics. Our study suggests that in chemistry, secondary science teachers need to take at least 30 credit hours in chemistry at a 3.2 GPA in order to pass a test of common chemistry misconceptions, but in physics the total number of credit hours could also include mathematics coursework (i.e., a minor degree). However, choice of coursework matters, as not all courses include the necessary science competencies that align with secondary science content standards.

CONCLUSION

To develop science teachers fluent in inquiry-based teaching approaches, TPPs should focus on elements such as building preservice teachers' self-efficacy and strong SMK, as well as opportunities to plan and practice lessons that elicit students' thinking and use of scientific practices. Additionally, it is important to prepare teachers in developing effective assessment practices and instructional strategies to explore and address students' misconceptions to generate more normative understanding and proficient achievement. Only 42% of middle-school and 49% of high-school science teachers have more than 10 years of teaching experience (Banilower et al., 2013), and schools with higher percentages of students who qualify for free and reduced lunch are more likely to have less experienced teachers than schools with fewer students in poverty (Banilower et al., 2013). It is more important than ever to ensure that newly certified teachers do not have significant deficiencies that will make their induction period unnecessarily challenging.

Science teacher preparation standards are essential, but in themselves insufficient to ensure that teacher education programs produce highly-qualified teachers. In an era of systemic science education reform, teacher education policies should be informed by careful, empirical research that demonstrates the relationships between teacher preparation factors, such as quantity of teacher SMK and mastery of such content to the quality of future science instruction. TPPs, state agencies, and national accreditors that attend to the research base and connect to the larger issues of science education reform, such as the performance expectations of the *Next Generation Science Standards* and models of reform-based science teaching, are far more likely to educate teachers who are prepared to teach all students in diverse settings and support more cohesive systems for teacher preparation.

ACKNOWLEDGMENTS

This work was funded by two National Science Foundation grants, NSF #1035358 and NSF #1540797.

NOTES

1. U.S. Department of Education, Institute of Education Sciences, 2015 Science State Snapshot Report: Nebraska, retrieved from https://nces.ed.gov/nations reportcard/subject/publications/stt2015/pdf/2016157NE8.pdf
2. In 2013, NCATE re-formed into the Council for the Accreditation of Educator Preparation (CAEP), which became one of UNL's several accreditors.
3. The MOSART biology (9–12) test was not available until after we collected our data. However, tests at two levels allowed us to compare SMK needed to teach at the middle school level versus more advanced high school science content.
4. With similar courses we reviewed course descriptions to determine equivalency (e.g., *General Biology I* and *Introduction to Life Science I*).
5. Due to space constraints we refer readers to conference presentations (Lewis, et al., 2018) and an article (under review) that provides greater detail on these analyses.
6. Since the writing of this chapter we completed a new analysis of physics minimum credit hours and included teacher candidates' mathematics coursework and GPA. This work is currently in preparation.
7. Other independent variables that were removed from the model were science credit hours (total and by subject) and GPA by subject since they did not have a significant effect on inquiry-based instruction in physical science lessons.
8. Since the writing of this chapter our new analyses, Lewis et al. (under review) suggest that mathematics coursework and mathematics GPA is also important to include in determining minimum amount of coursework and mastery levels.
9. Once sufficiently powered we will be analyzing teacher candidates' and undergraduate life sciences majors' performance on the new MOSART biology (9–12) test and investigate the relationship between middle school and high school content mastery.

REFERENCES

Baker, D., Beard, R., Bueno-Watts, N., Lewis, E., Özdemir, G., Perkins, G., . . . Yaşar-Purzer, S. (2008). *Discourse in inquiry science classrooms* (DiISC): *Reference Manual*, Technical Report No. 001. The Communication in Science Inquiry Project (CISIP): Arizona State University.

Banilower, E. R., Smith, P. S., Weiss, I. R., Malzahn, K. A., Campbell, K. M., & Weis, A. M. (2013). *Report of the 2012 National Survey of Science and Mathematics Education*. Chapel Hill, NC: Horizon Research.

Banilower, E. R., Trygstad, P. J., & Smith, P. S. (2015). The first five years: What the 2012 National Survey of Science and Mathematics Education reveals about novice science teachers and their teaching. In J. A. Luft & S. L. Dubois (Eds.), *Newly hired teachers of science: A better beginning* (pp. 3–29). Rotterdam, The Netherlands: Sense.

Bell, B., & Cowie, B. (2001). *Formative assessment and science education.* Boston, MA: Kluwer.

Bianchi, J. (2012). Teaching while still learning to teach: Beginning science teachers' views, experiences, and classroom practices. In B. J. Fraser, K. Tobin, & C. J. McRobbie (Eds.), *Second international handbook of science education* (pp. 389–399). Dordrecht, The Netherlands: Springer.

Bransford, J., Darling-Hammond, L., & LePage, P. (2007). Introduction. In L. Darling-Hammond & J. Bransford (Eds.), *Preparing teachers for a changing world: What teachers should know and be able to do* (pp. 1–39). San Francisco, CA: Jossey Bass.

Brown, T. E., LeMay, H. E., Bursten, B. E., & Murphy, C. (2008). *Chemistry: The central science.* Upper Saddle River, NJ: Prentice Hall.

Bybee, R. W. (2011). Science education policy and student assessment. In G. E. DeBoer (Ed.), *The role of public policy in K–12 science education* (pp. 211–240). Charlotte, NC: Information Age.

Calabrese-Barton, A. (1998). Reframing "Science for all" through the Politics of Poverty. *Educational Policy, 12*, 525–541.

Carter, P., & Darling-Hammond, L. (2016). Teaching diverse learners. In D. H. Gitomer & C. A. Bell (Eds.), *Handbook of research on teaching* (pp. 593–638). New York, NY: The American Educational Research Association.

Cochran-Smith, M., & Villegas, A. M. (2016). Research on teacher preparation: Charting the landscape of a sprawling field. In D. H. Gitomer & C. A. Bell (Eds.), *Handbook of research on teaching* (pp. 439–548). New York, NY: The American Educational Research Association.

Council of Chief State School Officers. (2011). Interstate Teacher Assessment and Support Consortium (InTASC) Model core teaching standards: A resource for state dialogue. Washington, DC: Author.

Crawford, B. A. (2007). Learning to teach science as inquiry in the rough and tumble of practice. *Journal of Research in Science Teaching, 44*(4), 613–642.

Crawford, B. A. (2014). From inquiry to scientific practices in the science classroom. In N. G. Lederman & S. K. Abell (Eds.), *Handbook of research on science education* (pp. 515–541). New York, NY: Routledge.

Duffy, G. G., Miller, S., Parsons, S., & Meloth, M. (2009). The interplay of scientific inquiry and metacognition: More than a marriage for convenience. In D. J.

Hacker, J. Dunlosky, & A. C. Graesser (Eds.), *Handbook of metacognition in education* (pp. 175–205). New York, NY: Routledge.

Evans, B. R. (2011). Content knowledge, attitudes, and self-efficacy in the mathematics New York City Teaching Fellows (NYCTF) Program. *School Science and Mathematics, 111*(5), 225–235.

Feldman, A. (2000). Decision making in the practical domain: A model of practical conceptual change. *Science Education, 84*(5), 606–623.

Guskey, T. R. (1988). Teacher efficacy, self-concept, and attitudes toward the implementation of instructional innovation. *Teaching and Teacher Education, 4*(1), 63–69.

Hamza, K. M., & Wickman, P. O. (2008). Becoming a scientist: The role of undergraduate research in students' cognitive, personal, and professional development. *Science Education, 92*(1), 141–164.

Hashweh, M. Z. (2002). Effects of subject-matter knowledge in the teaching of biology and physics. *Teaching and Teacher Education, 3*(2), 109–120.

Hill, H. C., Rowan, B., & Ball, D. L. (2005). Effects of teachers' mathematical knowledge for teaching on student achievement. *American Educational Research Journal, 42*(2), 371–406.

Jones, G., & Leagon, M. (2014). Science teacher attitudes and beliefs: Reforming practice. In N. G. Lederman & S. K. Abell (Eds.), *Handbook of research in science education* (Vol. 2; pp. 830–847). New York, NY: Routledge.

Kikas, E. (2004). Teachers' conceptions and misconceptions concerning three natural phenomena. *Journal of Research in Science Teaching, 41*(5), 432–448.

Lakshmanan, A., Heath, B., Perlmutter, A., & Elder, M. (2011). The impact of science content and professional learning communities on science teaching efficacy and standards-based instruction. *Journal of Research in Science Teaching, 48*(5), 534–551.

Lederman, N. G., & Abell, S. K. (Eds.). (2014). *Handbook of research on science education* (vol. 2). New York, NY: Routledge.

Lee, O., & Luykx, A. (2007). Science education and student diversity: Race/ethnicity, language, culture, and socioeconomic status. In N. G. Lederman & S. K. Abell (Eds.), *Handbook of research on science education* (pp. 171–197). Mahwah, NJ: Erlbaum.

Leonard, M. J., Kalinowski, S.T., & Andrews, T. C. (2014). Misconceptions yesterday, today, and tomorrow. *CBE Life Sciences Education, 13*(2), 179–186. http://doi.org/10.1187/cbe.13-12-0244

Lewis, C. C. (1995). *Educating hearts and minds: Reflections on Japanese preschool and elementary education.* Cambridge, England: University Press.

Lewis, E., Baker, D., Bueno Watts, N., & van der Hoeven Kraft, K. (2016). Science teachers' professional growth and the Communication in Science Inquiry Project. In T. Norton (Ed.), *Professional development: Recent advances and future directions* (pp. 1–57). Hauppauge, NY: Nova Science.

Lewis, E. B., Musson, A., & Lu, J. (2014, March). *Educating highly qualified science teachers: Challenges and perspectives.* Paper set presented at the 2014 annual meeting of the National Association for Research in Science Teaching (NARST): Pittsburgh, PA.

Lewis, E. B., Rivero, A., Lucas, L., Musson, A., & Helding, B. (under review). *Beginning science teachers' subject matter knowledge and misconceptions for teaching physical sciences.*

Lewis, E. B., Rivero, A., Lucas, L., Tankersley, A., & Helding, B. (2018, March). *Beginning science teachers' subject matter knowledge, misconceptions, and emerging inquiry-based teaching practices.* Paper set presented at the annual meeting of the National Association for Research in Science Teaching (NARST): Atlanta, GA.

Lewis, E. B., Rivero, A., Musson, A., Lu, J., & Lucas, L. (2016, April). *Building exemplary teaching practices: Following the paths of new science teachers.* Paper set presented at the annual meeting of the National Association for Research in Science Teaching (NARST): Baltimore, MD.

Loughran, J. J. (2014). Developing understandings of practice: Science teacher learning. In N. G. Lederman & S. K. Abell (Eds.), *Handbook of research in science education* (Vol. 2; pp. 811–829). New York, NY: Routledge.

Lucas, L., & Lewis, E. B. (2017). *Modeling inquiry-oriented instruction of beginning secondary science teachers.* In O. Finlayson, E. McLoughlin, S. Erduran, & P. Childs (Eds.), *Electronic proceedings of the ESERA 2017 conference: Research, practice, and collaboration in science education: Part 13 pre-service science teacher education* (co-ed by Maria Evagorou & Marisa Michelini; pp. 1742–1752). Dublin, Ireland: Dublin City University.

Marshall, J. C., Horton, B., Smart, J., & Llewellyn, D. (2009). *EQUIP: Electronic quality of inquiry protocol: Reviewed from Clemson University's inquiry in Motion Institute.* Retrieved from https://www.clemson.edu/education/research/centers-institutes/inquiry-in-motion/research-evaluation/equip.html

McDermott, L. C. (1990). A perspective on teacher preparation in physics and other sciences: The need for special science courses for teachers. *American Journal of Physics, 58,* 734.

McGinnis, J. R., Parker, C., & Graeber, A. O. (2004). A cultural perspective of the induction of five reform-minded beginning mathematics and science teachers. *Journal of Research in Science Teaching, 41*(7), 720–747.

McGinnis, J. R., & Stefanich, G. P. (2007). Special needs and talents in science learning. In N. G. Lederman & S. K. Abell (Eds.), *Handbook of research on science education* (pp. 287–317). Mahwah, NJ: Erlbaum.

Minner, D. D., Levy, A. J., & Century, J. (2010). Inquiry-based science instruction—What is it and does it matter? Results from a research synthesis years 1984 to 2002. *Journal of Research in Science Teaching, 47*(4), 474–496.

Miles, M. B., Huberman, A. M., & Saldana, J. (2014). *Qualitative data analysis: A methods sourcebook* (3rd ed.). Washington, DC: SAGE.

Murphy, C. (2005). The role of subject knowledge in primary trainee teachers' approaches to teaching in the topic of area. In D. Hewitt & A. Noyes (Eds.), *Proceedings of the Sixth British Congress of Mathematics Education held at the University of Warwick* (pp. 113–119). Lyon, France: INRP.

National Commission on Mathematics and Science Teaching for the 21st Century. (2000). *Before it's too late: A report to the nation from the National Commission on Mathematics and Science Teaching for the 21st Century.* Washington, DC: U.S. Department of Education.

National Commission on Teaching and America's Future. (2016). *What matters now: A new compact for teaching and learning.* Arlington, VA: NCTAF. Retrieved from https://eric.ed.gov/?id=ED572506

National Council for the Accreditation of Teacher Education. (2008). *Professional standards for the accreditation of teacher preparation institutions.* Washington, DC: Author.

National Research Council. (1996). *National science education standards.* Washington, DC: The National Academies Press. https://doi.org/10.17226/4962

National Research Council. (2010). *Preparing teachers: Building evidence for sound policy.* Committee on the Study of Teacher Preparation Programs in the United States, Center for Education. Division of Behavioral and Social Sciences and Education. Washington, DC: The National Academies Press.

National Research Council. (2012). *A framework for K–12 science education: Practices, crosscutting concepts, and core ideas.* Washington, DC: The National Academies Press. Retrieved from https://doi.org/10.17226/13165

National Research Council. (2013). *Next generation science standards: For states, by states.* Washington, DC: The National Academies Press.

Nehm, R. H., & Ridgway, J. (2011). What do experts and novices "see" in evolutionary problems? *Evolution: Education and Outreach, 4*(4), 666–679.

NGSS Lead States. (2013). *Next generation science standards: For states, by states.* Washington, DC: The National Academies Press.

Osborne, J. (2007). Science education for the twenty first century. *Eurasia Journal of Mathematics, Science and Technology Education, 3*(3), 173–184.

Osborne, J. (2014). Scientific practices and inquiry in the science classroom. In N. G. Lederman & S. K. Abell (Eds.), *Handbook of research on science education* (pp. 579–599). New York, NY: Routledge.

Özmen, H. (2010). Determination of science student teacher's conceptions about ionization energy. *Procedia–Social and Behavioral Sciences, 9,* 1025–1029.

Piburn, M., & Sawada, D. (2000). *Reformed Teaching Observation Protocol* (RTOP) Reference Manual (Report No. IN00-3). Retrieved from www.public.asu.edu/~anton1/AssessArticles/Assessments/Biology%20Assessments/RTOP%20Reference%20Manual.pdf

Roehrig, G. H., & Luft, J. A. (2004). Research report: Constraints experienced by beginning secondary science teacher in implementing scientific inquiry lessons. *International Journal of Science Education, 26*(1), 3–24.

Russell, T., & Martin, A. (2014). Learning to teach science. In N. G. Lederman & S. K. Abell (Eds.), *Handbook of research on science education* (pp. 871–888). New York, NY: Routledge.

Sadler, P. M., Coyle, H., Miller, J. L., Cook-Smith, N., Dussault, M., & Gould, R. R. (2010). The astronomy and space science concept inventory: Development and validation of assessment instruments aligned with the K–12 national science standards. *Astronomy Education Review, 8*(1), 010111.

Sadler, P., & Sonnert, G. (2016). Understanding misconceptions: Teaching and learning in middle school physical science. *American Educator, 40*(1), 26–32.

Tekkaya, C. (2002). Misconceptions as barrier to understanding biology. *Journal of Hacettepe University Education Faculty, 23,* 259–266. Retrieved from https://dergipark.org.tr/en/download/article-file/87939

Treagust, D. (2010). General instructional methods and strategies. In S. K. Abell & N. G. Norman (Eds.), *Handbook of research on science education* (Vol. 2; pp. 373–391). New York, NY: Routledge.

Treagust, D. F., & Tsui, C. Y. (2014). General instructional methods and strategies. In N. G. Lederman & S. K. Abell (Eds.), *Handbook of research on science education* (Vol. 2; pp. 303–320). New York, NY: Routledge.

Tschannen-Moran, M., & Hoy, A. W. (2001). Teacher efficacy: Capturing an elusive construct. *Teaching and Teacher Education, 17,* 783–805.

U.S. Department of Education, Institute of Education Sciences. (2015). *Science state snapshot report: Nebraska.* Retrieved from https://nces.ed.gov/nationsreport-card/subject/publications/stt2015/pdf/2016157NE8.pdf

van Driel, J. H., Berry, A., & Meirink, J. (2014). Research on science teacher knowledge. In N. G. Lederman & S. K. Abell (Eds.), *Handbook of research on science education* (Vol. 2; pp. 848–870). New York, NY: Routledge.

Veal, W. R., & Allan, E. (2014). Understanding the 2012 NSTA science standards for teacher preparation. *Journal of Science Teacher Education, 25*(5), 567–580.

Wiggins, G. (1998). *Educative assessment. Designing assessments to inform and improve student performance.* San Francisco, CA: Jossey-Bass.

Windschitl, M. A., & Stroupe, D. (2017). The three-story challenge. *Journal of Teacher Education, 68*(3), 251–261.

Windschitl, M., Thompson, J., Braaten, M., & Stroupe, D. (2012). Proposing a core set of instructional practices and tools for teachers of science. *Science Education, 96*(5), 878–903.

Yip, D. (1998). Identification of misconceptions in novice biology teachers and remedial strategies for improving biology learning. *International Journal of Science Education, 20*(4), 461–477.

CHAPTER 5

MEASURING DIVERSITY IN TEACHER CANDIDATE PRACTICUM PLACEMENTS AND ITS RELATIONSHIP TO OUTCOMES

Zafer Unal
University of South Florida St. Petersburg

Yasar Bodur
Georgia Southern University

Aslihan Unal
Georgia Southern University

The ethnic composition of American classrooms has been changing. According to the National Center for Educational Statistics *The Condition of Education 2017*, in Fall 2014, the percentage of White students in public elementary and secondary schools fell just below 50% for the first time—a

Linking Teacher Preparation Program Design and Implementation to Outcomes for Teachers and Students, pages 131–151

decrease from 58% in only a decade. During the same time period, the percentage of Hispanic students increased from 19% to 25%. Such changes are projected to continue (McFarland et al., 2017). Teacher preparation programs (TPPs) in colleges and universities have been responding to the need to prepare teachers for an increasingly diverse student population by altering requirements for courses, curriculum, fieldwork experiences, and other policies to include a diversity and multicultural education focus (Cochran-Smith & Zeichner, 2005; Finley, 2000). One of the primary methods for developing teachers capable of working with diverse student populations is through field experiences that place teacher candidates in schools with diverse populations. As Goldhaber, Krieg, and Theobald (2016) concluded, internship context had implications for teacher candidates and their students once they have their own classrooms; teachers were more effective when they taught in classrooms that were demographically similar to those in which they completed their student teaching.

The literature defines "diversity" in many ways, but its most typical definition tends to reflect equal employment opportunity (EEO) laws. EEO defines diversity in terms of differences among groups of people and individuals based on race, gender, national origin, religion, and disability status (Wheeler, 1994). On the other hand, Griggs (1995) provides a different perspective for describing diversity in two dimensions: primary and secondary. While the primary dimension includes human differences that are inborn and not possible to change such as race, age, gender, physical abilities, the secondary dimension includes factors that can be changed such as educational background, geographic location, income, marital status (Griggs, 1995). According to Interstate Teacher Assessment and Support Consortium (InTASC), diversity is inclusive of individual differences, such as personality and interests, and group differences, such as race, ethnicity, and language (2011). Others simply define diversity with a focus on all the characteristics that make one individual different from another (Carr, 1993; Caudron, 1992; Thomas, 1992; Triandis, 1994).

The Council for the Accreditation of Educator Preparation (CAEP) recognizes diversity as an important aspect of teacher preparation; the major indicator of this is that CAEP standards make reference to preparing teachers to make a positive impact on the learning and development of *all* P–12 students. Furthermore, CAEP treats diversity, along with technology, as a cross-cutting theme rather than a standard by itself. What this signifies is that diversity must be considered in all aspects of teacher preparation, from recruitment to clinical practice to content and pedagogical knowledge, skills, and dispositions of teacher candidates.

National accreditation and state approval agencies require that TPPs deliver high quality field experiences before teacher candidates start teaching in their own classrooms (AACTE, 2010; CAEP, 2013). These agencies provide general guidelines for quality of field experiences for TPPs. For example, CAEP's (2013) Standard 2 describes the need for P–12 school and university partnerships for designing clinical experiences; preparing and maintaining high quality clinical partners; and providing clinical experiences of sufficient depth, breadth, diversity, coherence, and duration. Quality of the clinical experiences in teacher preparation is recognized as an important factor in preparing teacher candidates to make a positive impact on all P–12 students.

Field experiences are commonly considered an important and powerful component of TPPs (Anderson & Stillman, 2013; Hollins & Torres-Guzman, 2005; Kyndt, Donche, Gijbels, & Van Petegem, 2014; McIntyre, Byrd, & Foxx, 1996; Steadman & Brown, 2011). These firsthand experiences in schools and classrooms allow teacher candidates to apply and reflect on their content knowledge, pedagogical skills, and professional dispositions with the guidance of a university supervisor and cooperating teacher (Cochran-Smith & Zeichner, 2005; Cuenca, Schmeichel, Butler, Dinkelman, & Nichols, 2011; Retallick & Miller, 2007; Sorensen, 2014). While the specifics of field experiences vary depending on individual TPP requirements, a typical field experience consists of three components: (a) observing the classroom and the cooperating teacher, (b) becoming involved with daily classroom tasks including some teaching assignments, and (c) taking over full-time teaching responsibility for a specific number of hours (Bacharach, Heck, & Dahlberg 2010; Henderson, Beach, & Famiano, 2009; Ronfeldt & Reininger, 2012). One or more cooperating teachers and a university supervisor typically observe and guide the teacher candidate during the field experience, providing feedback and support (Ambrosetti & Dekkers, 2010; Rubenstein, Thoron, & Estepp, 2014; Smalley, Retallick, & Paulsen, 2015). The performance and professional behavior of the teacher candidate is typically evaluated by the cooperating teacher and university supervisor multiple times during these experiences (Ambrosetti & Dekkers, 2010).

Although diversity of clinical experiences is important, as explained in CAEP's Standard 2, what is considered "diverse" is not always clear. Our understanding is that one way to ensure diversity in clinical experiences is to place teacher candidates in diverse schools and classrooms. Yet, still, there is no clarity on how diverse is diverse enough. Our goal in this chapter is twofold: (a) to describe how we applied a specific formula in our quality assurance system to determine if a given field placement can be considered diverse, and (b) to describe the ways in which we conducted research using the placement diversity data produced by the application of the formula.

CONTEXT AND PROJECT DESCRIPTION

This study was conducted at a TPP in a higher education institution in Florida in which all undergraduate and graduate TPPs are approved by the Florida Department of Education (FLDOE) and nationally accredited through CAEP. The TPP has been using an in-house developed quality assurance system to collect and analyze its institutional data for accreditation purposes since summer 2013. Data include but are not limited to program matrices, student assessment portfolios, state test scores, internship data, a graduation checklist, and completer and employer surveys. Program matrices include programs of study and alignment matrices between guiding standards and program assessments. For the internship data, the TPP records every field placement in its quality assurance system including teacher candidate demographics, school/classroom information and demographics, and information about the designated cooperating teacher and university supervisor. Also recorded are every field evaluation completed by the cooperating teacher and university supervisor for each teacher candidate.

Teacher candidates in the TPP are required to complete one or multiple field experiences depending on their program. For example, the Bachelor of Science in Education program requires three field experiences: (a) Integrated Clinical Experience K–5: one semester, 2 days per week; (b) Integrated Clinical Experience 6–12: one semester, 2 days per week; and (c) Integrated Final Internship: one semester in elementary classroom, 5 days a week. These field experiences are coded in the quality assurance system for each program.

The system also contains contact information of each university supervisor and cooperating teacher and allows these individuals to view information about teacher candidates under their purview. Supervisors use the system to submit their evaluation of the teacher candidates they supervise.

Before each field experience, teacher candidates are required to submit an online application form providing detailed information about their eligibility for internship. When the internship office receives these applications, staff validates the candidate's eligibility, and then works with the internship advisor to place the candidates. Even though candidates are allowed to submit preferences for the county/district of their placements, the final decision is made by the internship office. Once all teacher candidates are placed in a classroom, the placements are entered into the quality assurance system.

RECORDING DATA ABOUT PLACEMENT DIVERSITY

The TPP collects demographic data at the classroom and/or school level for each placement for program improvement and accreditation purposes.

These demographic data include information about students including: (a) gender, (b) ethnicity, (c) socioeconomic status (free/reduced lunch), (c) English language learner (ELL) status, and (e) exceptional student education (ESE) status. The TPP uses three methods to collect school/classroom demographic data to determine the diversity level of practicum placements for its teacher candidates. Table 5.1 describes these methods.

Using Method 1, the institution collects classroom demographic data from teacher candidates after the placement has been completed. At the beginning of each field practicum, including student teaching, teacher candidates are asked to fill out an online classroom demographics form where they simply record numbers of students in different diversity categories. Such data do not include any information identifying individuals and data collection is conducted according to the MOUs (memorandum of understanding) between the TPP and the school districts. The collection of data with this method is very useful since the data are at the classroom level, which ensures that the data can help determine whether the teacher candidates are placed in diverse classrooms.

Method 2 resembles Method 1 in the kind of data collected. The institution collects classroom-level specific data from cooperating teachers and university supervisors at the end of the semester. This method helps verify student-provided data. Like Method 1, the data are specific but cannot be used in field placement decisions due to the timing of the data collection.

Because in Methods 1 and 2 the data are collected only after the placements are made, these data do not allow the internship office to move teacher candidates to other classrooms in the cases where the original classroom is not considered diverse enough. In addition, it is very difficult to collect classroom demographic data before the school starts since classroom demographic data are usually not open to the public. In order to help the internship office identify placement diversity in time to inform placement, the TPP developed a third method where state and national school demographics data are exported from National Center for Educational

TABLE 5.1 Data Collection Methods for School/Classroom Demographics

Data	Data Collection	Advantages	Disadvantages
Method 1	Collected from teacher candidates	Data at the classroom level	Data collected after placement
Method 2	Collected from university supervisors & cooperating teachers	Data at the classroom level	Data collected after placement
Method 3	Collected from national & state school database (NCES & state databases)	Data collected before placement	Data at the school level

Statistics (NCES) to the TPP's quality assurance system. The advantage of this method is that diversity data can be obtained before practicum placements are completed; thus, these data can be used in placement decisions. One potential drawback of the third method is that the data exported from NCES may not always be completely accurate due to factors such as school closings and student transfers. Currently, the quality assurance system is set up to use all three methods; however, we find the third method to be more useful in making practicum placement decisions.

Table 5.2 shows an example of a school diversity placement report for a TPP during the spring 2016 semester using Methods 1 and 2. Even though

TABLE 5.2 Basic Placement Data With School Demographics

District	Pinellas								Hill[a]	Her[b]	Pas[c]
School	Sandy Lane Elem.	Mount Vernon Elem.	Meadow Middle	Pinellas Park High	Tyrone Middle	Paul B. Stephens	Blanton Elem.	Chiles Elem.	West Hern. Middle	River Ridge Middle	
# Placements	12	13	13	13	13	12	12	14	13	12	
	Percentages										
Gender											
Male	58	52	52	51	50	67	54	53	51	52	
Female	42	48	48	49	50	33	46	47	49	48	
Ethnicity											
White	16	46	60	58	50	72	52	39	72	82	
Black	49	32	15	12	21	11	17	16	17	2	
Hispanic	25	11	14	19	19	12	19	22	8	9	
Asian	1	5	7	7	11	1	9	17	1	3	
Hawaiian	0	0	0	0	0	0	0	0	0	0	
American Indian	0	0	1	0	0	0	0	0	0	0	
2 or more	9	6	3	4	3	4	4	6	2	4	
Socioeconomic											
Free & Reduced Lunch	74	52	38	43	62	38	54	36	51	35	
Percent of ELL Students	12	5	6	3	7	7	5	13	2	1	
Percent of ESE Students	5	5	5	6	5	5	5	6	2	2	
Diverse?	NA	NA	NA	NA	NA	NA	NA	NA	NA	NA	

[a] Hillsboro
[b] Hernando
[c] Pasco

the school diversity placement report has useful information, it does not provide a standard way of judging the degree to which a school is diverse in terms of student demographics for practicum placements. While field experiences in diverse settings are recommended for accreditation purposes, there are no guidelines on what is considered diverse. For example, CAEP (2013) lists diversity as one of the attributes of high-quality field experience. However, it does not describe what is meant by diversity in the case of field experiences.

Calculating Diversity With Simpson's Diversity Index

In order to offer a standard way to judge the degree to which a school is diverse, we used the Simpson's diversity index formula. Currently, the most common approach to measuring diversity in education is to count the percentage of students in various demographic categories (e.g., race, ethnicity, gender, and age) for a given population. In placement diversity reports, most of the TPPs simply list the percentage for demographic categories for each student placement. The use of proportion is the most common approach because of its simplicity and lack of a viable alternative. However, the use of these metrics cannot describe adequately whether a school is diverse. For example, a school with 50% males and 50% females can be said perfectly diverse in terms of gender. On the other hand, it is not possible to determine if a school should be considered diverse with 25% male and 75% female population in terms of gender. Along the same lines, how do we determine if a school that serves a student population that is 75% White is diverse or not?

In this study, we used Simpson's diversity index to calculate the diversity of a school as a single number for each demographic category (ethnicity, gender, socioeconomic status, ELL status, and ESE status). Simpson's Diversity Index is a measure of diversity used in the natural sciences which takes into account the number of species present, as well as the relative abundance of each species. As species richness and evenness increase, so does diversity. Although this index has been used in ecological studies, researchers in education have used it to study the extent of ethnic diversity in educational settings (Graham, Bellmore, Nishina, & Juvonen, 2009; Lee, Howes, & Chamberlain, 2007). The diversity index is an arithmetic mean weighted by its own observed probability with a score that ranges from 0 to 1. When used with school data, the closer a school's diversity index number is to 1, the more diverse the student population. Schools whose enrollment is made up of mostly one ethnic group will score closer to 0 using this formula indicating that students are less likely to encounter others from different ethnic backgrounds. The diversity index formula is presented as:

$$\text{Diversity Index (D)} = 1 - \frac{\sum n_i(n_i - 1)}{N(N-1)}$$

n_i = total number in each category
N = total number of the population

Simpson's diversity index has been used in numerous demographic studies. For example, Reese-Cassal (2015) used the diversity index formula to compute ethnic diversity and reported that the United States had a 2010 diversity index of 0.60, based on census counts. The diversity index based on 2014 updates was 0.62, and it is expected to rise to 0.65 in 2019. A diversity index of 0.65 translates to a probability of 65% that two people randomly chosen from the U.S. population would belong to different racial or ethnic groups.

Application of Simpson's Diversity Index Within the Quality Assurance System

Once the placement data are entered (i.e., student teacher, placement school, cooperating teacher, and university supervisor), the TPP's quality assurance system is able to (a) retrieve the school/district demographics data from its database, (b) apply Simpson's diversity index Formula to calculate school and district diversity values, and (c) compare the school diversity index score with that of the district in order to determine the extent to which the school is more or less diverse. (For ease of reading, we stated the Simpson's diversity index as a percentage rather than as a decimal in our tables.)

When the Simpson's diversity index is applied within the field placement section of the quality assurance system, the previous school diversity report provided in Table 5.2 becomes more useful for comparison. Most importantly, the quality assurance system shows whether the school population is more or less diverse when compared to its district. We consider a school "diverse" if the school's diversity index score is equal to or higher than the district's diversity index score in a given demographic category. Table 5.3 illustrates how diversity index score is used in the quality assurance system.

If a school has diversity index scores that are consistently equal or higher than those for its district across all demographic categories, then it is considered diverse. In addition to placement reports aggregated by the program, the TPP is able to use the same data to create individual teacher candidate reports. These individual placement reports provide information to help the internship office, program advisors, and assessment coordinators to determine whether a teacher candidate has had field practicum in a higher diversity school. The system allows the internship office to ensure that before graduation, a teacher candidate has been placed in a higher diversity school at least once in each

TABLE 5.3 Placement Data With School Diversity Index

District	Pinellas							Hill[a]	Her[b]	Pas[c]
School	Sandy Lane Elem.	Mount Vernon Elem.	Meadow Middle	Pinellas Park High	Tyrone Middle	Paul B. Stephens	Blanton Elem.	Chiles Elem.	West Hern. Middle	River Ridge Middle
# Placements	12	13	13	13	13	12	12	14	13	12
Percentages										
Gender										
School	49.3	49.9	49.9	50.3	49.9	43.7	49.8	49.8	49.9	51.8
District	47.1	47.1	47.1	47.1	47.1	47.1	47.1	48.9	49.9	49.9
Ethnicity										
School	65.4	67.1	59.2	62.3	67.1	45.5	65.2	74.5	42.4	32.6
District	60.2	60.2	60.2	60.2	60.2	60.2	60.2	70.1	70.1	51.7
Socioeconomic										
School	49.1	49.9	46.6	49.2	49.1	49.5	49.6	49.3	45.2	49.9
District	49.0	49.0	49.0	49.0	49.0	49.0	49.0	48.8	46.0	49.8
ELL										
School	13.6	9.5	7.1	11.2	10.3	7.2	11.5	22.6	3.9	1.9
District	8.8	8.8	8.8	8.8	8.8	8.8	8.8	21.1	5.8	7.6
ESE										
School	11.9	9.4	9.8	13.2	9.7	8.0	13.5	9.8	9.8	3.9
District	9.4	9.4	9.4	9.4	9.4	9.4	9.4	9.7	11.3	5.8
Diverse?	Yes	Yes	No	Yes	Yes	No	Yes	Yes	No	No

Note: The numbers in this table represents the diversity scores—not the percentages. Each school diversity score is then compared with that of its district to determine whether schools are diverse.

[a] Hillsboro
[b] Hernando
[c] Pasco

demographic category. Figure 5.1 shows a screenshot of diversity of practicum placements for two different teacher candidates with fictitious names.

As Figure 5.1 indicates, both teacher candidates have been placed in higher diversity settings in each demographic category by the time they graduated. The bubbles in the figure indicate whether or not a placement had higher diversity than the district in a given diversity category. With this information available for each teacher candidate, the TPP is able to build diversity reports for specific programs and individual teacher candidates.

Student	Level I (K–5) Internship	Level II (6–12) Internship	Final Internship Part I (Elementary)	Final Internship Part II (ESE)
Name: Heather Blue Program: B.S. in Education Level: Undergraduate Email: hblue@usfsp.edu	Semester: Spring 2011 District: Pasco School: Odessa Elementary Grade: 3 Supervisor: G. Stires Coop. Teacher: J. Henry # of PBA Evaluations: 3 # of Internship Evaluations: 3 School Diversity: Ge: ● Et: ● So: ● EL: ● ES: ● Placement Details & Evaluations	Semester: Fall 2011 District: Pasco School: Crews Lake Middle Grade: ESE-Middle Supervisor: T. Keys Coop. Teacher: J. Crumley # of PBA Evaluations: 3 # of Internship Evaluations: 3 School Diversity: Ge: ● Et: ● So: ● EL: ● ES: ● Placement Details & Evaluations	Semester: Spring 2012 District: Pasco School: New River Element. Grade: 4 Supervisor: B. Braun Coop. Teacher: L. Carlson # of PBA Evaluations: 3 # of Internship Evaluations: 3 School Diversity: Ge: ● Et: ● So: ● EL: ● ES: ● Placement Details & Evaluations	Semester: Spring 2012 District: Pasco School: New River Element. Grade: ESE-Elementary Supervisor: B. Braun Coop. Teacher: G. Allan # of PBA Evaluations: 3 # of Internship Evaluations: 3 School Diversity: Ge: ● Et: ● So: ● EL: ● ES: ● Placement Details & Evaluations
				OK
Name: George Blue Program: B.S. in Education Level: Undergraduate Email: gblue@usfsp.edu	Semester: Spring 2011 District: Pinellas School: Blantan Elementary Grade: Kindergarten Supervisor: D. McCaffrey Coop. Teacher: C. Keene # of PBA Evaluations: 3 # of Internship Evaluations: 3 School Diversity: Ge: ● Et: ● So: ● EL: ● ES: ● Placement Details & Evaluations	Semester: Fall 2011 District: Pinellas School: Pinellas Park High Grade: ESE-High Supervisor: N. Medley Coop. Teacher: E. Gulino # of PBA Evaluations: 3 # of Internship Evaluations: 3 School Diversity: Ge: ● Et: ● So: ● EL: ● ES: ● Placement Details & Evaluations	Semester: Spring 2012 District: Pinellas School: Skyview Element. Grade: 4 Supervisor: B. Braun Coop. Teacher: K. Zwissler # of PBA Evaluations: 3 # of Internship Evaluations: 3 School Diversity: Ge: ● Et: ● So: ● EL: ● ES: ● Placement Details & Evaluations	Semester: Spring 2012 District: Pinellas School: Marjorie Kinnan El. Grade: ESE-Elementary Supervisor: B. Braun Coop. Teacher: K. Stauffer # of PBA Evaluations: 3 # of Internship Evaluations: 3 School Diversity: Ge: ● Et: ● So: ● EL: ● ES: ● Placement Details & Evaluations
				OK

Figure 5.1 Candidate placement report.

METHODS

The application of the school diversity index formula on placement data has created many possibilities for new research. The new system enabled the institution to build real-time, dynamic reports for multiple purposes including: (a) generating placement diversity reports, like above, aggregated by individual teacher candidate, field practicum course, and program; (b) providing information about placement diversity for state approval and national accreditation; and (c) supporting research as a decision-making tool for program improvement. With the new system, we used the available data to investigate the following research questions:

1. Is there a relationship between student teacher placement diversity and student teacher evaluation scores?
2. Is there a relationship between student teacher placement diversity and employment placement diversity?
3. Is there a relationship between student teacher placement diversity and graduate/employer satisfaction?

Data and Instruments

Data were collected from multiple groups of teacher candidates, in a traditional teacher preparation program at a medium size institution in an urban center in Florida, during their last semester of student teaching during the 2011–2012 through 2015–2016 school years. The total number of participants across years was 387. While student teachers were placed in 27 different schools in four different districts, we used data from student teachers placed in ten different schools in the four districts. Data included teacher candidate scores on three assessments: the Professional Behavior Evaluation (PBE) form, the Internship Evaluation (IE) form, and Teacher Work Sample (TWS). Each measure is described in the next section.

Diversity of practicum placement was calculated based on the result of the Simpson's diversity index. If a student teacher was placed in a school that was considered diverse (relative to the district) in terms of all five demographic categories, that placement was considered a 5-star placement. To further illustrate, if a student teacher was placed in a school that was considered diverse in three of the five demographic categories based on the Simpson's diversity index formula, that placement was considered a 3-star placement. Star level of placements were correlated with teacher candidates' scores on the three assessments mentioned above.

The Professional Behavior Evaluation Form

The TPP in this study adopted a set of professional behaviors and dispositions that the faculty considered essential for prospective teachers. The PBE form is used for assessing teacher candidates' professional attitudes, values, and beliefs demonstrated through both verbal and non-verbal behaviors as they interact with students, families, colleagues, and communities. The instrument has a total of 20 questions focusing on behaviors such as time management, demonstrating ethical behaviors, demonstrating enthusiasm, demonstrating collaboration with colleagues, and working with parents. Candidates are evaluated before the end of the field experience by both their cooperating teacher and university supervisor along a 5-point scale: *unacceptable, emergent, bridging, proficient, mastery*. According to the program policy, failing performance on one or more of the indicators leads to an individualized plan for improvement and, in extreme cases, leads to removal from the teacher preparation program. Any teacher candidate who scored lower than proficient on one or more indicators was considered exhibiting failing performance. Cronbach's alpha indicated an acceptable level of internal consistency (20 items; $\alpha = 0.79$).

The Internship Evaluation Form

The IE form is a questionnaire grounded in the six Florida Educator Accomplished Practices (FEAPs) set by the Florida Department of Education. The FEAPs are Florida's core standards for effective educators and provide valuable guidance to Florida's public-school educators and educator preparation programs throughout the state about what educators are expected to know and be able to do. The instrument has 38 questions focusing on domains such as instructional design and lesson planning, learning environment, instructional delivery and facilitation, assessment, continuous professional improvement, and professional responsibility and ethical conduct. Each candidate is evaluated before the end the field experience by both the cooperating teacher and the university supervisor along a 5-point Likert scale (*unacceptable, emergent, bridging, proficient*, and *mastery*). According to the program policy, demonstrating failing performance on one or more of the items leads to an individualized plan for improvement or repetition of the course and, in extreme cases, leads to removal from the teacher preparation program. Internal consistency of the instrument was assessed using Cronbach's alpha, which indicated an acceptable level of reliability (38 items; $\alpha = 0.73$).

Teacher Work Sample

The TWS is a performance-based narrative prepared by the student teacher with a focus on demonstrating increased student learning. It is used as a performance assessment tool during student teaching to measure teacher candidate effectiveness. This assessment is evaluated with a rubric that includes 43 items focusing on eight domains: contextual factors, learning goals/objectives, assessment plan, design for instruction, instructional delivery, instructional decision making, analysis of student learning, and reflection/self-assessment. This assignment is evaluated separately by the university supervisor, cooperating teacher, and a faculty from the program along a 5-point Likert scale. Scores from each rater are averaged to compute a final score. Internal consistency of the instrument was assessed using Cronbach's alpha, which indicated a high level of reliability (43 items; $\alpha = 0.87$).

Employment Placement Diversity

The Florida Department of Education (FDOE) provides employment data for each teacher preparation institution that offers one or more state-approved initial teacher preparation programs. The data provided by FDOE includes the list of graduates from the institution working at public schools in Florida. These data include the names of the graduates, the schools where they are employed, their positions at the school (e.g., teacher, substitute, or reading coach), the subject area, and the grade level they teach. These data are imported into the quality assurance system and used for program evaluation, graduation follow-up surveys, and accreditation reports.

Graduate and Employer Satisfaction

In fulfillment of section 1004.04(5), Florida Statutes, the FDOE conducts an annual graduate satisfaction survey of individuals who completed a Florida state-approved TPP or a district alternative certification program and are employed in an instructional position in a Florida school district. The FDOE sends an email in the fall of the second year of employment containing a link to a web-based survey to completers requesting that they complete a brief online survey on perceptions of and satisfaction with their preparation program. The FDOE also surveys the employers (principals) of program completers to assess their perceptions of each completer's readiness for the teaching profession. Employer Satisfaction Survey results are analyzed to assist FDOE, districts, and institutions in making decisions for improving TPPs. Both the Graduate Satisfaction Survey and the Employer Satisfaction Survey are streamlined to focus on the Florida Educator Accomplishment Practices (FEAP). The Graduate Satisfaction Survey has 39 questions focusing on the effectiveness of the teacher preparation program on the six FEAP domains (i.e., instructional design and planning, the learning environment, instructional delivery and facilitation, assessment, continuous professional development, and professional responsibility and conduct), and the Employer Satisfaction Survey includes 36 questions focusing on principals' perception of each completer's readiness for the teaching profession in the same six domains. Cronbach's alpha values showed acceptable levels of reliability for both instruments (Graduate Satisfaction Survey: $\alpha = 0.79$, Employer Satisfaction Survey: $\alpha = 0.81$).

RESULTS

After all the data were collected, they were entered into SPSS 23.0 for analysis. Results of our analyses are organized by each research question and presented below.

Relationship Between Student Teacher Placement Diversity and Teacher Candidates' Evaluation Scores

Table 5.4 presents average teacher candidate scores on the PBE, IE, and TWS evaluation based on the diversity star rating of their student teaching placement. These data represent multiple cohorts of teacher candidate performance over a span of 5 years from fall 2011 to spring 2016.

As the table indicates, most of the teacher candidates (80%) had 5-star placements. While the teacher candidate performance does not look very different based on the diversity star rating of the placement on the PBE, on the IE and the TWS evaluation teacher candidates who had placements that were diverse in fewer demographic categories performed better. In other words, teacher candidates who had more diverse placements tended to receive lower scores on their performance evaluation.

TABLE 5.4   Descriptive Statistics: Teacher Candidate Performance During Student Teaching by Placement Diversity (2011–2016)

Instruments		Placement Diversity		
		5-Star Placement	4-Star Placement	3-Star Placement
Professional Behavior Evaluation Form ($n = 380$)	N	305	52	23
	M	4.76	4.78	4.71
	SD	2.08	1.91	1.76
Internship Evaluation Form ($n = 380$)	N	305	52	23
	M	4.14	4.39	4.77
	SD	1.21	0.96	0.86
Teacher Work Sample Assignment ($n = 380$)	N	305	52	23
	M	4.12	4.41	4.76
	SD	1.81	1.54	1.09

[*] The 1 and 2-star placements ($n = 7$) were omitted due to placements being less than 5.

In order to make better sense of the data, we conducted a correlation analysis between the diversity star ratings and candidate performance on the internship assessments using Kendall's tau. Diversity of student teaching placements and teacher candidate performance were negatively correlated. This was especially true for the PBE ($n = 380$, $\tau_b = -0.203$, p < 0.03), IE ($n = 380$, $\tau_b = -0.604$, p < 0.02), and TWS evaluation ($n = 380$, $\tau_b = -0.622$, $p < 0.01$), which had higher correlation coefficients. A one star increase in diversity was associated with a 0.2 decrease on the PBE and 0.6 decrease on IE and TWS.

Relationship Between Student Teacher Placement Diversity and Employment Placement Diversity

To assess the relationship between the student teaching placement diversity and employment placement diversity, we used Kendall's tau. The correlation analysis indicated that the diversity of the student teaching placement and the diversity of the schools where program graduates were employed had a significant, positive correlation ($n = 75$, $\tau_b = 0.59$, $p < .01$). In other words, teacher candidates who completed their internship in more diverse schools tended to obtain employment in more diverse public schools in the state.

Relationship Between Student Teacher Placement Diversity and Graduate/Employer Satisfaction

Table 5.5 presents average graduate and employer survey scores by placement diversity. As Table 5.5 indicates, teacher candidates who had more diverse placements tended to have higher mean scores both in graduate satisfaction and employer satisfaction.

We also conducted Kendall's tau to investigate the relationship between the diversity of internship placement and graduate and employer satisfaction. The Kendall's tau indicated a strong positive relationship between the placement diversity and program completer ($n = 105$, $\tau_b = 0.61$, $p < 0.01$) and employer satisfaction, ($n = 75$, $\tau_b = 0.59$, $p < 0.01$). In other words, teacher candidates who completed their internship in more diverse schools had a tendency to be more satisfied with their preparation. Similarly, employers tended to show more satisfaction with graduates who completed their teacher preparation in more diverse placements.

DISCUSSION

Diversity of field experiences has been recognized as a critical element in teacher education as indicated by the inclusion of diversity of field experiences in teacher preparation accreditation standards. However, there is not an agreed upon understanding of what is meant by diverse field experiences. What makes a field practicum site diverse? This study aimed to contribute to the teacher preparation community's collective understanding of how to determine if a given practicum should be considered diverse. In doing so, our main argument is that local demographic data (i.e., demographic data for the school district) could be the basis for determining the diversity level of a practicum placement. We argue that using Simpson's diversity index with district and school demographic data for such decisions creates opportunities for TPPs to approach the question of field placement diversity in a systematic way. Our experience with this system indicates that it is easy to implement and allows us to use the data for program improvement and accreditation purposes.

The second part of the study focused on relationships between internship placement diversity and teacher candidate performance, graduate job placement, and employer and graduate satisfaction. We found that there was a negative correlation between internship placement diversity and teacher candidate performance on practicum assessments, such that student teachers placed in diverse schools tend to receive lower scores in their IEs and TWSs compared to those who were placed in less diverse schools. This finding aligns with the literature suggesting that teaching diverse students can be more challenging than teaching students in homogeneous settings (Wilson, Floden, & Ferrini-Mundy, 2002). Teaching in diverse settings requires responsiveness to diversity such as positive attitude, appreciation, accommodation of differences among students, and planning and use of a variety of instructional strategies and learning activities (Sleeter & Grant, 1994).

We also found a significant positive relationship between practicum placement diversity and employment placement diversity such that students placed in more diverse schools for field placements tended to work in more diverse schools after program completion. This result may be due to the fact that teacher candidates develop a network of relationships during their internship and seek employment after graduation relying on these relationships. This point is supported by the research of Krieg, Theobald, and Goldhaber (2016) who found that location of a teacher candidate's student teaching is the biggest predictor of the location of their first job. Furthermore, the positive relationship could be due to the fact that teacher candidates feel prepared and are more willing to take the challenge of teaching in diverse schools because of the diversity level of their practicum placements. Either way, considering the difficulties associated with staffing highly diverse schools, placing teacher candidates in highly diverse schools may contribute to solving staffing problems in high diversity settings.

Finally, we found strong positive relationships between placement diversity and satisfaction of both program completers and employers. In other words, teacher candidates who were placed in diverse schools during their internship tended to be more satisfied with the preparation they received. Similarly, employers of teachers who had diverse field placements expressed more satisfaction with the performance of the graduates. It may be argued that those who were placed in more diverse schools in their internship may have come into the TPP with positive attitudes toward diversity and the practicum placement reinforced these attitudes. However, we do not have the data to substantiate such arguments.

Curricular Implications

Working with a quality assurance system where diversity is defined using Simpson's Diversity Index allowed our teacher preparation institution to engage in more informed program improvement efforts in this area. Our findings prompted important curricular changes. The fact that teacher candidates who were placed in higher diversity schools received lower scores on performance assessments suggested that they may have been insufficiently prepared to work with diverse students. As a result of these findings, the following curricular changes were made to better prepare teacher candidates for diverse placements.

- Classroom Management: Addition of a 2-week module on "Classroom Management for Diverse Students"
- Instructional Design: Expansion of the topic "Differentiated Instruction for Diverse Learners"
- Standard Based Education: Addition of a 2-week module on "Culturally Responsive Practices" and "Working with Diverse Students"
- Multiple courses: Replacement of faculty-selected course activities with new "Case/scenario Based Activities" on working with diverse students

These changes started being implemented in fall 2017. As in any potential program improvement, we will examine data similar to what we reported here to assess the impact of these curricular changes and continue with revisions based on new findings. Further actions to be implemented in the near future based on these findings include training assessors on the instruments and examining the instruments for sensitivity to the context in which teacher candidates complete their internship.

Limitations

Our goal in this study was to describe our experience using Simpson's diversity index formula in determining the diversity level of field experience placements. Although the study revealed meaningful findings, it had limitations. First, because our analyses were correlational, we were not able to make causal interpretations. Second, while the sample size of this investigation might allow for institutional generalization, conducting the same study with a larger sample size at multiple institutions and a broader range of schools including lower diversity placements might help with broader generalization. Finally, the diversity index is a relative measure of diversity and may not work in all settings. For example, the school diversity index calculated in this study is most useful in a district that meets some minimum threshold of diversity and that has schools with varying levels of diversity. On the other hand, it would be challenging for this diversity index to work well in a homogeneous district or in a district where schools have a roughly equivalent degree of diversity. In those cases, teacher preparation programs might consider possible alternatives to this index, such as school diversity relative to state diversity, or an objective standard of diversity with a preset diversity score. Furthermore, Simpson's diversity index formula is useful in calculating the diversity level of a school relative to a standard like district's diversity; however, in teacher education, diversity of field experience placements may be defined in other ways. For example, a rural and an urban school with similar demographics may produce the same diversity index score but still be very different due to being rural or urban. Therefore, other general ways of defining diversity should be considered when using the Simpson's diversity index formula.

CONCLUSION

When all the findings are put in perspective together, it seems reasonable that teacher candidates who had more diverse practicum placements obtained jobs in diverse schools and were satisfied with their preparation because of the relevance of the practicum experiences to their employment site; because these teacher candidates experienced diverse classrooms in their teacher preparation, they were better prepared to seek employment in diverse schools. As indicated by our analyses, diverse placements were related positively to the outcome measures of graduate and employer satisfaction. Teacher preparation programs should provide teacher candidates with the information and experiences necessary for successful employment in increasingly diverse public schools. Because there is a greater likelihood that teachers will be working with students whose cultural backgrounds differ greatly from their own (Dilworth, 1992; Fox & Gay, 1995), it is of great importance that teachers become aware of individual cultural perspectives and that they have an opportunity to experience various forms of diversity.

Finding a system to define (or measure) diversity in field placements can lead to program improvements that may not be obvious without placement diversity data. Therefore, we encourage TPPs to consider diversity of their practicum placements in a way that produces meaningful and usable data and to test the relationship between aspects of placement diversity and completer outcomes. Given the strong emphasis of CAEP on data-informed program improvement, such efforts would be useful for accreditation purposes as well. In order to help all teacher education programs in the United States, the authors of this chapter created a website (www.schooldiversity.com) that allows users to see diversity index score of all schools in the United States.

Our study points to the necessity of further studies to better understand the dynamics of how practicum diversity and other variables such as the cooperating teacher characteristics and achievement levels of school children in diverse placements work together. While the index used here weighted five types of diversity equally, future work might explore whether some types of diversity matter more than others for future outcomes. Furthermore, collecting qualitative data in the form of interviews from teacher candidates who had different levels of practicum diversity placements may shed light on the perceived value of diverse field experiences. To address causal questions about the impact of practicum placement diversity on teacher satisfaction, employer satisfaction, and particularly teacher retention and effectiveness, future research could include experimental studies in which candidates are randomly assigned to varying levels of diversity.

REFERENCES

American Association of Colleges for Teacher Education. (2010). *Reforming teacher education: The critical clinical component.* Washington, DC: Author.

Anderson, L. M., & Stillman, J. A. (2013). Student teaching's contribution to preservice teacher development: A review of research focused on the preparation of teachers for urban and high-needs contexts. *Review of Educational Research, 83*(1), 3–69.

Ambrosetti, A., & Dekkers, J. (2010). The interconnectedness of the roles of mentors and mentees in pre-service teacher education mentoring relationships. *Australian Journal of Teacher Education, 35*(6), 42–55.

Bacharach, N., Heck, T., & Dahlberg, K. (2010). Changing the face of student teaching through co-teaching. *Action in Teacher Education, 32*(1), 3–14.

Carr, C. (1993). Diversity and performance: A shotgun marriage? *Performance Improvement Quarterly, 6*(4), 115–126.

Caudron, S. (1992). U. S. West finds strength in diversity. *Personnel Journal, 71*(3), 40–44.

Cochran-Smith, M., & Zeichner, K. M. (2005). *Studying teacher education: The report of the AERA panel on research and teacher education.* Mahwah, NJ: Erlbaum.

Council for the Accreditation of Educator Preparation. (2013). *CAEP accreditation standards.* Washington, DC: Author.

Cuenca, A., Schmeichel, M., Butler, B., Dinkelman, T., & Nichols, J. (2011). Creating a "third space" in student teaching: Implications for the university supervisor's status as outsider. *Teaching and Teacher Education, 27*(7), 1068–1077.

Dilworth, M. (1992). *Diversity in teacher education: New expectations.* San Francisco, CA: Jossey-Bass.

Finley, S. (2000). Transformative teaching for multicultural classrooms: Designing curriculum and classroom strategies for master's level teacher education. *Multicultural Education, 7*(3), 20–27.

Fox, W., & Gay, G. (1995). Integrating multicultural and cultural principles in teacher education. *Peabody Journal of Education, 70*(3), 64–81.

Goldhaber, D., Krieg, J. M., & Theobald, R. (2016). *Does the match matter? Exploring whether student teacher experiences affect teacher effectiveness and attrition.* CALDER Working Paper 149.

Graham, S., Bellmore, A., Nishina, A., & Juvonen, J. (2009). "It must be me": Ethnic diversity and attributions for peer victimization in middle school. *Journal of Youth and Adolescence, 38*(4), 487–499.

Griggs, L. B. (1995). Valuing diversity: Where from . . . where to? In L. B. Griggs & L. L. Louw (Eds.), *Valuing diversity: New tools for a new reality* (pp. 1–14). New York, NY: McGraw-Hill.

Henderson, C., Beach, A., & Famiano, M. (2009). Promoting instructional change via co-teaching. *American Journal of Physics, 77*(3), 274–283.

Hollins, E., & Torres-Guzman, M. T. (2005). Research on preparing teachers for diverse populations. In M. Cochran-Smith & K. M. Zeichner (Eds.), *Studying teacher education: The report of the AERA panel on research and teacher education* (pp. 477–548). Mahwah, NJ: Erlbaum.

Interstate Teacher Assessment and Support Consortium. (2011). *InTASC model core teaching standards: A resource for state dialogue.* Retrieved from https://www.ccsso.org/

Krieg, J., Theobald, R., & Goldhaber, D. (2016). A foot in the door: Exploring the role of student teaching assignments in teachers' initial job placements. *Educational Evaluation and Policy Analysis, 38*(2), 364–388.

Kyndt, E., Donche, V., Gijbels, D., & Van Petegem, P. (2014). Workplace learning within teacher education. The role of job characteristics and goal orientation. *Educational Studies, 40*(5), 515–532.

Lee, L., Howes, C., & Chamberlain, B. (2007). Ethnic heterogeneity of social networks and cross-ethnic friendships of elementary school boys and girls. *Merrill-Palmer Quarterly, 53*(3), Article 3. Retrieved from https://digitalcommons.wayne.edu/mpq/vol53/iss3/3/.

McFarland, J., Hussar, B., de Brey, C., Snyder, T., Wang, X., Wilkinson-Flicker, S., . . . Hinz, S. (2017). *The condition of education 2017* (NCES 2017–144). U.S. Department of Education. Washington, DC: National Center for Education

Statistics. Retrieved from https://nces.ed.gov/pubsearch/pubsinfo.asp?pubid =2017144

McIntyre, D. J., Byrd, D. M., & Foxx, S. M. (1996). Field and laboratory experiences. In W. R. Houston, M. Haberman, & J. Sikula (Eds.), *Handbook of research on teacher education: A project of the Association of Teacher Educators* (pp. 171–193). New York, NY: Macmillan.

Reese-Cassal, K. (2015). *2015/2020 Esri Diversity Index.* Retrieved from http:// downloads.esri.com/support/whitepapers/other_/2015_USA_ESRI_Diversity _Index_Methodology.pdf

Retallick, M. S., & Miller, G. (2007). Early field experience documents in agricultural education. *Journal of Agricultural Education, 52*(3), 100–109.

Ronfeldt, M., & Reininger, M. (2012). More or better student teaching? *Teaching and Teacher Education, 28*(8), 1091–1106.

Rubenstein, E. D., Thoron, A. C., & Estepp, C. M. (2014). Perceived self-efficacy of preservice agriculture teachers towards specific SAE competencies. *Journal of Agriculture Education, 55*(4), 72–84.

Sleeter, C. E., & Grant, C. (1994). M*aking choices for multicultural education: Five approaches to race, class and gender.* Englewood Cliffs, NJ: Prentice Hall.

Smalley, S. W., Retallick, M. S., & Paulsen, T. H. (2015). Cooperating teachers' perspectives of student teaching skills and activities. *Journal of Agricultural Education, 56*(3), 123–137.

Sorensen, P. (2014). Collaboration, dialogue and expansive learning: The use of paired and multiple placements in the school practicum. *Teaching and Teacher Education, 44*, 128–137.

Steadman, S. C., & Brown, S. D. (2011). Defining the job of university supervisor: A department-wide study of university supervisors' practices. *Issues in Teacher Education, 20*(1), 51–68.

Thomas Jr., R. R. (1992). Managing diversity: A conceptual framework. In S. E. Jackson & Associates (Eds.), *Diversity in the workplace* (pp. 306–317). New York, NY: Guilford Press.

Triandis, H. C. (1994). *Culture and social behavior.* New York, NY: McGraw-Hill.

Wheeler, M. L. (1994). *Diversity training* (# 1083–94RR). New York, NY: The Conference Board.

Wilson, S., Floden, R., & Ferrini-Mundy, J. (2002). Teacher preparation research: An insider's view from the outside. *Journal of Teacher Education, 53*(3), 190–204.

CHAPTER 6

SIGNATURE PRACTICES IN AN URBAN RESIDENCY PROGRAM

How Are These Practices Evident in the Graduates' Classrooms?

Jennifer Collett
Lehman College, City University of New York

Nancy Dubetz
Lehman College, City University of New York

Harriet Fayne
Lehman College, City University of New York

Anne Marie Marshall
Lehman College, City University of New York

Anne Rothstein
Lehman College, City University of New York

Linking Teacher Preparation Program Design and Implementation to Outcomes for Teachers and Students, pages 153–179
Copyright © 2020 by Information Age Publishing
153

Elementary school teachers face multiple challenges through the varied roles they must take up in schools. Among these challenges is the critical and difficult task of preparing young children to build foundational academic skills. Teachers must be prepared to instruct across a multitude of subjects, from science and mathematics to supporting students' early literacy development. Due to these academic demands, many elementary school teachers enter the teaching force lacking the necessary knowledge to effectively instruct across all areas. Research focused on science and mathematics instruction has shown how novice teachers hold insufficient knowledge to instruct in these areas, and subsequently, struggle to garner a level of self-confidence in their instruction (Ball, 1990a, 1990b, 1990c; Banilower, Smith, Weiss, Malzahn, & Weis, 2013; Hills et al., 2008; Reys & Fennell, 2003).

Another challenge to effective teacher preparation in elementary school is to create structures where teachers learn how to support the academic achievement of a diverse range of learners. For example, over the past decade, the U.S. population of English learners has continued to rise. Currently, over 9% of all school-age children in U.S. public schools are labeled as such (National Center for Educational Statistics, 2017). Thus, teachers are faced with the task of differentiating instruction to meet the needs of students with varying linguistic and academic backgrounds.

While these challenges have persisted for decades, standardized student achievement data have made these challenges more visible to the public eye. For example, the National Assessment of Educational Progress (NAEP) has highlighted discrepancies across math and reading levels of U.S. students (Hemphill & Vanneman, 2010). Such discrepancies have been one of the driving forces motivating the changes that are being made in how local schools address the ways in which teachers instruct across content areas, as well as how teacher preparation programs equip novice teachers with the pedagogical and academic skills to meet the needs of young learners.

Mathematics Achievement with Teachers of High-Need Urban Populations (MATH UP) was created to attempt to address these challenges. MATH UP was an 18-month residency, elementary school teacher-preparation program. From 2011–2015, MATH UP was implemented at Lehman College, a 4-year college within the City University of New York (CUNY). While enrolled in graduate-level classes, MATH UP teacher candidates completed a yearlong internship in a local Bronx classroom. Graduate courses covered content-specific areas of instruction including math, science, and literacy, as well as special education, child development, and language development. Across all aspects of the program including the graduate courses and internship, teacher candidates were exposed to sets of practices to deepen their understandings of formative assessment, math instruction, and strategies to support English learners.

The chapter investigates how three specific sets of practices were implemented across the following instructional areas:

1. the Keeping Learning on Track© (KLT) program,
2. standards-based mathematics instruction, and
3. effective instruction of English learners.

Each set of practices focuses on a particular type of instruction, and thus, is referred to as a *signature practice.* For example, the set of signature practices referred to as *standards-based mathematics instruction* focused on that specific content area, while the set of signature practices, *effective instruction of English learners,* targeted the specific population of students classified as English learners. For this reason, there was a need to use distinct research methods to investigate how and to what degree the MATH UP graduates implemented each set of signature practices in their instruction as credentialed teachers. This chapter reports on three separate investigations that explored how MATH UP graduates implemented these three sets of signature practices when they transitioned into the classroom as the lead, credentialed teacher of record.

The chapter begins with a brief literature review on the need for signature practices to be taught in teacher-preparation programs, and then moves to a description of the MATH UP program. The findings section is divided into three subsections, which are aligned to each set of signature practices. In each subsection the signature practice under investigation is defined, research methods used to carry out the investigation are outlined, and the findings associated with the set of signature practices are described. Drawing from findings related to the three sets of signature practices, the chapter concludes with a discussion and implications.

LITERATURE REVIEW

With increasing concerns about the ability of teacher preparation programs to respond to the growing population of learners from varied linguistic, ethnoracial, and economic backgrounds, it is imperative that research highlights evidence-based practices that support student achievement. Researchers have referred to these practices in multiple ways including high-leverage practices (Ball & Fornazi, 2011), core practices (McDonald, Kasemi, & Schneider Kavanagh, 2013), or general pedagogical practices/instructional routines (Hiebert & Morris, 2012). In this chapter we use the term *signature practices.* We refer to signature practices as a cluster of instructional routines to help graduates become successful instructors.

Grossman (2010) suggests preservice teachers need consistent, structured, and meaningful experiences in classrooms to effectively implement signature practices as novice teachers. Over the past decade in teacher education research, there has been a movement to identify and define signature practices (Ball & Fornazi, 2011). Creating ways to measure such practices across instruction is important in understanding the extent to which these practices are actually applied by new teachers. Examining how signature practices are introduced and supported during preservice experiences may shed light on factors that enable teachers to apply signature practices as teachers of record.

For these reasons, the MATH UP program served as an ideal context to investigate how teacher candidates execute signature practices once they graduate, because MATH UP candidates interned in classrooms with mentor teachers for one academic year. Methods courses and professional development sessions, attended by both teacher candidates and mentor teachers, infused the set of signature practices in varied ways so they could be immediately implemented in practice.

Three sets of signature practices were introduced and reinforced across MATH UP coursework and systematically assessed in the practicum classrooms. The first of these signature practices included formative assessment strategies associated with the *Keeping Learning on Track*© (KLT) program. The second set of signature practices, standards-based mathematics instruction, emphasized both mathematical content knowledge and pedagogical knowledge for effective instruction. The final set of signature practices is referred to as effective instruction of English learners.

Background on Mathematics Achievement With Teachers of High-Need Urban Populations (MATH UP)

Between 2011 and 2015, MATH UP recruited four cohorts of culturally and racially diverse individuals. Of the 70 individuals participating in the MATH UP program, more than 60% of the total population identified as Latinx. Among MATH UP teacher candidates, approximately two-thirds were between the ages of 21 and 29, 16% were between the ages of 30 and 35, and 18% were older than 35. Each MATH UP cohort moved through the program together, taking courses and participating in additional professional activities as a group while they served as co-teachers in five partner schools located in the Bronx.

The MATH UP course of study included 18 months of graduate coursework leading to initial certification in Childhood Education—Grades 1–6, with an optional certification extension in bilingual education. Upon entering the program, MATH UP teacher candidates participated in two courses during the initial spring semester. Candidates participated in a full-time residency and simultaneously completed coursework across the content areas of math, science, literacy, social studies, the arts, as well as a special education course. While all candidates took courses on teaching English learners, those pursuing childhood education certification with a bilingual extension took separate language arts and social studies methods courses that focused on teaching content in both Spanish and English.

A critical difference between the MATH UP program and Lehman's traditional teacher education program was the residency component. More specifically, MATH UP teacher candidates participated in a 1-year internship with a mentor teacher, while those teacher candidates enrolled in the traditional program completed a 15-week student-teaching placement. During the teaching residency component of the program, MATH UP teacher candidates worked collaboratively with mentor teachers. Mentor teachers had at least 5 years of teaching experience, received excellent ratings in prior evaluations at their respective K–6 schools, and were willing to mentor a teacher candidate for an academic year. To foster a collaborative relationship between the MATH UP teacher candidate and mentor teacher, both individuals participated in a weeklong professional development institute that introduced and/or reinforced central program components, including the three sets of signature practices that are the focus of this chapter.

By fall of the 2016–2017 academic year, all four MATH UP cohorts graduated from the program and entered the teaching force. To gain a deeper understanding of how MATH UP graduates infused the signature practices into their instruction, this chapter explores how, and to what degree, these signature practices were implemented during the graduates' initial years of teaching. A varied set of research methods was used to collect data to answer the following questions.

1. How did MATH UP graduates incorporate signature practices— that is KLT, standards-based mathematics instruction, and effective instruction of English learners—once they became teachers of record?
2. What methods of formative assessment from the KLT curriculum were used to monitor student understanding? Why did MATH UP graduates make these instructional choices in assessing students?
3. How did MATH UP graduates plan and carry out standards-based mathematics instruction across their classroom?
4. How did the MATH UP graduates differentiate instruction to meet the needs of English learners?

GRADUATES INCORPORATING SIGNATURE PRACTICES ACROSS INSTRUCTION

Investigation 1: Keeping Learning on Track©

Effective instruction is driven by assessment. Thus, a teacher preparation program needs to equip teacher candidates with a repertoire of tools to assess student learning. The MATH UP program adopted the KLT program to teach candidates varied means of formative assessment.

Novice teachers' use of formative assessment strategies is often infrequent and uneven (Borgioli, Ociepka, & Coker, 2015). MATH UP teacher candidates were introduced to a repertoire of formative assessment strategies that would provide them with direct and ongoing evidence of student learning. The KLT program was integrated into the MATH UP coursework and clinical experiences. KLT is a research-based program comprised of over 100 assessment techniques based on key strategies designed to empower student learning (Educational Testing Service, 2009). The fundamental idea guiding KLT implementation is that effective instruction must be aligned to students' needs, which are continually assessed across a given minute, day, and week. Thus, in a KLT classroom, instruction across content areas is driven by a formative assessment cycle based on three questions: Where is the learner right now? Where is the learner going? How does the learner get there?

As mentioned, KLT consists of over 100 types of formative assessments, ranging from informal whole class assessments that monitor student understanding in a given lesson to formal, rubric-based assessments. Examples of the breadth of formative assessments in the KLT program include the following:

- Thumbs-up/thumbs down: A gestural signal that students use to indicate whether or not they understand the information the teacher is trying to convey.
- Think-pair-share: A technique that encourages each student to generate answers to open-ended or higher order questions through small group discussion.
- Use of individual whiteboards for students to write down and display solutions to a problem.
- Providing students with graphic organizers to make their thinking visible.
- Co-constructing assessment rubrics with students to support their understanding of the skill under instruction.

Interns, mentors, and faculty were introduced to KLT strategies during the summer professional development institute. College faculty modeled the more informal, responsive assessment strategies in graduate classes. To ensure these practices were transferred into the teacher candidates' residency classroom, a MATH UP field consultant documented each candidate's use of the strategies in the classroom and recommended how other strategies could be incorporated in future instruction.

Methods

A sample of 12 participants was selected to investigate how MATH UP graduates implemented KLT formative assessment structures in their classroom. These 12 participants were deliberately chosen. Upon graduation from the MATH UP program, six participants were hired to teach at a MATH UP partner school, while the remaining six participants were also MATH UP graduates but hired by other Bronx schools. All schools where graduates were hired had similar demographics.

Observational data were collected and analyzed to understand how participants implemented KLT techniques to support instruction. The 12 participants were observed five times across their initial 2 years as credentialed teachers of record. Observations occurred twice during the initial year, and three times during the following year. For each 45-minute lesson observation, a trained observer recorded field notes in nine, 5-minute intervals. The observer then used these notes to complete a systemic observational protocol, the *Classroom Observation Protocol* (see Appendix A). (The *Classroom Observation Protocol* was created in partnership with Research for Better Schools [RBS] affiliated with The Research & Evaluation Group [http://www.phmcresearch.org]). The *Classroom Observation Protocol* was developed and used to collect data on how MATH UP graduates assessed student learning across instruction. After each classroom observation, observers held brief post-observation conferences with the teacher and collected work samples. In addition, evaluators from RBS, a collaborative partner with the MATH UP program, conducted telephone interviews with all 12 participants at the end of each of the two academic years (Richardson, Feighan, & Rudolph, 2016, 2017).

Findings

Results indicated that MATH UP teachers continued to consistently use some of the formative assessment techniques introduced and reinforced during the MATH UP program. Moreover, information gleaned from the interview and observational data underscored how the graduates used KLT strategies. Despite the fact that a multitude of KLT strategies ranging from student questioning, articulating the learning expectations with students, providing student feedback, and supporting students' independence in their learning were introduced and reinforced across the MATH UP program, participants tended to use only a few of the KLT strategies. As indicated in Table 6.1, by the fifth observation, half of the teachers had used three or more KLT strategies. The four KLT strategies most often observed were focused on gestural cues and conversation protocols to engage students in small group discussions. These strategies included: (a) use of individual whiteboards to display student thinking, (b) thumbs-up/thumbs-down, (c) think-pair-share partner discussion protocol, and (d) popsicle sticks. In other words, those formative assessments observed most often were implemented during whole class discussion, indicating that some graduates continued to engage in very teacher-directed, procedural teaching. Table 6.2 outlines those KLT strategies observed with greatest frequency across observations. It is important to note that those KLT strategies that were not

TABLE 6.1 Frequency of KLT Technique Use

Number of KLT Techniques Observed	Observation Cycles[a]				
	First	Second	Third	Fourth	Fifth
No KLT Techniques	0	1	1	4	2
One KLT Technique	2	4	3	1	1
Two KLT Techniques	5	4	4	4	3
Three or More KLT Techniques	5	3	4	3	6

[a] A total of 12 teachers were observed one time in each cycle. In each cell, the number reflects the frequency of teachers using KLT techniques.

TABLE 6.2 Frequency of KLT Strategy Use

Type of KLT Strategies Observed	Observation Cycles[a]				
	First	Second	Third	Fourth	Fifth
Whiteboards	16	2	11	1	12
Thumbs Up, Thumbs Down	16	2	11	5	16
Think, Pair, Share	10	11	9	15	8
Popsicle Sticks (with or without wait time)	9	4	7	7	3
Other	6	1	2	0	0
Phone-a-Friend	4	5	3	1	0
Exit Tickets	2	0	3	0	0
Total KLT instances	63	25	46	29	39

[a] During each 45-minute observation each of the 12 teachers was observed at 9 timed intervals and the use of KLT strategies was recorded. The frequency recorded across each observation is the number of times out of 108 possible instances that all 12 teachers used KLT strategies. So for the first observation there were 63 instances out of 108 possibilities. For the second observation there were 25 instances out of 108 possibilities. In the third, fourth and fifth observations the ratios were 46/108, 29/108 and 39/108 respectively.

observed, or rarely observed, included strategies that were focused on sharing learning expectations with students.

To provide further information in understanding why teachers made such instructional moves in using the KLT strategies, interviews were conducted. Teachers shared the following sentiments about their use of the practices:

> [The KLT techniques] give you a very quick check on the kids to seek what they're understanding [and] what they're not understanding, so you can better meet the needs of all the children. It just gives you that quick formative assessment—right there, on the spot, assessment—to see what further needs to be done to make sure all the kids are understanding what you're teaching.

> [KLT techniques] are easy. They're just clean in a sense. The popsicle sticks take away from the constantly calling on one student. It leaves all students accountable. With ABC cards you get to have a quick assessment of who knows what and the nonverbal cues definitely keep the noise down in the classroom. So KLT strategies really just help. They make the classroom run smoothly.

Aligning observational data with interview data reveal important findings in how and why teachers favored certain KLT strategies in their instruction. First, the KLT practices were used for their intended purpose, to assess student learning. Teachers may have relied more heavily on those strategies considered "informal" modes of formative assessment because of how they internalized the strategies into their practice. Namely, participants understood the KLT strategies as a "quick check," or an "easy" way to assess student understandings. This could explain why the more time-intensive KLT strategies, such as co-constructing grading rubrics with students and modeling the rubric's use, were not observed across instruction.

Another important finding was in how graduates identified the KLT strategies as a tool to foster student engagement and motivation, and a tool to hold "all students accountable" to learning. For new teachers, like those in our study, this could create a false assumption that when a student is "on-task," she is learning. Confounding engagement with learning became strikingly apparent during one observation of a fractions lesson. In the lesson, the teacher used the KLT strategy "think, pair, share" to provide students an opportunity to share their thinking about comparing two fractions. Observations indicated that students were engaged in the discussion about fraction sizes. The researcher noted that in partner discussions students' thinking revealed incorrect notions about fractions, however these partial understandings were never made public or addressed in the lesson. For this reason, we felt the need to investigate how graduates were using the mathematics content knowledge nurtured in the MATH UP program to drive instruction. This motivated the following investigation on mathematics instruction.

Investigation 2: Standards-Based Mathematics Instruction

One of the central tenets of the MATH UP program was to provide teachers with the necessary mathematical content knowledge and pedagogical knowledge to become effective and self-confident math instructors at the elementary school level. Methods courses emphasized the use of participatory activities to create student-centered instruction including hands-on experiences, group projects, inquiry-based activities, and methods of student self-assessment. For this reason, the second set of signature practices under investigation was associated with math content and pedagogical knowledge.

In order to deepen mathematical knowledge in regard to content and pedagogy, MATH UP teacher candidates were required to take three math methods courses. The courses are listed below:

- Children's Concepts of Mathematics in Grades 1–6
- Studies in the Teaching of Elementary mathematics
- Practicum in Developing Remedial Programs for Children Experiencing Difficulties in Learning Mathematics

The first two courses were offered in the campus-based *Mathematics Discovery Lab*. The lab was a room equipped with math manipulatives, math games, and math extension materials that were used during course sessions and made available for interns to use in their classrooms. During the third course interns prepared math lessons and activities, as well as completed a structured field experience where they delivered these lessons to struggling students enrolled in an after-school program.

The project also offered noncredit, content workshops that could be attended by current teacher candidates, MATH UP graduates, as well as mentor teachers from the partner schools. Topics included: (a) fractions concepts and operations, (b) ratio and proportional reasoning, (c) operations and algebraic thinking, and (d) visual display of quantitative information. Teacher candidates explored students' mathematical development underlying the progressions outlined in the Common Core State Standards in Mathematics (CCSSM).

Methods

During the MATH UP graduates' second year of teaching, a new protocol was created to understand how graduates accessed their math content knowledge to drive instruction. The protocol was created from the pedagogical model of high-leverage practices (Ball & Fornazi, 2011) developed by the Teacher Education Initiative at the University of Michigan (http://www.teachingworks.org/work-of-teaching/high-leverage-practices).

Two high-leverage practices were selected because of their alignment to the goals, practices, and foci of the MATH UP program, as well as the likelihood that explicit evidence of these high-leverage practices would be visible given the data sources of observations and interviews. The high-leverage practices were the following:

- Lesson Design. Teachers should design lessons, or a sequence of lessons, that have a spirit of inquiry and provide opportunities for students to practice and master foundational concepts.
- Analysis of Instruction. Teachers should be in a constant state of reflection, which requires a level of self-analysis of the given instruction so that continual changes and shifts can be made to improve the instruction.

To provide data on how the two high-leverage practices—lesson design and analysis of instruction—were enacted in math classrooms, observation and interview data were collected from 12 participants, the same MATH UP graduates participating in the prior investigation. One of the authors, a Lehman faculty member who researches math learning among elementary school-aged children, conducted all data collection aligned to this investigation.

Each participant was observed instructing one math lesson, approximately 45 minutes in length. Rich ethnographic notes captured key components of the lesson including teacher and student discourse as well as the varying participation structures. For the observed lesson, the 12 teachers submitted four artifacts including: (a) the lesson plan, (b) a copy of any related curriculum materials, (c) six samples of student work from the observed lesson, and (d) the teacher's feedback and reflections on this student work. The artifacts were used to structure a follow-up teacher interview. Interview questions were used to understand the teacher's pedagogical decisions and practices related to the observed lesson, as well as overall reflections on math learning and instruction. Data were coded using a set of thematic codes (Saldaña, 2013) created from analyzing the math content covered across the three math methods courses completed by all MATH UP teacher candidates.

Findings

Two general themes surfaced from the data. Findings indicated how the graduates: (a) exploited the use of manipulatives in their math instruction, and (b) provided students with varied strategies to solve problems. In analyzing the data, the majority of MATH UP graduates discussed the importance of using manipulatives; this practice was clearly evident in the observed lessons. Another common theme that surfaced across the interview data was the belief among MATH UP graduates that students should be exposed and encouraged to use multiple strategies for solving math problems. Below are examples of these findings from two participants.

Example 1—Javier. Javier was teaching 6th grade mathematics at the time of the observation and interview. When asked what he learned about being an effective math teacher in the MATH UP program, Javier's reflections focused on three fundamental ideas around mathematics instruction. These included: (a) the need for multiple problem-solving techniques, (b) the role of manipulatives, and (c) the need to help students construct meaning. These three ideas were themes across the three math courses in the MATH UP program. In his interview, Javier described the approach he used to help students see multiple ways to solve problems.

> When it comes to approaching the problem, I try my best to include context, you know, and methods of how to approach a problem, not only in one way, in multiple ways. When we work on a problem, I'll show them this is [step] number one, this is [step] number two, and this is [step] three. These are the three different ways of approaching it.

Javier also showed evidence of applying these ideas in his classroom during the lesson observation. During Javier's lesson, students were working on solving equations with variables. He connected the idea of isolating a variable by having a student stand physically alone as a representation of the mathematical situation. By doing this, he was helping students make meaning of the mathematics by using a student as a manipulative.

In addition, during part of the lesson, students engaged in multiple approaches to solving a problem that yielded the same result. This too highlighted how multiple strategies can be used to solve any one given problem. While solving the problem $6x + 12 = 2x + 4$, Javier posed a question to the class around whether a specific order of operations was needed to solve the problem correctly. In other words, he pushed the class to analyze if it mattered whether students began solving the problem by subtracting the $6x$ or the $2x$. Students expressed uncertainty in how to begin to solve the problem, and whether order of operations was critical for a correct solution. As a result, Javier asked students to solve the problem both ways, and the students discovered that the different strategies to solving the problem resulted in the same final answer.

Example 2—Kristina. Kristina was a kindergarten teacher at the time of the investigation. In her reflections, Kristina shared the sentiment that an effective mathematics teacher was one who infused engagement and fun into student learning, and one who modeled multiple strategies to solve a problem. Kristina explained how teachers should work to make mathematics relevant to students' lives by helping students construct connections to the real world.

During an observed lesson, Kristina began by using a song to engage students in the math content. The songs' lyrics included the verse, "get our voices and brains ready for math." The lesson focused on decomposing numbers into their place value parts (e.g., 14 can be thought of as 14 ones, or one ten and four ones). During the lesson, students used multiple manipulatives, including Unifix cubes and counters, to solve word problems based on real world examples. Unifix cubes are plastic connecting cubes commonly used in elementary mathematics classrooms. Kristina's understanding of how manipulatives could be used as an instructional tool was evident as she encouraged students to use base-ten block materials to decompose numbers into their place value parts as she consistently asked students a series of open-ended questions to determine their understanding of the content. The lesson concluded with students completing an exit ticket that asked them to solve two real-world story problems focused on place value.

In reflecting on the lesson goals, and in assessing student work, Kristina explained how she provided opportunities for students to practice and demonstrate understanding of tens and ones with the support of manipulatives. She expressed these ideas in the following way:

> When I do teach math, I love manipulatives. I like seeing students work with them. I think it's really important for them to be able to work with manipulatives then one day move away from them when they start really understanding and grasping the concept of math and how numbers work.

Across the data points of observations and interviews, it was clear how Kristina appropriated manipulatives as an instructional tool to support student learning, believing that manipulatives fostered a level of critical and abstract mathematical thinking.

In the final section, we look at how MATH UP teachers used a set of signature practices to support the learning of a diverse group of students, focusing specifically on English learners.

Investigation 3: Effective Instruction for English Learners

Preparing teachers to create classrooms where students are continually assessed and able to engage in inquiry-based practices is critical. However, it is also crucial to look more deeply at how these practices and assessments are meeting the needs of varied learners. For this reason, the third investigation examined the ways in which MATH UP graduates implemented instructional methods to meet the needs of English learners.

One of the MATH UP program's overarching goals was that all graduates would be fully prepared to teach special populations of learners, including English learners. English learners constituted 20% to 30% of the student population in the partner elementary schools where candidates completed their internships. A set of signature practices for English learners was created from literature on multilingual practices (Baker, 2007; deJong, 2012; Garcia, 2012) and the Sheltered Instruction Observation Protocol (SIOP) model (Echevarria, Vogt, & Short, 2014), which is a set of techniques to support English learners in learning content-specific material and practices that promote multilingual learning (Baker, 2007; deJong, 2012).

All MATH UP interns participated in a two-course sequence designed to meet the instructional and language needs of English learners. In the first course, all teacher candidates were introduced to theories of bilingual development and research-based instructional strategies that used the learner's home language as a resource for instruction (Baker, 2007; deJong, 2012; Garcia, 2012). This course was co-taught by a teacher educator and a first-grade bilingual teacher. Teacher candidates applied what they were learning as they worked with one child and prepared a case study. The second course built upon the first course but was more practice-based and focused on teaching grade level content in a second language. An experienced elementary school teacher was the instructor for this course. Each class focused on a component of the SIOP model and its features (Echevarria et al., 2014). Teacher candidates were exposed to different SIOP instructional strategies by viewing teaching videos and identifying the specific instructional and environmental features that supported English learners. Then, in small groups teacher candidates reviewed teaching scenarios to evaluate how the teacher used particular SIOP features, and how effective these features were implemented. Finally, teacher candidates demonstrated learning of the SIOP model by developing a five-lesson sequence that incorporated key components of the model, and responded to the language needs of the case study child with whom they had worked while completing the first course. The teacher candidate selected one of the five lessons for a peer-teaching simulation.

Methods

To evaluate how MATH UP graduates developed skills to be effective teachers of English learners, we undertook an investigation of how 14 instructional strategies were used in the graduates' classrooms. The 14 instructional strategies were aligned to the SIOP features and effective instruction of English learners, and clustered around five core teaching practices:

1. frontloading and reinforcing academic language,
2. making content comprehensible for English learners at varying levels of academic proficiency,

3. designing linguistically responsive assessments,
4. using learner resources to scaffold learning in a new language, and
5. promoting oral language development.

Appendix B shows alignment between the five core teaching practices, 14 instructional strategies, and SIOP features, and identifies where each practice was introduced in preservice coursework.

To explore the use of signature practices to meet the needs of English learners, a larger sample size than the previous two investigations was used. This sample size included a total of 30 graduates, the same 12 participating in the prior two investigations and 18 additional graduates. It was possible to use a larger sample size because more graduates volunteered to be in the study since it required fewer participatory hours. Of the 30 graduates who volunteered to participate in the study, 43% ($N = 13$) completed the bilingual extension teaching certification program. Five of these graduates were hired to teach in bilingual programs in their first years of teaching. The remaining 25 graduates were hired to teach in classrooms where English was the medium of instruction.

The data set included 55 sets of descriptive field notes from lesson observations during the MATH UP graduates' first 2 years of teaching. On average, all participants were observed once during their first year of teaching, and again the following year. Observed lessons were 45 to 60 minutes in length. Each set of descriptive field notes generated during the observed lessons were divided into five segments: (a) introduction/motivation, (b) teacher demonstration, (c) guided practice, (d) independent or group practice, and (e) closure. Each segment was coded with a set of 38 descriptive and structural codes (Saldaña, 2013) capturing the 14 instructional strategies that were embedded in the five core teaching practices and emphasized in the course sequence described earlier. Once all data were coded, frequencies of core practices and instructional strategies were generated for analysis.

Findings

In this subsection, we describe the signature practices aligned to teaching English learners that were evident in MATH UP graduates' classrooms during their first 2 years of teaching. Table 6.3 and Table 6.4 outline the percentage of occurrences for the most and least frequently used instructional practices to meet the needs of English learners. As mentioned, the 14 strategies were clustered into the five core teaching practices.

In reviewing frequencies across data types, patterns emerge that add to our understanding of how MATH UP graduates infused instructional strategies and differentiation methods to meet the learning needs of English learners. As Table 6.3 indicates, the five most frequently used strategies are

TABLE 6.3   Most Frequently Used Instructional Strategies for English Learners

Core Practice	Instructional Strategy	Percentage
1. Frontloading and Reinforcing Academic Language	Instructional Strategy 3: Repeated use of targeted academic language throughout a lesson	87.3%
2. Making Content Comprehensible for English Learners at Varying Levels of Academic Proficiency	Instructional Strategy 6: Using visual representations of technology and multimedia	85.5%
3. Designing Linguistically Responsive Assessments	Instructional Strategy 7: Frequently checking for understanding using verbal and non-verbal assessments	98.2%
4. Using Learner Resources to Scaffold Learning in a New Language	Instructional Strategy 10: Using learner resources to scaffold learning in a new language	50.9%
5. Promoting Oral Language Development	Instructional Strategy 13: Creating peer-mediated and interactive activities	70.9%

TABLE 6.4   Least Frequently Used Instructional Strategies for English Learners

Core Practice	Instructional Strategy	Percentage
1. Frontloading and Reinforcing Academic Language	Instructional Strategy 2: Communicating language objectives to learners	5.5%
2. Making Content Comprehensible for English Learners at Varying Levels of Academic Proficiency	Instructional Strategy 5: Using gestures and Para verbal cues	5.5%
3. Designing Linguistically Responsive Assessments	Instructional Strategy 8: Designing assessments in English by proficiency levels to reduce language demands	5.5%
4. Using Learner Resources to Scaffold Learning in a New Language	Instructional Strategy 11: Using English learners' home language to teach content in English	20.0%
5. Promoting Oral Language Development	Instructional Strategy 12: Building in hands-on activities using supplementary materials, to enhance English learners' opportunities to participate	14.6%

represented across the five core teaching practices. Table 6.4 shows those strategies that were never implemented in certain classrooms, and rarely observed in general.

As noted, for each core teaching practice there were instructional strategies that were used with high levels of frequency, while other instructional strategies were seldom observed. For example, with the core teaching practice *designing linguistically responsive assessments*, the instructional strategy "frequently checking for understanding using verbal and nonverbal assessments" was observed approximately 98% of the time. However, this was in great contrast to how rarely the instructional strategy, "designing assessments in English by proficiency levels to reduce language demands," was observed. There were three instances of this strategy being used across the 55 observations, equating to 5.5% of the time. It is important to note that some instructional strategies were more time consuming to implement, which may explain why they were rarely observed. In addition, some strategies aligned to the aforementioned KLT strategies (e.g., the KLT strategy of thumbs up, thumbs down) were used as a way to frequently check for understanding using a nonverbal assessment (Instructional Strategy 7), meaning that students may have been more inclined to use them because they were more embedded in their practice.

To illustrate how some frequently used instructional strategies were enacted in a classroom, the following example is drawn from field notes of a participant's classroom. The participant, Ms. Miller, was in her second year of teaching a third-grade classroom with five students classified as English learners. These five students were from different home language backgrounds and were performing at intermediate to advanced levels of English proficiency. The example presents Ms. Miller teaching a math lesson on counting arrays. English was the language of instruction.

The lesson began with Ms. Miller displaying two pieces of information on the overhead projector. The first was the learning target—*I can use an array model and friendly numbers to help me solve multiplication problems.* The second was a math problem—*Jayden has 9 toy trucks. Each toy truck has 6 wheels. How many wheels do the toy trucks have in all?* Ms. Miller read the learning target aloud and pointed to the words as she read, "I can use an array model and friendly numbers to help me solve multiplication problems." She then asked students to write the learning target in their notebooks, and to explain the definition of array, by posing the question, "What do we mean by array?" To which several children called out answers that defined an array as putting objects in a specific order and that an array looks like a "box." In response to students' definition of a box, Ms. Miller continued to probe students' prior knowledge by asking, "What does that box have in it?" Several students then volunteered the answer that "friendly numbers" are in the box and these friendly numbers refer to numbers that "end with a digit five and a digit zero."

In this first part of the lesson Ms. Miller drew upon two core teaching practices. First, Ms. Miller used the core teaching practice *frontloading and reinforcing academic language* as she communicated the language objectives to the learner. Ms. Miller also used core teaching practice *using learner resources to scaffold learning in a new language* by drawing upon students' existing knowledge of arrays and problem-solving strategies by using the terminology "friendly numbers."

As the lesson continued, Ms. Miller again used the overhead projector and invited a student, Josephine, to draw an array that would solve the initial multiplication problem, requiring students to multiply nine and six. Josephine correctly drew an array by writing the numbers one to nine down the side of the paper, one to six across the top of the paper, and drawing little circles to represent the row and column. Ms. Miller concluded this part of the lesson with the question, "Is it nine groups of six or six groups of nine?" To which children correctly called out, "Nine groups of six."

In this interaction, Ms. Miller drew on the core teaching practice *making content comprehensible for English learners at varying levels of academic proficiency* as she asked Josephine to make a visual of the array. Before transitioning students to independent practice, Ms. Miller informally assessed student learning. This was accomplished by asking students to self-assess their learning of arrays using an assessment chart where Level 0 indicated that the student did not understand the concept even with help and Level 4 that indicated the student could solve the problem independently. Five students that self-assessed at Levels 0 or 1 stayed on the rug to receive additional instructional support; two of these students were English learners. In using this self-assessment, Ms. Miller drew upon the core teaching practice *designing linguistically responsive assessments* as she checked for student learning using verbal forms of assessment through the chart.

DRAWING CONCLUSIONS FROM THE THREE INVESTIGATIONS

To frame the overall conclusions and implications for improving teacher-preparation programs, it is important to return to the larger question guiding this chapter: How did MATH UP graduates incorporate signature practices (i.e., KLT, standards-based mathematics instruction, and effective instruction of English learners) once they became teachers of record? Findings indicate varied results. Some of the more commonly used sets of signature practices introduced in the MATH UP program were observed being used with high frequency during teachers' first years in the classroom. For example, MATH UP graduates clearly transferred tenets of effective math instruction learned in the program to their classrooms. Findings indicate how the graduates provided students with varied math strategies to solve problems, modeled mathematical thinking through the use of manipulatives, and allowed students a space to reflect on their learning. However, other signature practices were seldom observed in the graduates' classroom.

In regard to the set of signature practices associated with formative assessments, while three strategies from the KLT program were routinely observed, there were many strategies that did not transfer into the graduates' classroom. An example of a practice not observed was developing shared assessment rubrics with students to help the students and teacher evaluate learning. Rather, those formative assessment practices observed with greatest frequency were ones that brought a level of participation and engagement to the classroom. In addition, teachers did not consistently use the information from these assessments to differentiate instruction. In other words, MATH UP graduates seemed to internalize the formative assessment practices at a routine-based, or mechanical level. For example, partner discussions were often observed, but teachers appeared to use discussion more as a means to engage students in whole class instruction and increase student participation than to gather information to drive instruction.

Focusing specifically on the set of practices aligned to effective instruction for English learners, findings highlight that while the MATH UP graduates developed a strong foundation in understanding and implementing some signature practices to teach English learners, they did not apply all practices they were exposed to as MATH UP teacher candidates. There are several possible explanations for this. First, it may be that some practices were emphasized more so than others in the coursework, or it may be that some practices were reinforced in other courses and/or the internship classrooms where teacher candidates were learning to teach. Another explanation might be that some practices are more complex to embed in prescribed curricula and instructional materials, requiring additional support and professional development to implement in the new contexts in which graduates found themselves teaching. Finally, it is important to consider that even though practices like developing linguistically responsive assessments that include the use of students' home language are encouraged by school administrators and curriculum coaches in partner schools where the graduates completed their teacher preparation, those from other schools might not endorse such practices.

Context is key when researching teacher practice, meaning that it was important to understand the demographics of the schools where the graduates became teachers to make sense of why they were making certain instructional choices, and thus using some strategies with greater frequency. A salient example of a practice that the program emphasized in coursework but teachers did not translate into practice as well as we had hoped was the use of English learners' home language. When we reviewed field notes, we discovered that very few graduates had students new to the United States in their classrooms, which might explain why there was such infrequent use of the home language as a resource. In those classrooms where there were students new to the United States, we found examples of teacher's explicit use of student's home language to ensure comprehension. In classrooms where the home language was not shared by teacher and student, we found an example of a teacher using Google translate to work with the student. These findings suggest that graduates were aware of the need to supplement their instruction with added strategies for these students; however, it also suggests that teachers may have limited understanding of the value of the home language for students at intermediate and advanced levels of proficiency, or limited confidence in using home language in a school culture that discourages teachers from using this resource.

This study provides an example of how distinct research methods may be used to examine implementation of signature practices, focusing on how MATH UP graduates sustained certain instructional strategies as they transitioned into the role of a teacher. Our goal was to look at instruction that cut across content areas for a varied set of learners, and thus, we collected data focused on instruction aligned to formative assessments, meeting the needs of English learners, and implementing effective math instruction. Given the breadth of our study and research questions we recognized that methods needed to be altered when investigating each signature practice. For example, a specific protocol, *Classroom Observation Protocol,* was co-constructed with our collaborators from the organization Research for Better Schools to answer the research question regarding which methods of formative assessment from the KLT curriculum were used to monitor student understanding. While the *Classroom Observation Protocol* generated important findings about how MATH UP teachers used formative assessment to drive instruction, we quickly realized that the same protocol fell short of providing rich data to answer the second and third questions aligned to mathematics instruction and differentiating instruction to meet the needs of English learners. Thus, a revised protocol of aligning observation data to teacher interviews was used to examine how the MATH UP graduates designed inquiry-based math lessons and reflected on their pedagogical choices.

Implications

The results from this study have implications for implementation of teacher preparation programs and conducting future research. Teaching sets of signature practices in a teacher preparation program is the first step. However, these findings suggest that teaching signature practices is necessary, but not sufficient. Preservice and beginning teachers need opportunities for continuous reflection and analysis or instructional coaching to ensure consistent, high-quality implementation of signature practices.

In working with recent graduates of teacher preparation programs, surveys, observations, and teachers' self-reports provide information on the techniques teachers were using in their classroom. However, these protocols fell short in working with graduates to critically reflect on their practice in order to make consistent and thoughtful instructional change. Our work has suggested that sustained interactions with graduates are more powerful and serve to encourage graduates to continue to use student-focused strategies to improve instruction and student outcomes. Currently, we are designing reunions and exploring social media outlets in order to provide continuing support and professional development opportunities to sustain use of best practices. For example, we have established a link on our website that highlights clips from graduates' classrooms and identifies the effective practices that are being modeled to meet the needs of English learners.

In addition, we are working with eight graduates to design and execute action research projects. In these projects, teachers are reflecting on their own practice and designing weeklong interventions where they are disrupting elements of their practice, meaning that the teachers are identifying the instructional frustrations they face in the classroom, and constructing new interventions to support student learning. While such moves may be labor intensive and require additional funding, sustained partnerships between teacher education programs and high-need districts that bridge preservice and in-service instruction has the potential to strengthen the quality and retention of new teachers.

Finally, additional research is needed to explore relationships between the instructional and pedagogical practices teacher candidates are taught in their preservice programs and how these skills are translated to the classroom. This research will benefit teacher preparation program evaluation and critical stakeholders including the partnering schools that work with these programs. To fully understand why teachers make certain instructional decisions, it is necessary to look more closely at the school demographics and the curricula or instructional mandates that were imposed on these new teachers. Likewise, future research needs to explore the relationships between these instructional practices and student outcomes to further validate these practices, as well as improve the efficacy of such practices to support student learning.

APPENDIX A
Classroom Observation Protocols

MATH-UP Intern Classroom Observation Protocol   Page 1 of 2 | May/June 2014

Observer Initials: _____   Observation date: _____   ☐ PS 1   ☐ PS 55   ☐ PS 58   ☐ PS 73   ☐ PS 114

Intern: _____   Subject: _____   Grade: ☐ 1   ☐ 2   ☐ 3   ☐ 4   ☐ 5

Is coop teacher present?   ☐ Yes   ☐ No   No. of Boys: _____   Girls: _____

Is there another adult present?   ☐ Yes   ☐ No   What is his or her role?   ☐ ICT teacher   ☐ Para   ☐ Other _____

Is the *Learning Intention* posted or shown (e.g., SMARTboard or overhead)?   ☐ Yes   ☐ No

Write/type the *Learning Intention*: _____

Is the *Learning Intention* read to/with the students?   ☐ Yes   ☐ No

 If yes, who reads the *Learning Intention*? ☐ Intern   ☐ Coop Teacher   ☐ Student(s)   ☐ Other   ☐ n/a

Is the *Learning Intention* discussed with the students (i.e., students participate in the discussion)?   ☐ Yes   ☐ No

---

Record the co-teaching model, instructional mode, math lesson code, KLT technique, and level of engagement used in each 5-minute interval (enter as many of each as applicable; separate codes with commas).

Intervals:→	Minutes 0–5	Minutes 5–10	Minutes 10–15	Minutes 15–20	Minutes 20–25	Minutes 25–30	Minutes 30–35	Minutes 35–40	Minutes 40–45
Co-teaching model (if <u>no</u> co-teaching, enter "--")									
Instructional mode									
Literacy lesson codes									
KLT technique(s)									
Level of engagement LE = low (≥80% of students off-task) ME = mixed HE = high (≥80% of students on-task)									

Questions for the observer to answer after the observation

Was a SMART Board used?   ☐ Yes   ☐ No   If yes, were "smart" or interactive features used?   ☐ Yes   ☐ No

If yes, please describe how the SMART Board was used: _____

Were hands-on materials or manipulatives used?   ☐ Yes   ☐ No   What type(s) of manipulatives? _____

If hands-on materials or manipulatives were used, were there enough that each student involved in the lesson can actually manipulate or use them (either individually or in groups)?   ☐ Yes   ☐ No

If any students were pulled aside, ask the intern why those students were chosen and for what purpose.

What reading and writing materials were used by the students (e.g., textbook, workbook, pencil, blank paper)?

Please indicate the amount of instruction that was driven by the intern and the proportion of class management/disciplining that was done by the intern (if there is no discernible class management/disciplining, please write "n/a").

Amount of instruction the intern drove/directed: _____   Proportion of CM/disciplining the intern completed: _____

*Scale: **0** = intern drove no teaching and engaged in no disciplining; **1** = intern drove a little instruction / engaged in a small proportion of disciplining; **2** = intern drove about half the instruction / half of the disciplining; **3** = intern drove much of the instruction / engaged in a large proportion of disciplining; **4** = intern drove all the instruction / all the disciplining.*

Co-Teaching Codes (short descriptions in "Friend CoTeaching Models.doc")

ITCO	Intern teaches, cooperating teacher observes	PT	Parallel teaching
CTIO	Co-op teacher teaches, intern observes	ST	Station teaching
ITCA	Intern teaches, cooperating teacher assists	Alt	Alternative teaching (large group/small group)
CTIA	Co-op teacher teaches, intern assists	TT	Team teaching

Instructional Mode Codes

AD	Administrative Tasks	A	Assessment (formal: quiz, test)	CD	Class discussion
DP	Drill and practice (on paper, vocally, or computer)	HOA	Hands-on activity/ Manipulatives	I	Interruption
LC	Learning center/station	L	Lecture/whole-class instruction/ video (mostly teacher talk)	QA	Question and Answer (at least 60% time on student talk)
SGD	Small-group discussion or work	SP	Individual student presenting or reading aloud	TIS	Teacher interacting with students individually (students working independently)
TM	Teacher modeling a problem/process for all students (or all students in SG)	TRA	Teacher reading aloud (to a small group or the whole class)	V	Visualization (teacher asks students to picture or visualize a concept)

Literacy Lesson Codes

Hi-L	High-level questions: students are asked to deduce from reading or listening. Not factual questions.	SA	Short answer—open-ended, but with very limited responses expected (e.g., whom did Scout sit with at Tom's trial?)
MC	Multiple-choice questions.	SQ	Students develop their own questions about a topic
RG	Students reading, discussing, or writing in groups	SS	Student(s) share(s) ideas about text, content, ideas
RA	Students reading or writing on their own	YN	Yes/No Questions

Hints for high-level questions—Asking students to think beyond the literal

• Why? What if? and How? ("How do you know this word is 'banana' and not 'boat'?" "Why do you think Tom ran away even though Atticus said they had a chance for a successful appeal?") "What is your evidence from the text?"

• Are students being asked only to read the lines themselves or also to read between the lines?

• Questions that help students make connections to their own lives, other books, TV shows or movies, and/or other disciplines.

• Questions stems such as these:

What is similar (or different) about . . ?	What would happen if . . ?	Is it always true that . . ?
How do you know that . . ?	How would you prove _____ . . ?	How can you find out . . ?
How would you explain _____ to a younger student or sibling?		Do you agree or disagree with _____'s answer . . ?

Common KLT Techniques & Codes

ABCD cards—**ABC:** Students answer multiple-choice or true-false questions by displaying index-sized cards.

Basketball—**BSK:** Questions and responses move from teacher to student to student to student, etc., rather than teacher-student-teacher-student.

Entrance ticket—**ENT** *or Exit ticket*—**EXT:** Students write a summary, a question, or some other content-related text on a paper to give to the teacher before class (ENT) or before leaving class or moving to the next subject (EXT).

Graphic organizers—**GO:** Use of graphic organizers to stimulate thought, develop ideas, or organize learning.

Phone-a-friend—**PAF:** Student can "phone-a-friend" if they are called on and can't provide an answer.

Popsicle sticks—**POP:** Teacher writes names of students on Popsicle sticks and uses them to call on students. *Wait time* is crucial: teacher will ask a question, pause, and then call on a student (so all students think about their answers *before* they know who will be called on). Write **"POP+"** if there's "wait time" before calling on a student.

Rubrics—**RUB:** Rubrics are made available to students (at higher levels, students help develop the rubrics and/or use them to evaluate their own or each others' work).

Student Reflection—**REF:** At the end of a lesson, students write reflections about what they've learned. Can be handed in (often as EXT) or written in a journal or notebook that the teacher will see later.

Student Review—**REV:** At the end of a lesson, a student(s) provide(s) a summary of what the class was expected to learn.

Think, pair, share—**TPS** (also called turn and talk/share with group): students are asked about something. They think about their answer, then discuss with another student, and then report out their answers to the class.

Thumbs up—**TU:** Students indicate whether they agree with a statement or answer (thumbs-up), disagree (thumbs-down), or either aren't sure or think an answer depends on other factors or is sometimes true (thumb pointed sideways).

Traffic light cups—**CUPS:** Students use green, yellow, and red cups to indicate whether they are working fine alone (green), can work for the time being but have a question (yellow), or need help before they can continue (red).

Two stars and a wish—**2S1W:** Teacher assessment of assignment noting two strengths and one wish for improvement.

Whiteboards—**WB:** Students show their answers using small whiteboards.

Other—**OTH:** Another KLT technique (please describe in written comments)

MATH-UP Intern Classroom Observation Protocol, Page 2 of 2 March 2014

Co-Teaching Codes (short descriptions in "Friend CoTeaching Models.doc")

ITCO	Intern teaches, cooperating teacher observes	PT	Parallel teaching
CTIO	Co-op teacher teaches, intern observes	ST	Station teaching
ITCA	Intern teaches, cooperating teacher assists	Alt	Alternative teaching (large group/small group)
CTIA	Co-op teacher teaches, intern assists	TT	Team teaching

Instructional Mode Codes

AD	Administrative Tasks	HOA	Hands-on activity/ Manipulatives	SGD	Small-group discussion or work
A	Assessment (formal: quiz, test)	I	Interruption	SP	Individual student presentation
CD	Class discussion	LC	Learning center/station	TIS	Teacher interacting with students individually (students working independently)
DP	Drill and practice (on paper, vocally, or computer)	L	Lecture/whole-class instruction/ video (mostly teacher talk)	TM	Teacher modeling a problem or process so all students (or all students in SG) can see
		QA	Question and Answer (at least 60% time on student answers)	V	Visualization (teacher asks students to picture or visualize a concept)

Math Lesson Codes

Hi-L	High-level questions: students are expected to/required to think about their responses	SA	Short answer—open-ended, but with very limited responses expected
MC	Multiple-choice question	SQ	Students develop their own questions about a topic
PSG	Students solve extended problems in groups	SS	Student(s) share(s) ideas about topic, problems, answers
PSA	Students solve extended problems alone	YN	Yes/No Questions

Hints for high-level questions—

• Why questions? ("Why are do you think you are correct?" "Why does 2 + 2 = 4?" "Why did you start the problem that way?")

• Questions that help students make connections to their own lives, other math content, and/or other disciplines.

• Questions stems such as these:

What is similar (or different) about . . ?	What would happen if . . ?
Is it always true that . . ?	How do you know that . . ?
How would you prove _____ . . ?	How many different ways can you think of to . . ?
How can you find out . . ?	Do you agree or disagree with _____'s answer . . ?
How would you explain _____ to a student in a lower grade?	

Common KLT Techniques & Codes

ABCD cards—**ABC:** Students answer multiple-choice or true-false questions by displaying index-sized cards.

Basketball—**BSK:** Questions and responses move from teacher to student to student to student, etc., rather than teacher-student-teacher-student.

Entrance ticket—**ENT** or *Exit ticket*—**EXT:** Students write a summary, a question, or some other content-related text on a paper to give to the teacher before class (ENT) or before leaving class or moving to the next subject (EXT).

Graphic organizers—**GO:** Use of graphic organizers to stimulate thought, develop ideas, or organize learning.

Phone-a-friend—**PAF:** Student can "phone-a-friend" if they are called on and can't provide an answer.

Popsicle sticks—**POP:** Teacher writes names of students on Popsicle sticks and uses them to call on students. *Wait time* is crucial: teacher will ask a question, pause, and then call on a student (so all students think about their answers *before* they know who will be called on). Write "POP+" if there's "wait time" before calling on a student.

Rubrics—**RUB:** Rubrics are made available to students (at higher levels, students help develop the rubrics and/or use them to evaluate their own or each others' work).

Student Reflection—**REF:** At the end of a lesson, students write reflections about what they've learned. Can be handed in (often as EXT) or written in a journal or notebook that the teacher will see later.

Student Review—**REV:** At the end of a lesson, a student(s) provide(s) a summary of what the class was expected to learn.

Think, pair, share—**TPS** (also called turn and talk/share with group): students are asked about something. They think about their answer, then discuss with another student, and then report out their answers to the class.

Thumbs up—**TU:** Students indicate whether they agree with a statement or answer (thumbs-up), disagree (thumbs-down), or either aren't sure or think an answer depends on other factors or is sometimes true (thumb pointed sideways).

Traffic light cups—**CUPS:** Students use green, yellow, and red cups to indicate whether they are working fine alone (green), can work for the time being but have a question (yellow), or need help before they can continue (red).

Two stars and a wish—**2S1W:** Teacher assessment of assignment noting two strengths and one wish for improvement.

Whiteboards—**WB:** Students show their answers using small whiteboards.

Other—**OTH:** Another KLT technique (please describe in written comments)

APPENDIX B
Alignment of Core Teaching Practice (CTP), Instructional Strategy (IS), and Sheltered Instruction Observation Protocol (SIOP) Feature

MATH UP Graduate Course	Core Teaching Practice (CTP) & Instructional Strategy (IS)	Sheltered Instruction Observation Protocol (SIOP) Feature
CTP #1: Frontloading and Reinforcing Academic Language		
Course #2 ESL Methods	CTP #1, IS 1 - Teaching key academic vocabulary and important linguistic forms necessary for English learners to understand content before introducing content matter	Key Vocabulary Emphasis (F9)
Course #2 ESL Methods	CTP #1, IS 2 - Communicating language objectives to learners	Language Objectives Supported by Lesson Delivery (F24)
Course #2 ESL Methods	CTP #1, IS 3 - Repeatedly use of targeted academic language throughout a lesson	Clearly Defined Language Objectives (F2) Comprehensive Review of Key Vocabulary (F27)
CTP #2: Making Content Comprehensible for English Learners at Varying Levels of Academic Proficiency		
Course #2 ESL Methods	CTP #2, IS 4 - Teacher modeling where teacher demonstrates how to perform an activity, a procedure, or how to work with a group. Teacher uses think alouds to demonstrate a process or task, using explicit language to indicate that she is modeling a practice. (e.g. "I'm going to show you what this looks like.")	Variety of Techniques (F12)
Course #2 ESL Methods	CTP #2, IS 5 - Using gestures (e.g., circling arms, pointing), facial expressions, and Para verbal cues (e.g., enunciating, slowing down speech rate, or raising volume of voice when emphasizing and important word or idea)	Appropriate Speech (F10) Appropriate Pacing (F26)
Course #2 ESL Methods	CTP #2, IS 6 - Using visual representations of content (e.g., manipulatives, graphic organizers), technology and multimedia	Variety of Techniques (F12) Supplementary Materials (F4)

CTP #3: Designing Linguistically Responsive Assessments		
Course #2 ESL Methods	CTP #3, IS 7 - Frequently checking for understanding using verbal (structuring questions for different levels of language proficiency) and non-verbal assessments (e.g., thumbs up)	Regular Feedback on Student Output (F29)
Course #2 ESL Methods	CTP #3, IS 8 - Designing assessments in English by proficiency levels to reduce language demands, (e.g., use of graphic organizers, sentence starters, cloze structures.)	Regular Feedback on Student Output (F29)
Course #2 ESL Methods Course #1 Bilingualism	CTP #3, IS 9 - Assessing content learning in a learner's home language	Regular Feedback on Student Output (F29)
CTP #4: Using Learner Resources to Scaffold Learning in a New Language		
Course #2 ESL Methods	CTP #4, IS 10 - Connecting English learners' existing content and language knowledge to new learning	Concepts linked to background experiences (F7) Links explicitly made between past learning/new concepts (F8)
Course #1 Bilingualism	CTP #4, IS 11 - Using English learners' home language to teach content in English (e.g., encouraging the use of translanguaging as a resource to facilitate communication of content knowledge), providing multilingual text or translations, or pointing out connections between languages (e.g., teaching cognates)	Opportunity for Students to Clarify Key Concepts in L1 as needed with aide, peer or L1 text (F19)
CTP #5: Promoting Oral Language Development		
Course #2 ESL Methods	CTP #5, IS 12 - Building in hands-on activities using supplementary materials, to enhance English learners' opportunities to participate	Hands-On Materials (F20) Meaningful Activities (F6)
Course #2 ESL Methods	CTP #5, IS 13 - Creating peer-mediated and interactive activities where English learners have opportunities to talk in order to maximize English learners' language use (e.g., cooperative learning structures, turn and talks)	Interaction & Discussion (F16) Grouping Configurations (F17)
Course #2 ESL Methods	CTP #5, IS 14 - Applying verbal scaffolding through teacher directed activities like extended dialogues involving teacher and student(s) in which teachers asks questions to expand the dialogue between teacher and student, paraphrases, reforms, or recasts what the learner says, and provides corrective feedback on language	Scaffolding (F14) Questioning Promoting Higher Order Thinking (F15)

REFERENCES

Baker, C. (2007). *A parents' and teachers' guide to bilingualism*. Clevedon, England: Multilingual Matters.

Ball, D. L. (1990a). Breaking with the experience in learning to teach mathematics: The role of preservice methods course. *For the Learning of Mathematics, 10*(2), 10–16.

Ball, D. L. (1990b). Prospective elementary and secondary teachers' understandings of division. *Journal for Research in Mathematics Education, 21*(2), 132–144.

Ball, D. L. (1990c). The mathematical understandings that prospective teachers bring to teacher education. *Elementary School Journal, 90*(4), 449–466.

Ball, D. L. (1993). With an eye on the mathematical horizon: Dilemmas of teaching elementary school mathematics. *Elementary School Journal, 93*(4), 373–397.

Ball, D., & Fornazi, F. M. (2011, Summer). Building a common core for learning to teach and connecting professional learning to practice. *American Educator, 35*(2), 17–39.

Banilower, E. R., Smith, S. P., Weiss, I. R., Malzahn, K. M., & Weis, A. M. (2013). *Report of the 2012 National Survey of Science and Mathematics Education.* Chapel Hill, NC: Horizon Research.

Borgioli, G. M., Ociepka, A., & Coker, K. (2015). A playbill: Rethinking assessment in teacher education. *Journal of the Scholarship of Teaching and Learning, 15*(3), 68–84.

deJong, E. J. (2012). *Foundations of multilingual education: From principals to practice.* Philadelphia, PA: Caslon.

Echevarria, J., Vogt, M. E., & Short, D. (2014). *Making content comprehensible for elementary English learners: The SIOP Model.* Boston, MA: Allyn & Bacon.

Educational Testing Service. (2009). *Research rationale for Keeping Learning on Track program.* Princeton, NJ: Northwest Evaluation Association.

Garcia, O. (2012). Theorizing translanguaging for educators. In C. Celick & K. Seltzer (Eds.), *Translanguaging: A CUNY-NYSIEB guide for educators* (pp. 1–6). New York, NY: CUNY-NYSIEB.

Grossman, P. (May, 2010). *Learning to practice: The design of clinical experience in teacher preparation. Policy Brief of the Partnership for Teacher Quality.* Washington, DC: American Association of Colleges of Teacher Education.

Hemphill, F. C., & Vanneman, A. (2010). *Achievement gaps: How Hispanic and White students in public schools perform in mathematics and reading on the National Assessment of Educational Progress* (NCES 2011–459). Washington, DC: National Center for Education Statistics, Institute of Education Sciences, U.S. Department of Education.

Hiebert, J., & Morris, A. K. (2012). Teaching, rather than teachers, as a path toward improving classroom instruction. *Journal of Teacher Education, 63*(2), 92–102. doi:10.1177/0022487111428328

Hill, H. C., Blunk, M., Charalambous, C., Lewis, J., Phelps, G., Sleep, L., & Ball, D. L. (2008). exploratory study. *Cognition and Instruction, 26*(4), 430–511.

McDonald, M., Kazemi, E., & Schneider Kavanagh, S. (2013). Core practices and pedagogies of teacher education: A call for a common language and collective activity. *Journal of Teacher Education, 64*(5), 378–386.

National Center for Educational Statistics. (2017). *English language learners in public schools.* https://nces.ed.gov/programs/coe/indicator_cgf.asp

Reys, B. J., & Fennell, F. (2003). Who should lead mathematics instruction at the elementary school level? *Teaching Children Mathematics, 9*(5), 277–282.

Richardson, M., Feighan, K., & Rudolph, A. (2016). *Mathematics achievement with teachers of high-need urban populations—MATH UP evaluation extension reports.* Philadelphia, PA: Research for Better Schools at PMHC.

Richardson, M., Feighan, K., & Rudolph, A. (2017). *Mathematics achievement with teachers of high-need urban populations—MATH UP evaluation extension reports.* Philadelphia, PA: Research for Better Schools at PMHC.

Saldaña, J. (2013). *The coding manual for qualitative researchers* (2nd ed.). Thousand Oaks, CA: SAGE.

CHAPTER 7

PREPARING AND KEEPING OUR BEST

Linking a Measure of Preservice Teacher Quality to Professional Outcomes

Margarita Pivovarova
Arizona State University

Robert Vagi
Independent Research Consultant

Wendy Barnard
Arizona State University

A large body of research suggests that recruiting and retaining excellent teachers into the profession is vital for students' academic success (Hanushek, 2011). Consequently, preparing, recruiting, and retaining high quality teachers are long-standing policy issues and concerns for schools and school districts. In this chapter, we examine the trajectories of improvement for preservice teachers and demonstrate how teaching quality during

Linking Teacher Preparation Program Design and Implementation to Outcomes for Teachers and Students, pages 181–210
Copyright © 2020 by Information Age Publishing
181

preservice is related to entry into the profession after graduation and retention on the job 2 years after. Studies of personal development trajectories are not uncommon in the psychology literature, but these are relatively new to teacher education. In this chapter, we use an approach to studying improvement trajectories that is novel to teacher preparation literature (i.e., growth mixture modeling) to understand how rates of change in preservice teacher quality differ across preservice teachers and to identify individual characteristics of preservice teachers associated with different rates of growth. We also use a discrete-time hazard model to provide evidence on the relationship between preservice quality and retention.

On March 27, 2017, President Donald Trump signed a bill that overturned controversial regulations put in place by the Obama administration that sought to hold teacher preparation programs accountable for the quality of their graduates (Iasevoli, 2017). Although they never fully went into effect, the U.S. Department of Education's teacher preparation regulations marked the culmination of years of discussion and debate surrounding the role that teacher preparation programs play in ensuring that every child has access to an excellent teacher (U.S. Department of Education, 2016). While the policy landscape has shifted recently, this debate highlighted the important role that teacher preparation programs play in training and supporting high-quality teachers.

Given recent interest in the relationship between teacher preparation and teacher quality, teacher preparation programs may benefit from a better understanding of the relationships that underlie preservice teacher quality and teachers' decisions to enter into and remain in the profession. Although many studies have examined why teachers enter and leave the profession, relatively few studies have investigated the relationship between teacher retention in the profession and preservice teacher quality (Feng & Sass, 2011; Krieg, 2006).

Teacher preparation, recruitment, and replacement are all costly processes, with teacher replacement being particularly burdensome to the public education system (Barnes, Crowe, & Schaefer, 2007; Levy, Joy, Ellis, Jablonski, & Karelitz, 2012). To replace a teacher, schools must provide additional training to a new hire (Levy et al., 2012). The district must also spend resources to recruit new teachers, interview them, process newly hired teachers, and train them to abide by school and district policies (Barnes et al., 2007; Levy et al., 2012). The total financial costs associated with teacher attrition vary by district and can range from $4,000 per teacher in small rural districts to $18,000 per teacher in large urban districts (Barnes et al., 2007). Research also indicates that these costs are the most damaging in high-poverty districts where teacher turnover is highest and where resources for social and academic support are scarce (Darling-Hammond,

2003). In addition to administrative and financial costs, research has demonstrated that unstable learning environments as a result of teachers leaving schools negatively affect student achievement, particularly in schools with many low-performing and Black students (Ronfeldt, Loeb, & Wyckoff, 2013).

Despite the fact that a growing body of literature examines how teacher quality changes over time (Clotfelter, Ladd, & Vigdor, 2007; Harris & Sass, 2011; Kraft & Papay, 2014; Ladd & Sorensen, 2015; Papay & Kraft, 2015; Papay, West, Fullerton, & Kane, 2012; Rockoff, Jacob, Kane, & Staiger, 2011; Wayne & Youngs, 2003), less is known about preservice teacher quality and how it is related to important outcomes throughout teachers' professional careers, including teachers' growth and retention.

RESEARCH QUESTIONS

In this chapter, we investigate the relationship between teacher preparation, teacher quality, and subsequent employment and retention. Specifically, we ask the following research questions:

1. How do preservice teacher quality ratings change over time during their preparation?
2. Which characteristics of preservice teachers are related to growth in their quality ratings?
3. What is the relationship between preservice teachers' quality ratings and their subsequent entry and retention in teaching?

To answer these questions, we use data from an apprenticeship-style teacher preparation program in a large state flagship university. This program is representative of other teacher preparation programs of its kind across many major universities in the country.

In the following sections we describe our data, explain our methodological approaches and analyses, present our findings, and conclude with implications for teacher preparation programs.

DATA

We use data collected as part of an evaluation of a teacher preparation program that emphasizes intensive, school-based pre-professional training. Students in their senior year of college spend an entire academic school year teaching in a P–12 school under the guidance of a mentor teacher. In addition, university faculty provide preservice teachers with classes at their school site to ground instruction in the practical aspects of teaching. Further, and critical for our research questions, preservice teachers are provided with regular and rigorous feedback by university-trained site coordinators.

In addition to information collected by the university, our data also included teachers' employment histories, which were provided by the state department of education for each year after graduation. These data span the 2012–2013 through 2015–2016 school years.

Data for the analyses in this chapter include information about preservice teachers' academic performance, demographics, and observational ratings of teaching performance during their student teaching year. For each teacher candidate in the program, we know their gender and ethnicity, the degree-type they were granted, and whether they were first-generation college students and out-of-state students; we also have information about their age at entry into student teaching and their high school grade-point average (GPA). These data were available for those teacher candidates in the program who had successfully completed their yearlong student teaching residency and graduated with a traditional teaching degree.

Measure of Teaching Quality

Our main variable of interest in this study was an indicator of preservice teachers' teaching quality. The quality measure was computed from a composite of several indicators of teaching quality, which use a one to five scale with 1 indicating *poor performance* and 5 indicating *exemplary performance*. These indicators come from two widely used teacher evaluation instruments: 8 indicators from the TAP Observational Rubric (National Institute for Excellence in Teaching, 2011) and 9 indicators from Danielson's *Framework for Teaching* (2007), for a total of 17 indicators (Table 7.1 lists all indicators used in the analyses). The TAP Observational Rubric was chosen as a way to both measure quality of teaching and as a coaching tool for faculty to prepare preservice teachers to be "classroom ready" by showing proficiency in core areas such as instruction and ability to maintain a positive classroom environment. Items selected by college faculty were those deemed most crucial for effective classroom instruction. Items from Danielson's Professional Responsibilities domain were added as a complement to the TAP Observational Rubric, as the Danielson items examine professional duties beyond classroom instruction. Taken together, the components focused on examining teacher quality holistically in a way that moved beyond theoretical best practices to classroom application.

TABLE 7.1   Professional Responsibilities and Classroom Practice Indicators

Professional Responsibilities (Danielson Framework)	Classroom Practice (TAP Observation Rubric)
Showing Professionalism a. Relationships with others in schools and the profession b. Fulfilling professional responsibilities *Growing and Developing Professionally* a. Growing in content knowledge and pedagogical skill b. Continued professional growth *Maintaining Accurate Records* a. General record keeping b. Maintains information on student progress in learning *Communicating with Families* a. Communicates instructional program information to parents (i.e., academic standards, grade level expectations, curriculum) b. Communicates individual student performance to parents c. Advocacy/resources for students	a. Standards and objectives b. Presenting instructional content c. Activities and materials d. Academic feedback e. Instructional plans f. Managing student behavior g. Teacher content knowledge h. Teacher knowledge of students

Danielson's Framework for Teaching

The first set of indicators (nine indicators listed in the first column of Table 7.1) deals with teachers' professionalism and is taken from Domain 4: Professional Responsibilities of Danielson's *Framework for Teaching* (2007). Our measure of teacher quality includes four of the six subdomains identified in Danielson's *Framework for Teaching*: showing professionalism, growing and developing professionally, maintaining accurate records, and communicating with families. Each subdomain includes between two and three indicators for a total of nine total professional responsibilities indicators.

Evidence of the validity and reliability of the *Framework for Teaching* is documented in Benjamin (2002) and Milanowski (2004, 2011). For instance, using feedback from a panel of preservice teachers, cooperating teachers, and university supervisors, Benjamin (2002) found strong evidence of the instrument's reliability (i.e., 96% agreement among raters). Additionally, the measures produced internally consistent ratings ($\alpha = 0.84–0.93$). Finally, the structural validity of the measures was established through confirmatory factor analysis (NFI = 0.89; CFI = 1.00; GFI = 0.91). Milanowski (2004, 2011) found a moderate degree of criterion-related validity between ratings from a modified version of the framework and a value-added measure based on student achievement on standardized tests.

TAP Observational Rubric

The second set of indicators (eight indicators listed in the second column of Table 7.1) focuses on teachers' classroom practices. This measure is a modified version of the TAP Observational Rubric (National Institute for Excellence in Teaching, 2011). Indicators of practice include alignment of instruction with standards and objectives, presentation of instructional content, quality of activities and materials, academic feedback, instructional plans, management of student behavior, teacher content knowledge, and teachers' knowledge of students (see Table 7.1, Column 2). Similar to the Professional Responsibilities indicators, preservice teachers were rated on each indicator using a one to five scale, with 1 representing *poor performance* and 5 representing *exemplary performance*. A few studies have assessed the validity and reliability of the TAP Observational Rubric. Morgan, Hodge, Trepinski, and Anderson (2014) examined the stability of TAP scores over time and found that TAP scores remained stable or improved over time for 56% of their sample with 31% showing erratic score patterns. Using a larger sample ($n = 2,482$), Barnett and Wills (2015) also assessed the stability of TAP scores over time and found estimates of stability were large and statistically significant ($r = 0.56$–0.70). Additionally, Barnett and Wills (2015) assessed the convergent validity of TAP scores by correlating them with classroom-level value-added measures of teacher effectiveness. These estimates were both positive and statistically significant ($r = 0.18$–0.24).

Combined Measure of Teaching Quality

To obtain an overall measure of preservice teacher quality, the scores on all of the professionalism and classroom practice indicators (17 indicators) were summed, resulting in a minimum score of 17 and a maximum score of 85. To make these scores more interpretable, they were then divided by the total number of indicators (17), which resulted in a mean scale score that is on the same scale as the original indicators (1 = *overall unsatisfactory performance*, 5 = *overall exemplary performance*; Cohen, Cohen, Aiken, & West, 1999). Figure 7.1 presents the distribution of the fourth and final mean observational scores in our sample.

Mentor teachers evaluated preservice teachers on the set of 17 indicators using a one to five scale. Mentor teachers and faculty observers underwent rigorous training to ensure that their ratings were valid and reliable.

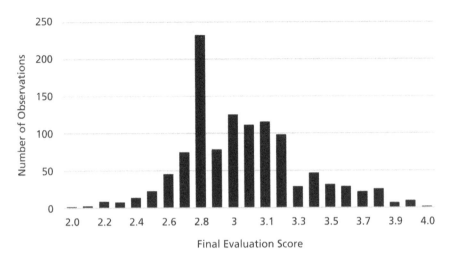

Figure 7.1 Distribution of teacher quality rating scores ($n = 1,126$).

Preservice teachers received four formal evaluations during the course of student teaching that included scores on each indicator. After the observation was completed, preservice teachers received detailed feedback that they were expected to address prior to their next observation. At the end of each evaluation period, teacher candidates received a summary score that was computed as an average of all of the indicators described above, ranging from one to five. A score of 1 or 2 indicated low quality performance, whereas a score of 4 or 5 was indicative of a master teacher. A score of 3 indicates proficient teaching behaviors; however, the expectation is that novice teachers score on average 2.5. Teacher candidates are expected but not required to obtain at least a 3 on each indicator during their final observation before graduation.

Sample

Our data represent 1,283 teachers from three academic years (2011–2012, 2012–2013, and 2013–2014) from five cohorts who graduated from a teacher preparation program housed in a large state university that emphasizes intensive, school-based professional training before entry into profession. This sample consists of all teachers from these five cohorts who graduated with a teaching degree, met minimum professional qualifications as rated by their supervisors, and for whom complete data were available. All teacher candidates in our sample experienced two full semesters of student teaching, but their beginning and completion calendar periods did not always overlap. A breakdown of these cohorts with the respective

TABLE 7.2 Descriptions of Cohorts

Semester in Which Student Teaching Began	Number of Preservice Teachers	Percentage of Preservice Teachers	Observed Decision for Entry Into the Profession	Possible Years in Which Retention Can Be Observed
Fall 2011	354	31.4%	Yes	3
Spring 2012	123	10.9%	Yes	2
Fall 2012	284	25.2%	Yes	2
Spring 2013	123	10.9%	Yes	1
Fall 2013	242	21.5%	Yes	1
Total	**1,126**	**100.0%**		

numbers of teacher candidates in each is listed in Table 7.2. Roughly 78% of teachers in our sample began student teaching in a fall semester with the remainder (22%) beginning during a spring semester. In the analyses, we focus on whether or not a teacher entered into, continued in, and/or left the profession after graduating. While we have up to 4 years of teachers' employment history, we only observe the decision to stay or leave the profession for a maximum of 3 years. To determine whether a teacher stayed or left, we need a subsequent year of the data. For example, if a preservice teacher is employed in both 2014–2015 and 2015–2016, then we know that they did not choose to leave the profession in 2014–2015. To analyze their decisions to enter and stay in the profession, we treat the school year after graduation as the first year in which teachers could be employed. Although teachers who graduate in the fall semester can technically be employed in the spring, we focus on the school year after graduation as this reflects the normal hiring cycle of schools.

Descriptive statistics for our sample of teachers are presented in Table 7.3. The majority of teachers are female (90%), and they are predominantly White (70%). Half of the teachers graduated with an elementary education degree. About 16% of teacher candidates are from out of state, and almost half of all teacher candidates (48%) are first generation college students. The four measures of observational scores demonstrate that on average, preservice teachers' quality improved over time.

We restricted the samples based on the available information required for the analysis. The bottom panel of Table 7.3 lists three analytic samples with the respective sample sizes that we used for the analyses described below.

METHODS

To answer our research questions, we use three quantitative approaches. For our first research question, we use latent growth curve modeling

TABLE 7.3 Descriptive Statistics for Analytic Sample in Analysis of Entry Into the Profession

Variable	Mean or Percent	Standard Deviation
Mean Composite Score, First Observation	2.42	0.41
Mean Composite Score, Second Observation	2.66	0.36
Mean Composite Score, Third Observation	2.86	0.29
Mean Composite Score, Fourth and Final	3.05	0.32
Degree Type		
Early Childhood (%)	12.4%	
Elementary (%)	50.4%	
Secondary (%)	1.3%	
Special Education (%)	10.2%	
Special Education and Early Childhood (%)	3.8%	
Special Education and Elementary (%)	22.0%	
Gender		
Female (%)	90.1%	
Male (%)	9.9%	
Ethnicity		
American Indian (%)	1.6%	
Asian (%)	2.6%	
Black (%)	2.1%	
Hispanic/Latino (%)	21.3%	
Hawaiian/Two or More/Other (%)	2.6%	
White (%)	69.8%	
Other Teacher Characteristics		
First Generation College Student (%)	48.2%	
Out of State Student (%)	16.0%	
Age at Entry Into Student Teaching	23.8	5.81
High School GPA	3.5	0.37
Sample Size (N)		
GMM Analysis	1,283	
Logistic Analysis	1,126	
Discrete time hazard model analysis	865	

(LGCM) to identify differences in how the measure of preservice teacher quality improves over time. To address our second research question, we examine how these rates of change are related to preservice teacher characteristics like high school GPA, age, and first-generation college student status. Using that information, we apply growth mixture modeling (GMM) to identify possible latent classes of preservice teachers based on their improvement over time. In both the LGCM and GMM analyses, we estimate a linear latent growth curve model with time-invariant predictors. For our final research question, we use two analyses. In the first, we use logistic regression to understand the relationship between entry into the profession after graduation and preservice teacher characteristics and specifically preservice quality. In the second analysis, we estimate the probability that a teacher would stay in the profession in the first 2 years upon graduation using a discrete-time hazard model. We describe our methods in detail below.

Growth Modeling

LGCM is a commonly used method for examining rates of change in the outcomes or malleable characteristics of individuals. The use of LGCM and GMM in education research is still relatively new. So far, only a handful of studies have applied this technique to education-relevant phenomena. For instance, GMM has been used to describe engagement typologies of Canadian students (Janosz, Archambault, Morizot, & Pagani, 2008) and to identify typologies of high school students associated with dropping out of school (Bowers & Sprott, 2012; Muthén, 2004). To our knowledge, ours is the first analysis that uses GMM to identify a typology of teachers based on changes in quality ratings.

LGCM estimates latent growth functions for individual units when they are observed at multiple time points. In the case of a linear growth model, these rates of change are assumed to follow linear trajectories and, therefore, are expressed as linear functions. Parameters of these linear functions—slopes and intercepts—are assumed to vary randomly across units (in our case, preservice teachers). This variability allows researchers to test hypotheses related to systematic differences in individuals' rates of change. In the present study, we examine whether preservice teachers' demographic and academic characteristics (age, ethnicity, first generation college student and out-of-state status, and high school GPA) are associated with different rates of change in their observational scores.

We then identify and describe latent classes of preservice teachers whose changes in observation scores are similar over time. These classes are often referred to as development typologies. In order to do that, we make use of GMM, which is a form of finite mixture modeling that has recently gained popularity (Dolan, 2009; Jung & Wickrama, 2008; Muthén, 2004; Muthén et al., 2002). GMM is an extension of LGCM that allows for the identification of discrete subgroups in longitudinal datasets. In line with latent growth analyses using structural equation modeling (SEM), GMM estimates latent slopes and intercepts from a set of longitudinal observations. However, traditional latent growth curve analyses assume that the sample comes from a single population. GMM, on the other hand, assumes that a sample is drawn from multiple populations and that these groups are expressed in the non-normal distribution of slopes and intercepts.

GMM is an exploratory procedure that requires a priori specification of the number of subgroups in the data. The model uses an iterative procedure to determine the most likely class membership for each observation and to estimate a LGCM for each latent class. GMM analyses also provide model-fit indices that allow researchers to compare models with different numbers of latent classes. These fit indices are then used to determine the number of latent classes that are likely present in the data. Additionally, GMM allows researchers to examine differences between latent classes based on each observation's most likely class membership. We conducted each of these analyses using Mplus 7.

The first and perhaps most important step in GMM is to determine the number of latent classes (i.e., distinct groups) that are likely present in the data. Because this analysis is exploratory, we followed the method proposed by Ram and Grimm (2009) and examined a series of models with varying complexity and compared their fit statistics. Specifically, we estimated models where all parameters were constrained to be equal across classes (i.e., M1), where the means of the latent slopes and intercepts were allowed to vary across classes (i.e., M2), where the means and variances of the latent slopes and intercepts were allowed to vary across classes (i.e., M3), and where the means, variances, and covariances of the latent slopes and intercepts were allowed to vary across classes (i.e., M4). Following the recommendation of Tofighi and Enders (2007), we estimated these models without covariates to ensure that the number of classes is determined solely by the distributions of the latent slopes and intercepts. Our analysis indicated that the model with two classes (M2) provided the best model fit. Additionally, this model was able to adequately distinguish between latent classes and did not result in convergence or estimation problems.

Logistic Regression and Discrete-Time Hazard Modeling

To answer our third research question, we follow preservice teachers through their graduation and first 3 years of employment. In these analyses, we focus on whether a teacher entered into and remained in the profession for up to 2 years after graduating and relate these decisions to their quality scores using logistic regression and discrete-time hazard modeling. First, we estimate the relationship between the measure of preservice teacher quality and teachers' entry into the profession for all teachers in our analytic sample ($N = 1{,}126$). To do this, we estimate a series of logistic regressions with teachers' employment in a state public school during the year after graduation as the outcome. Logistic regression models account for the non-normal residual structure associated with discrete outcomes and produce coefficients that indicate the average relationship between each predictor and likelihood of entry into the profession. In our case, such relationships reflect the association between being employed at a public school in the state in the year after graduation (employed = 1) versus not being employed (not employed = 0). These analyses take the following form:

$$\log\left(\frac{p_{ic}}{1 - p_{ic}}\right) = \beta_1 w_i + \beta_2 X_i + \beta_3 C + e_{ic}$$

where

$$\log\left(\frac{p_{ic}}{1 - p_{ic}}\right)$$

is the conditional probability, or log odds, of a teacher i in cohort c entering the profession in the year after graduation; w_i is the composite indicator of teacher quality from teacher candidates' final student teaching observation; X_i is a set of time-invariant teacher characteristics; C is a set of dummy variables indicating preservice teacher's cohort, which also serve as a proxy for year-specific effects; and e_{ic} is an error term. We included preservice teacher demographics (gender, race or ethnicity, first generation college student, age at entry into student teaching) and preservice teacher academic achievement (high school GPA), as previous research indicated that these variables were likely related to teachers' decisions to enter and remain in the profession (Clotfelter et al., 2007; Rockoff et al., 2011; Wayne & Youngs, 2003). We also included teacher candidate cohort (semester when a teacher candidate began their preservice teaching experience) and a teacher candidate major in the program (e.g., early childhood, elementary, secondary, and special education). We also control for the Title I status schools where preservice teachers had their student teacher training. Although Title I status is a somewhat blunt indicator, previous research has demonstrated that teachers are significantly more likely to leave high-need and high-poverty districts and schools (Ingersoll, 2001; Ingersoll & Smith, 2004; Simon & Johnson, 2015).

In our second analysis, we focus only on those teachers who were employed in a public school in the year after graduation ($N = 865$). We make use of discrete-time hazard modeling to examine the relationship between preservice teacher quality and the likelihood that a teacher who enters the profession in the year after graduation will continue to be employed in the state public education system during the following 2 years. Discrete-time hazard modeling predicts the likelihood that an event of interest (in our case, leaving the teaching profession) occurs in a given time period conditional that the event did not occur in a previous period (Singer & Willett, 2003). Discrete-time hazard models also allow researchers to analyze data for which censoring occurs at different times, addressing the challenge of individuals in the data set who are observed for different amounts of time. We consider each school year as a discrete time period within which a teacher can choose to remain in or leave the profession once their contract term is completed. These decisions, however, can only be observed at the beginning of the following year. In other words, we can only know if a teacher chose to leave the profession during a given year if they are no longer employed in the following year. Also, we assign the year after which teachers have graduated as the first year in which an event can potentially occur. As described earlier, only those teachers who were employed during the year after graduating from the program are included in these analyses. Our models include the same set of covariates described above plus an indicator for each time period.

The outcome of interest in the second set of analyses is whether a teacher is employed in the state public education system within the first 3 years of employment (exit is coded as an indicator variable equal to 1). We identify leavers, or teachers who leave the profession during the observed period, as those who are listed as employed by the state department of education in 1 year but are not employed in the state public education system in the following year. This classification raises two potential issues. First, appearing in 1 year but not the next does not mean that teachers necessarily left the profession, only that they are no longer teaching in the state public education system. Previous research suggests that teacher labor markets are localized (Reininger, 2012) indicating that out-of-state teachers (i.e., teachers who moved from another state) are more likely to leave the state than those who are from the state in which they are employed. To account for this, we include a dummy variable indicating whether or not a teacher was ever listed as an out-of-state student for tuition purposes at the time of enrollment to the university. Because much of the coursework (including student teaching) requires students to reside in the state, these students were most likely to have moved from out-of-state to attend the university.

Teachers who leave the data set could also potentially leave the public school sector to work in a private school. Unfortunately, we are unable to account for this in our data, as private schools are not required to report employment data to the state. The second issue associated with this strategy is that some teachers exit the profession and then return at a later date. This subpopulation is relatively small in our sample (5%) and should not pose a significant problem to our estimation. We acknowledge, though, that treating this subpopulation in this way may potentially bias our estimates. To account for this, we compare models where returners are treated as if they entered and remained in the profession and where they did not. In addition, all models include the same control variables that are described above in the first set of analyses with the addition of a time-period dummy variable.

Our final retention model takes the following form:

$$\log\left(\frac{p_{ict}}{1-P_{ict}}\right) = \alpha_t T + \beta_1 w_i + \beta_2 X_i + \beta_3 C + \beta_4 \text{Title I}_{it} + e_{ict}$$

where

$$\log\left(\frac{p_{ict}}{1-P_{ict}}\right)$$

is the probability of teacher i from cohort c leaving the profession in year t conditional on the fact that they have not left previously, T is a set of dummy variables indicating time period (i.e., time period 1 = the first year in which a teacher was employed), w_i is our composite indicator for teacher quality measured at the final observation of preservice teachers' student teaching residency, X_i is a set of time-invariant teacher characteristics, C is a set of dummy variables indicating preservice teachers' cohort, Title I_{it} is a time-varying dummy variable indicating whether teacher i was employed at a Title I school in year t, and e_{ict} is an error term.

Before we proceeded with the estimation of the empirical models above, we evaluated the extent of multicollinearity, or interdependence among the control variables in our models, and its potential confounding effect on the estimates. As an initial step, we estimated bivariate correlations among all of the predictors; none exceeded 0.15. Additionally, we examined the tolerance and variance inflation factors (VIF) for each of the variables in our model. Similarly, these suggested that multicollinearity was not an issue in our models since all tolerance values were between 0.59–0.98 and VIF values ranged between 1.05 and 2.01.

RESULTS

Growth in Preservice Teacher Quality Ratings

Our model estimating the rate of growth for preservice teachers' observational scores is presented in Figure 7.2. This model estimates latent intercepts that are centered at preservice teachers' first observations and latent slopes derived from each of the four observations.

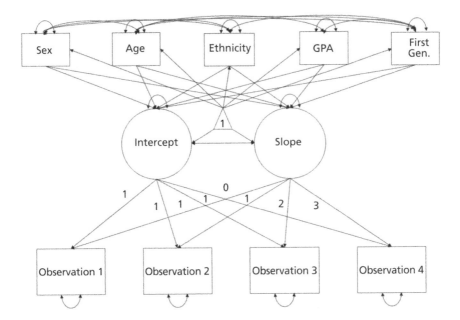

Figure 7.2 Latent growth curve model.

While average values of preservice teachers' scores suggest that they improve over time, to provide a formal test for this, we began by comparing an *intercept-only* model to a model that included both latent intercepts and slopes. This analysis suggested that allowing slopes and intercepts to vary improved the model fit significantly. Further, these analyses indicated a strong negative correlation between preservice teachers' initial evaluation scores (i.e., intercepts) and their rates of improvement (i.e., slopes; $r = -0.73$). In other words, preservice teachers with higher initial evaluation scores had, on average, lower rates of improvement with the opposite being true for initially low-performing teachers. We can rule out ceiling effect in this case since even the highest performing preservice teachers started with the scores sufficiently below the maximum score of five. In all models, the residual variances of the observed variables were constrained to be equal across observations.

Preservice Teacher Characteristics Affecting Growth in Their Quality Ratings

Next, we estimated a model that included teachers' gender, age, high school GPA, ethnicity, and first-generation college student status as covariates. Age and high school GPA were mean centered to make the intercepts interpretable. The results from this analysis are presented in Column 2 of Table 7.4. To determine if this model significantly improved the fit of our

TABLE 7.4   Results From Latent Growth Curve Models

Estimate	Model 1	Model 2	
Mean/Intercept			
Intercept	2.43***	2.44***	
Slope	0.22***	0.20***	
Variance/Correlation			
Intercept	0.10***	0.09***	
Slope	0.01***	0.01***	
ρ Intercept/Slope	−0.73***	−0.73***	
Coefficient on Intercept			
Age		0.00	(0.00)
GPA		0.16	(0.03)
Minority		−0.01	(0.02)
Male		−0.03	(0.04)
First Generation		−0.01	(0.02)
Coefficient on Slope			
Age		−0.002*	(0.00)
GPA		−0.01	(0.01)
Minority		−0.00	(0.01)
Male		−0.01	(0.02)
First Generation		0.01	(0.01)
Loglikelihood	1,229.21	7,911.81	
n	1,283	1,283	

* $p < .05$, ** $p < .01$, *** $p < .001$.

Note: Variances in Model 2 reflect the residual variances of the slopes and intercepts not accounted for by the predictors.

model, we estimated a comparison model that included the predictors but constrained their coefficients to equal zero. We then conducted a χ^2 difference test and concluded that the model with freely-estimated coefficients significantly improved the fit of the model ($\chi^2 (10) = 68.19$, $p < 0.01$).

Table 7.4 presents results from the analysis of teachers' growth trajectories and shows, of our predictors, high school GPA is significantly related to preservice teachers' initial evaluation score. Specifically, a one-unit increase (e.g., a change from a GPA of 3.0 to 4.0) in high school GPA is associated with an average increase of 0.16 in the initial evaluation score ($p < 0.001$). This transforms into a 0.19 standard deviation increase in the initial evaluation score for a one standard deviation increase in high school GPA. Additionally, preservice teachers' age is associated with slightly lower rates of improvement. For a 1-year increase in age, there is an average decrease of 0.002 in teachers' rate of improvement ($p < 0.05$). This transforms into a 0.08 standard deviation decrease in the rate of improvement for a standard deviation increase in teachers' age. Despite these statistically significant relationships, it is important to note that the model was only able to account for roughly 1% of the variance in the latent intercepts and less than 1% of the variance in the latent slopes.

Exploring a Typology of Preservice Teachers With Differential Growth in Quality Ratings and Factors Associated With Latent Class Membership

Figure 7.3 shows the estimated mean trajectories for each latent class and Table 7.5 displays the parameter estimates for each latent class. Looking at the estimated mean trajectories, we see that both classes begin student teaching with roughly the same evaluation scores (2.43 and 2.30). However, preservice teachers in Latent Class 2 improve at a much faster rate and finish student teaching with an evaluation score nearly two standard deviations above those in Latent Class 1 (3.69 vs. 2.98). We refer to Latent Class 2 as faster improving group.

Additionally, the faster improving group has slightly fewer men (7.6% vs. 10.6%) and slightly higher high school GPAs (3.69 vs. 3.55). Preservice teachers in both classes were roughly 24 years old, on average. Both groups had similar proportions of first-generation college students. Finally, Latent Class 1 had significantly more minority students (31.3%) than Latent Class 2 (18.6%).

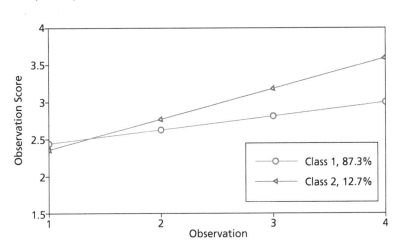

Figure 7.3 Estimated mean trajectories from the growth mixture model ($n = 1,283$).

TABLE 7.5 Descriptive Statistics by Latent Class

	Latent Class 1		Latent Class 2	
	Mean or Percent	SD	Mean or Percent	SD
Observation Score 1	2.43	0.40	2.30	0.33
Observation Score 2	2.65	0.35	2.74	0.39
Observation Score 3	2.82	0.27	3.19	0.31
Observation Score 4	2.98	0.25	3.69	0.19
Male (%)	10.6%		7.6%	
Age	24.1	6.05	23.5	4.89
GPA	3.55	0.38	3.69	0.28
Minority (%)	31.3%		18.6%	
First Gen. (%)	48.2%		50.0%	
n	1,120		163	
	(87.3%)		(12.7%)	

Next, we examined systematic differences between latent classes by predicting latent class membership from preservice teachers' gender, age, high school GPA, ethnicity, and first-generation status. The results from this analysis are presented in Table 7.6. In this model, the outcome is a binary variable representing each preservice teacher's most likely latent class where Latent Class 2 (faster improving group) is coded 1 and Latent Class 1 is coded 0. As such, the coefficient estimates are on the logit scale with odds-ratios presented for ease of interpretation.

Looking at these results, two coefficients are statistically significant at $p < 0.05$. Specifically, the odds of being in the faster improving group (i.e., Latent Class 2) increase four-fold for a one-unit increase in high school GPA (e.g., an increase from 3.0 to 4.0). In standard units, this equates to a

TABLE 7.6 Multinomial Logistic Regression With Latent Class as the Outcome

	Latent Class 2	
Variable	Coefficient	Odds Ratio
Male	−0.18 (0.53)	
Age	−0.04 (0.02)	
GPA	1.44*** (0.38)	4.20***
Minority	−0.95* (0.44)	0.39*
First Generation	0.31 (0.29)	

* $p < 0.05$, ** $p < 0.01$, *** $p < 0.001$
Notes: Latent class 1 is the reference group.

118% increase in the odds of being in Latent Class 2 for an increase of one standard deviation in high school GPA. The second statistically significant coefficient indicates that minority students are 61% less likely than White peers to be in faster improving group.

Relationship of Preservice Teacher Quality Ratings to Entry in the Profession

Our next question is whether those teachers who have higher overall scores on the observation measure are more likely to enter and stay in the profession. We begin by examining the relationship between preservice teacher quality and entry into the profession. In total, 865 (76.8%) of the 1,126 teachers in our sample were employed in a state public school in the year after graduation. Table 7.7 presents the results of logistic regression models where the outcome is a binary indicator for whether or not a teacher candidate was employed after their student teaching year (i.e., employed = 1). Model 1 contains only preservice teachers' observation scores and cohort fixed-effects. Model 2 adds teacher candidate characteristics while Model 3 includes a dummy variable for whether or not a preservice teacher taught at a Title I school. Because all "returners" were employed in the year after their student teaching, there was no need to account for their decision to return in these models. In the table, we report both the

TABLE 7.7 Coefficient Estimates From Logistic Regression Models Predicting Entry Into the Profession

Variable	Model 1		Model 2		Model 3	
	Coefficient	Odds Ratio	Coefficient	Odds Ratio	Coefficient	Odds Ratio
Mean Composite Score	0.74** (0.24)	2.09**	0.66* (0.27)	1.91	0.65** (0.26)	1.91**
Degree						
Early Childhood			−0.58* (0.25)	0.56	−0.58* (0.25)	0.56*
Secondary			1.32 (1.09)	3.73	1.36 (1.10)	3.88
Special Education			−0.41 (0.30)	0.67	−0.38 (0.30)	0.69
SPED and Early Childhood			−0.33 (0.40)	0.72	−0.29 (0.41)	0.75
SPED and Elementary			−0.40* (0.22)	0.67*	−0.41* (0.22)	0.67*

(continued)

TABLE 7.7 Coefficient Estimates From Logistic Regression Models Predicting Entry Into the Profession (Continued)

	Model 1		Model 2		Model 3	
Variable	Coefficient	Odds Ratio	Coefficient	Odds Ratio	Coefficient	Odds Ratio
Demographics						
Male			0.28 (0.30)	1.32	0.28 (0.30)	1.32
American Indian			0.93 (1.06)	2.53	0.92 (1.06)	2.50
Asian			−1.11** (0.41)	0.33**	−1.09** (0.41)	0.34**
Black			−0.11 (0.54)	0.90	−0.09 (0.54)	0.91
Hispanic/Latino			−0.02 (0.22)	0.99	−0.01 (0.22)	0.99
Hawaiian/Two or More/Other			−0.89 (0.41)	0.41**	−0.89* (0.41)	0.41*
Age at Entry					0.02 (0.02)	1.02
Other Teacher Characteristics						
High School GPA			0.08 (0.22)	1.08	0.08 (0.22)	1.08
First Generation			0.24 (0.17)	1.27	0.24 (0.17)	1.28
Out of State			−0.86*** (0.19)	0.42***	−0.86*** (0.19)	0.42***
School Characteristics						
Title I					−0.12 (0.19)	0.89
Deviance	1,068.46		1,016.61		1,016.22	
χ^2 change from empty model	9.09**		60.93***		61.32***	
Cox & Snell pseudo-R^2	0.01		0.05		0.05	
Nagelkerke pseudo-R^2	0.01		0.09		0.09	
N	1,126		1,126		1,126	

* indicates significance at $p < 0.10$, ** indicates significance at $p < 0.05$, and *** indicates significance at $p < 0.01$.

Note: All models include cohort fixed-effects.

regression parameters and also transformed parameters, or so-called "odds ratios." Because logistic regression transforms the outcome into log odds, the untransformed parameters are difficult to interpret. Therefore, it is common to also report the results as odds ratios since they are easier to interpret—they represent the amount that the odds in favor of the outcome are multiplied by per one-unit change in the predictor (for more details, see Cohen, Cohen, West, & Aiken, 2002).

According to the estimates from all three models, preservice teachers' mean composite score was significantly related ($p < 0.05$) to their decisions to enter the profession. Looking at the full model (i.e., Model 3), a one-point increase in preservice teachers' observation scores is associated with an average increase of 91% in the odds of entering the profession. In standard units, this transforms into a 29% increase in the odds of entering the profession for a one standard deviation increase in preservice teachers' evaluation scores. Although not the focus of this study, it should be noted that both ethnicity and out-of-state status were also significantly related to being employed in the state after graduation. Specifically, Asian students were 66% less likely to be employed in the state in the year after graduation when compared to White students. Similarly, out-of-state students were 58% less likely to be employed in the state after graduation. Finally, we should note that while some of the relationships identified in our analyses are statistically significant, the pseudo-R^2 values suggest that the model only reduces a small portion of the deviance (roughly 8%) when compared to intercept-only model (Cohen et al., 2002).

Relationship of Preservice Teacher Quality Ratings to Teacher Retention

Table 7.8 presents the results from the discrete-time hazard models with leaving the profession during the first 2 years of employment as the outcome. As in our first analysis, we estimate three successive models. As mentioned above, these models include only preservice teachers who were employed in the school year following their student teaching residency ($N = 865$).

The first two models in Table 7.8 include our variables of interest as predictors and treat all teachers who are not employed in a subsequent year after entering the profession as "leavers" (including those who return at a later date). As a robustness check, Model 3 treats those who leave but return in a later year as if they did not leave the profession. In all three models, we see that preservice teacher observation scores are strongly and significantly related to whether or not a teacher remains in the profession during the first 2 years

TABLE 7.8 Coefficient Estimates From Discrete-Time Hazard Models Predicting Teacher Retention

	Model 1		Model 2		Model 3	
Variable	Coefficient	Odds Ratio	Coefficient	Odds Ratio	Coefficient	Odds Ratio
Mean Composite Score	−0.81*** (0.29)	0.44**	−0.83*** (0.30)	0.44***	−1.28*** (0.41)	0.28***
Time Period						
Period 2	−0.35* (0.19)	0.70	−0.29 (0.20)	0.75	−0.87*** (0.28)	0.42***
Degree						
Early Childhood			0.13 (0.28)	1.13	0.01 (0.37)	0.99
Special Education			0.06 (0.29)	1.06	0.08 (0.38)	1.08
SPED and Elementary			−0.06 (0.34)	0.95	−0.47 (0.44)	0.62
Demographics						
Male			−0.62 (0.36)	0.54	−1.25** (0.62)	0.28
American Indian			0.74 (0.83)	2.09	0.24 (1.09)	1.27
Asian			0.64 (0.58)	1.89	0.97 (0.60)	2.63
Black			−1.09 (1.05)	0.34	−18.51 (73.0)	0.00
Hispanic/Latino			0.10 (0.26)	1.11	−0.48 (0.37)	0.62
Hawaiian/Two or More/Other			0.38 (0.58)	1.46	−0.53 (1.05)	0.59
Age at Entry			0.02 (0.02)	1.02	0.01 (0.02)	1.01
Other Teacher Characteristics						
High School GPA			−0.62** (0.27)	0.54**	−0.03 (0.37)	0.97
First Generation			0.19 (0.21)	1.21	0.33 (0.26)	1.39
Out of State			0.42 (0.28)	1.52	0.52 (0.34)	1.68
School Characteristics						
Title I			−0.65*** (0.21)	0.52***	0.36 (0.30)	1.44

(continued)

TABLE 7.8 Coefficient Estimates From Discrete-Time Hazard Models Predicting Teacher Retention (Continued)

Variable	Model 1		Model 2		Model 3	
	Coefficient	Odds Ratio	Coefficient	Odds Ratio	Coefficient	Odds Ratio
Deviance	761.98		738.02		488.44	
Cox & Snell pseudo-R^2	0.05		0.07		0.05	
Nagelkerke pseudo-R^2	0.11		0.15		0.15	
χ^2 change from an empty model	74.20***		98.16***		71.75***	
N	865		865		865	

* indicates significance at $p < 0.10$, ** indicates significance at $p < 0.05$, and *** indicates significance at $p < 0.01$.

Note: All models include cohort fixed-effects.

after graduation. Models 1 and 2 imply that a one-point increase in mean observation scores is associated with an average reduction in the odds of leaving the profession of 56%. In standard units, this transforms into a 17% reduction in the odds of leaving for one standard deviation increase in preservice teacher quality. However, as Model 3 suggests, this effect increases significantly when we treat returners as if they had not left the profession. Specifically, a one-unit increase in evaluations scores is associated with an average reduction in the odds of leaving of 72%. This transforms into a 22% decrease in the odds of leaving for a standard deviation increase in evaluation scores.

Again, though not the focus of this study, Table 7.8 suggests additional parameters achieve statistical significance; however, the results change depending on the specification of the model. For instance, when returners are treated as those who stay in the profession, men are 72% less likely to leave during their first 2 years of employment. This relationship, however, does not reach statistical significance when returners are treated as leavers. In other words, the relationship between gender and retention is likely explained by the relationship between gender and returning. In this case, it may be that men are more likely to take a year off between graduation and employment or that they temporarily leave the profession for a year.

IMPLICATIONS FOR TEACHER PREPARATION PROGRAMS

Our results suggest that preservice teacher quality ratings improve over time and at different rates. Additionally, we find that preservice teacher rates of improvement are largely related to their initial evaluation scores and that these initial scores are positively related to teachers' high school GPAs. These findings suggest that selection of high achieving students (as measured by high school GPA) into preparation programs contributes to initial teaching success and improvement in teaching (as measured by observation-based quality ratings).

Additionally, our analyses suggest that there is significant variability in preservice teachers' initial evaluation scores ($\sigma = 0.32$, $p < 0.001$). This variability indicates that some preservice teachers may benefit from targeted interventions prior to student teaching. For many preservice teachers, the student teaching experience may be the first time that their teaching is observed with such a high level of scrutiny. Therefore, finding ways to identify and coach low-performing preservice teachers prior to their student teaching experience may help them exceed performance standards rather than simply meeting them. This would not only benefit preservice teachers, but also the students they teach.

Although our analysis did not provide strong evidence identifying factors associated with low initial performance, it does suggest that lower high-school GPAs are associated with slightly lower initial evaluation scores. Although high school GPA may not be a definitive indicator of students' abilities, it may serve as a preliminary way of identifying teacher candidates who could benefit from targeted interventions prior to student teaching.

The finding that initial evaluation scores are strongly related to preservice teachers' rates of improvement ($r = -0.73$, $p < 0.001$) suggests that teachers with initially high evaluation scores tend to improve at slower rates than their lower-performing peers. While determining the cause of this relationship is beyond the scope of this study, it seems likely that it is related to the fact that successful student teaching is determined by a fixed score. For instance, preservice teachers who begin with high initial scores may be less motivated to improve since passing requires less effort. Therefore, our findings suggest that teacher preparation programs may benefit from focusing on ways to incentivize growth during student teaching rather than focusing on reaching proficiency.

The results from our latent class analyses may also be informative for teacher preparation programs. Specifically, our analyses identified two distinct groups of preservice teachers based on their rates of improvement over time. The first and largest group began with scores slightly below a passing score and finished with a score just above the passing mark. The second group, on the other hand, had similar initial scores but improved at a much faster rate, placing them nearly two standard deviations above their peers by the end of their student teaching. Further, we found that preservice teachers with higher high school GPAs and who were White were significantly more likely to be classified in the rapidly-improving group. This finding plausibly suggests presence of the raters' racial bias in the quality rating process that further implies the need to attend to this issue during the raters' training. In addition, teacher preparation programs might consider ways to support all preservice teachers, particularly those from underrepresented communities, as they pursue not only teaching competency but teaching excellence.

Identifying and recruiting teacher candidates who are most likely to improve as well as enter the profession ready to excel in the classroom should be a top priority for teacher preparation programs. To this end, our analysis suggests that high school GPA may be a useful indicator of teacher candidates' future success. Although determining the causes of these relationships is beyond the scope of this study, high school GPA may serve as a proxy for other important unobserved characteristics like motivation, academic competence, or a desire to be successful. On the other hand, GPA may reflect things like a preservice teacher's level of compliance or likeability, which may enter into grading beyond more objective measures. Whatever the case, this is particularly interesting in light of previous research that finds conflicting evidence relating academic indicators to teacher quality and student achievement (Ferguson & Womack, 1993; Kane, Rockoff, & Staiger, 2008).

In addition to changes in preservice teachers' observational scores, we examined the relationship between preservice teacher quality and entry into the profession. We estimated a number of statistical models with different sets of control variables and found that across all specifications, the average observational score had a statistically significant, positive relationship with preservice teachers' employment in a state public school the year after graduation.

Entry into the profession is an important outcome for graduates of teacher preparation programs, but even more critical to schools and students are high-quality teachers' decisions to remain in the profession. To this end, we found that ratings of preservice teacher quality are strongly and significantly related to whether or not a teacher enters into and remains in the profession during the first 2 years after graduation. This finding remains consistent across model specifications in our analysis, and echoes the results of previous studies that found positive relationships between teacher experience and retention (Ingersoll & Smith, 2004; Marvel, Lyter, Peltola, Strizek, & Morton, 2007).

These findings suggest that recruiting higher quality novice teachers into the profession may help reduce teacher attrition, at least during their first 3 years of employment and in the context of this particular state. To the extent that teacher preparation programs are able to produce high-quality graduates, teacher preparation programs may play an important role in reducing teacher turnover. Maximizing this benefit, however, may require greater collaboration between school districts and teacher preparation programs. For instance, schools (particularly those with high rates of attrition) may wish to recruit higher-quality preservice teachers, however, this would be difficult without knowing teachers' ratings during the hiring process. To help with this, teacher preparation programs might help by encouraging high-performing preservice teachers to seek employment at these schools as well as sharing data on preservice teacher quality. Further, state and local governments could offer incentives for these preservice teachers to work in high-attrition schools.

LIMITATIONS AND FUTURE RESEARCH

As with all research, there are limitations to our findings. For instance, our measure of preservice teacher quality relied on observed measures of teachers' practice. The current body of research has yet to provide conclusive evidence that these measures are related to key student outcomes, namely student achievement (Cohen & Goldhaber, 2016; Garrett & Steinberg, 2015; Steinberg & Garrett, 2016). More research is needed to determine the ability of observational measures of teacher quality to predict these and other student outcomes.

We also lack sufficiently detailed data to determine whether the specific measures used in this study are free from rater bias. To the extent that the raters of teacher quality are sensitive to nonteaching characteristics like preservice teachers' likeability, desire to please, or even race and gender, this measure may be capturing things unrelated to teacher quality. Although university supervisors were trained in the use of the observation rubric to ensure valid and reliable data, we were unable to test this. Future studies might consider ways of determining the extent to which these and other biases may be affecting preservice teacher evaluations.

Additionally, we are limited by the nature of the outcome variable in our analyses of entry and retention in the profession. While we have employment data for public schools in the state and the majority of preservice teachers likely go on to work in these schools, we cannot make definitive statements about their decisions to enter or leave the profession at large. For instance, preservice teachers who have chosen to remain in education but are working in private schools or are employed in other states will not appear in our data set. Our hope is that future studies can address this by gathering data about employment beyond the state and in multiple contexts.

Finally, we are limited by the highly contextual nature of the program. Many aspects of this program, both observed and unobserved, are likely unique to this context including the student and preservice teacher demographics, the local labor markets, and specific features of the training programs. To the extent that these characteristics are associated with our results, the findings from this study may not generalize to other contexts. While we feel that our analyses provide useful initial insight to teacher preparation programs, we encourage researchers to examine the extent to which our findings can be replicated in other settings.

CONCLUSION

Overall, our analyses in this chapter provide insight on teachers' rates of growth and retention. First, there is substantial variation with regard to both preservice teachers' initial evaluation scores and their subsequent rates of improvement, and this variation can be linked to preservice teachers' high school GPAs. Second, our findings suggest that recruiting higher quality novice teachers into the profession may help reduce teacher attrition, at least during their first 3 years of employment and in the context of this particular state.

TPPs are evaluated and ranked in part based on preservice teachers' entry into the profession and decision to remain in the profession. Entry of high-quality teachers into the profession and teacher retention may benefit the entire population of students served. Taken together, the findings presented in this chapter underscore the importance of measuring improvement trajectories of preservice teachers. Teacher preparation programs should consider evaluating their graduates based on performance measures as well as on the improvement in their quality over time. This is critical for university administrators of teacher preparation programs as they seek to develop approaches that prepare high quality teachers who enter and remain in the profession

REFERENCES

Barnes, G., Crowe, E., & Schaefer, B. (2007). *The cost of teacher turnover in five school districts: A pilot study.* Washington, DC: National Commission on Teaching and America's Future.

Barnett, J., & Wills, K. (2015). *Measuring and assessing classroom instruction: Properties of TAP observational rubric.* Santa Monica, CA: National Institute for Excellence in Teaching.

Benjamin, W. J. (2002, April). *Development and validation of student teaching performance assessment based on Danielson's Framework for Teaching.* Paper presented at the annual meeting for the American Educational Research Association, New Orleans, LA.

Bowers, A., & Sprott, R. (2012). Examining the multiple trajectories associated with dropping out of high school: A growth mixture model analysis. *The Journal of Educational Research, 105*(3), 176–195.

Clotfelter, C. T., Ladd, H. F., & Vigdor, J. L. (2007). *Teacher credentials and student achievement in high school: A cross-subject analysis with student fixed effects* (NBER Working Paper No. 13617). Cambridge, MA: National Bureau of Economic Research.

Cohen, P., Cohen, J., Aiken, L., & West, S. (1999). The problem of units and the circumstance for POMP. *Multivariate Behavioral Research, 34*(3), 315–346.

Cohen, J., Cohen, P., West, S. G., & Aiken, L. S. (2002). *Applied multiple regression/ correlation analysis for the behavioral sciences* (3rd ed.). Hillsdale, NJ: Erlbaum.

Cohen, J., & Goldhaber, D. (2016). Building a more complete understanding of teacher evaluation using classroom observations. *Educational Researcher, 45*(6), 378–387.

Danielson, C. (2007). *The framework for teaching: Evaluation instrument.* Princeton, NJ: The Danielson Group.

Darling-Hammond, L. (2003). Keeping good teachers: Why it matters, what leaders can do. *Educational Leadership, 60*(8), 6–13.

Dolan, C. V. (2009). Structural equation mixture modeling. In R. E. Millsap & A. Maydeu-Olivares (Eds.), *The SAGE handbook of quantitative methods in psychology* (pp. 568–591). Thousand Oaks, CA: SAGE.

Feng, L., & Sass, T. (2011). *Teacher quality and teacher mobility.* Washington, DC: The Urban Institute. Retrieved from http://www.urban.org/sites/default/files/ alfresco/publication-pdfs/1001506-Teacher-Quality-and-Teacher-Mobility .pdf

Ferguson, P., & Womack, S. T. (1993). The impact of subject matter and education coursework on teaching performance. *Journal of Teacher Education, 44*(1), 55–63.

Garrett, R., & Steinberg, M. P. (2015). Examining teacher effectiveness using classroom observation scores: Evidence from the randomization of teachers to students. *Educational Evaluation and Policy Analysis, 37*(2), 224–242.

Hanushek, E. (2011). Valuing teachers: How much is a good teacher worth? *Education Next, 11*(3), 40–45.

Harris, D., & Sass, T. (2011). Teacher training, teacher quality and student achievement. *Journal of Public Economics, 95*(7–8), 798–812.

Iasevoli, B. (2017, March 28). Trump signs bill scrapping teacher-prep rules. *Education Week.* Retrieved from http://blogs.edweek.org/edweek/teacherbeat/ 2017/03/trump_signs_bill_scrapping_tea.html

Ingersoll, R. M. (2001). Teacher turnover and teacher shortages: An organizational analysis. *American Educational Research Journal, 38*(3), 499–534.

Ingersoll, R., & Smith, T. (2004). What are the effects of mentoring and induction on beginning teacher turnover? *American Education Research Journal, 41*(3), 681–714.

Janosz, M., Archambault, I., Morizot, J., & Pagani, L. S. (2008). School engagement trajectories and their differential predictive relations. *Journal of Social Issues, 64*(1), 21–40.

Jung, T., & Wickrama, A. (2008). An introduction to latent class growth analysis and growth mixture modeling. *Social and Personality Psychology Compass, 2*(1), 302–317.

Kane, T. J., Rockoff, J., & Staiger, D. O. (2008). What does certification tell us about teacher effectiveness? Evidence from New York City. *Economics of Education Review, 27*(6), 615–631.

Kraft, M., & Papay, J. (2014). Can professional environments in schools promote teacher development? Explaining heterogeneity in returns to teaching experience. *Educational Evaluation and Policy Analysis, 36*(4), 476–500.

Krieg, J. W. (2006). Teacher quality and attrition. *Economics of Education Review, 25*(1), 13–27.

Ladd, H., & Sorensen, L. (2015). *Returns to teacher experience: Student achievement and motivation in middle school.* Washington, DC: American Institutes for Research.

Levy, A., Joy, L., Ellis, P., Jablonski, E., & Karelitz, T. (2012). Estimating teacher turnover costs: A case study. *Journal of Education Finance, 38*(2), 102–129.

Marvel, J., Lyter, D. M., Peltola, P., Strizek, G. A., & Morton, B. A. (2007). *Teacher attrition and mobility: Results from the 2004–2005 Teacher Follow-up Survey.* Washington, DC: National Center for Education Statistics.

Milanowski, A. (2004). The relationship between teacher performance evaluation scores and student achievement: Evidence from Cincinnati. *Peabody Journal of Education, 79*(4), 33–53.

Milanowski, A. T. (2011, April). Validity research on teacher evaluation systems based on the Framework for Teaching. Paper presented at the annual meeting of the American Education Research Association, New Orleans, LA

Morgan, G. B., Hodge, K. J., Trepinksi, T. M., & Anderson, L. W. (2014). The stability of teacher performance and effectiveness: Implications for policies concerning teacher evaluation. *Education Policy Analysis Archives, 22*(95), 1–21.

Muthén, B. O. (2004). Latent variable analysis: Growth mixture modeling and related techniques for longitudinal data. In D. Kaplan (Ed.), *The SAGE handbook of quantitative methodology for the social sciences* (pp. 345–370). Thousand Oaks, CA: SAGE.

Muthén, B. O., Brown, C. H., Masyn, K., Jo, B., Khoo, S. T., Yang, C. C., & Liao, J. (2002). General growth mixture modeling for randomized preventive interventions. *Biostatistics, 3*(4), 459–475.

National Institute for Excellence in Teaching. (2011). *TAP: The system for teacher and student advancement.* Santa Monica, CA: National Institute for Excellence in Teaching.

Papay, J. P., & Kraft, M. A. (2015). Productivity returns to experience in the teacher labor market: Methodological challenges and new evidence on long-term career improvement. *Journal of Public Economics, 130,* 105–119.

Papay, J. P., West, M. R., Fullerton, J. B., & Kane, T. J. (2012). Does an urban teacher residency increase student achievement? Early evidence from Boston. *Education Evaluation and Policy Analysis, 34*(4), 413–434.

Ram, N., & Grimm, K. (2009). Growth mixture modeling: A method of identifying differences in longitudinal change among unobserved groups. *International Journal of Behavioural Development, 33*(6), 565–576.

Reininger, M. (2012). Hometown disadvantage? It depends on where you're from teachers' location preferences and the implications for staffing schools. *Educational Evaluation and Policy Analysis, 34*(2), 127–145.

Rockoff, J., Jacob, B., Kane, T., & Staiger, D. (2011). Can you recognize an effective teacher when you recruit one? *Education Finance and Policy, 6*(1), 43–74.

Ronfeldt, M., Loeb, S., & Wyckoff, J. (2013). How teacher turnover harms student achievement. *American Educational Research Journal, 50*(1), 4–36.

Simon, N. S., & Johnson, S. M. (2015). Teacher turnover in high-poverty schools: What we know and can do. *Teachers College Record, 117*(3), 1–36.

Singer, J., & Willett, J. (2003). *Applied longitudinal data analysis.* New York, NY: Oxford University Press.

Steinberg, M. P., & Garrett, R. (2016). Classroom composition and measured teacher performance: What do teacher observation scores really measure? *Educational Evaluation and Policy Analysis, 38*(2), 293–317.

Tofighi, D., & Enders, C. (2007). Identifying the correct number of classes in a growth mixture model. In G. R. Hancock (Ed.), *Advances in Latent Variable Mixture Models* (pp. 317–341). Greenwich, CT: Information Age.

Wayne, A., & Youngs, P. (2003). Teacher characteristics and student achievement gains: A review. *Review of Educational Research, 73*(1), 89–122.

United States Department of Education. (2016). *Improving on teacher preparation: Building on innovation.* Washington, DC: U. S. Department of Education.

CHAPTER 8

TOWARD CAUSAL EVIDENCE ON EFFECTIVE TEACHER PREPARATION

Dan Goldhaber
American Institutes for Research

Matthew Ronfeldt
University of Michigan

A large body of quasi-experimental research shows that teachers can differ substantially from one another. Differences are evident in teachers' effects on students' test performance (Goldhaber, Brewer, & Anderson,1999; Nye, Konstantopoulos, & Hedges, 2004; Rivkin, Hanushek, & Kain, 2005), non-cognitive outcomes (Gershenson, 2016; Jackson, 2018; Kraft, 2019), as well as their impacts on students' ultimate educational attainment and other later life outcomes, such as employment probabilities and labor market earnings (Chamberlain, 2013; Chetty, Friedman, & Rockoff, 2014). It has thus become commonplace for researchers to cite teacher quality as the most important schooling factor influencing academic outcomes, and for policymakers to focus on ways to improve it. Over the past decade teacher preparation programs

Linking Teacher Preparation Program Design and Implementation to Outcomes for Teachers and Students, pages 211–236
Copyright © 2020 by Information Age Publishing
211

(TPPs) have received increased attention and scrutiny as a potential policy lever for improving the quality of the teacher workforce.[1]

Several states have begun to rate programs based on measures of how the teachers that they prepare perform in the classroom (NCTQ, 2017). At the federal level, the U.S. Department of Education previously signaled that understanding the effectiveness of teacher preparation was a national priority. Regulations in Title II of the Higher Education Act called for states and preparation organizations to collect data and publicly report on placement and retention of graduates in teaching positions, feedback from administrators about the competence of graduates, and the effectiveness of graduates in raising student achievement (U.S. Department of Education, 2014). These regulations were subsequently rescinded under the Trump administration, though a number of states do require such reporting. TPPs are also being scrutinized and rated by nongovernmental groups, similar to the longstanding practice of college and university ratings (Goldhaber & Koedel, 2018). The idea here is that such ratings may influence the selection of institutions by prospective teacher candidates and drive changes to the preparation practices of TPPs.

We argue there is relatively little known about whether and how teacher preparation *contributes* to teacher quality and, in turn, to student outcomes. This is consistent with a National Research Council (NRC) committee report on teacher preparation that concluded, "There is currently little definitive evidence that particular approaches to teacher preparation yield teachers whose students are more successful than others. Such research is badly needed" (NRC, 2010, p. 174). Since the publication of the NRC report there has been a significant increase in the number of large-scale studies linking features of preparation to graduate workforce outcomes. These much-needed studies have identified a number of features of preparation that are associated with better outcomes for recent graduates. However, as we elaborate below, existing research is unable to establish definitively that these features *cause* candidates to have better outcomes. Thus, while some progress has been made in understanding what might constitute effective teacher preparation, the NRC conclusion is nearly as valid today as it was a decade ago.

Indeed, despite the commonsense notion that preparation for formal classroom responsibilities should improve the readiness of teacher candidates, the value of formalized preservice teacher education in the *development* of teacher candidates is unclear from an empirical standpoint. As we go on to describe below, it is conceptually important to distinguish the role that TPPs may play (i.e., the causal impact of attending a particular TPP) in developing the skills, capacities, and attitudes of teacher candidates that may influence the candidates' or their students' outcomes when they become teachers from the *associations* between the outcomes of teachers or their students who are credentialed by different TPPs. TPPs can certainly influence the quality of the teacher workforce through their decisions about who to admit to (or retain in) their programs and through the development of those teacher candidates who are admitted, but research has not disentangled the ways in which programs affect the quality of teacher candidates. And the distinction between these two mechanisms (selection and development) matters. If the primary mechanism is teacher development, then improvement in the actual training of prospective teachers depends on knowing something about the efficacy of that training. If the primary mechanism is through selection processes, then we could probably find ways to select effective teacher candidates faster and at a lower cost than we do currently.

The lack of knowledge about how best to prepare prospective teachers is one of the most pressing unaddressed questions in education policy. And when it comes to improving teacher preparation, the stakes are high. Fifty states regulate and administer traditional and alternative teacher certification systems that cover more than 1,400 schools of education. About a third of the total dollar value, estimated to be about $40 billion, of the national investment in teacher training occurs prior to teachers entering the labor market.[2]

In the next section of this chapter, we briefly describe some of the recent research linking teacher preparation to in-service teacher and student outcomes. We then, in Section 3, describe why it is important to be quite cautious about interpreting findings from the existing research as reflecting impacts of preparation on candidates; here we delve deeper into the challenges of distinguishing between the development of teacher candidates while in TPPs from various types of selection (e.g., into and out of programs and into the workforce). In Section 4, we describe an *experimental* study, called the Improving Student Teaching Initiative (ISTI), focused on understanding whether specific initiatives connected with student teaching lead to better outcomes for teacher candidates. In describing ISTI, we emphasize that the research is designed to yield causal estimates of how specific aspects of student teaching may contribute to the effectiveness or retention of in-service teachers. Finally, in the conclusion we offer a few parting thoughts about other aspects of teacher education that merit more rigorous experimental research.

WHAT DOES EMPIRICAL EVIDENCE SUGGEST ABOUT TEACHER PREPARATION?

The last decade has witnessed an explosion of research on teacher preparation that links teachers' preservice programs or training in those programs with in-service teacher or student outcomes.[3] While these studies have made important contributions, which we elaborate below, there is still relatively little we can conclude from them about how teacher preparation actually *contributes* to teacher quality. In this section, we begin by reviewing studies that focus on the achievement test scores of students taught by graduates from preparation programs, but then consider studies examining the observation ratings and retention of graduates.

Teacher Preparation Program Research Using Student Tests as the Outcome

The studies that focus on student test scores typically try to isolate the effects of teachers on student test gains from other factors, such as the affluence of the families of students being taught or the resources of the school systems in which teachers are employed. These measures of teacher contributions are often referred to as "value-added," which is a statistical measure of the contribution that teachers make toward the gains in student test scores (see Goldhaber & Theobald [2013] for more information). It is these value-added measures that are linked to what we know about teachers' pathways into the profession or the programs granting teachers their teaching degrees, a key step toward obtaining the credentials required to be eligible to teach in public schools.

Much of the early work on teacher preparation compares teachers who enter the profession through traditional college- and university-based TPPs versus alternative routes such as Teach For America (e.g., Constantine et al., 2009; Glazerman, Mayer, & Decker, 2006; Kane, Rockoff, & Staiger, 2008; Xu, Hannaway, & Taylor, 2011). These studies tend to find little in the way of differential impacts on student test scores of being assigned to a traditional or alternatively prepared teacher, which is perhaps surprising given that alternatively prepared teachers typically receive far less pedagogical preparation than those who are traditionally prepared.[4] This has led some (e.g., Nemko & Kwalwasser, 2013) to suggest that there may be little value in some kinds (or amounts) of pedagogical preparation typically found in traditional TPPs.[5]

The fact that traditionally and alternatively prepared teachers do not appear to typically differ in terms of their value-added measures is consistent with the conclusion that the extra or different types of preparation received in traditional TPPs may not be terribly beneficial for the development of teacher candidate skills. However, it would be premature to jump to that conclusion. One reason, discussed more extensively in the next section, is that there are various types of "selection" inherent in determining which teachers from which programs (in this case traditional versus alternative) end up teaching which students.

Some studies randomly assigned students to graduates from either alternative or traditional routes to guard against conflating impacts of pathway with the kinds of students that graduates teach (e.g., Clark et al., 2013; Constantine et al., 2009; Glazerman et al., 2006). However, this type of random assignment does not protect against the possibility that teachers in traditional and alternative programs are themselves different *before* they enter their programs. For instance: Individuals apply (and/or are recruited) into a TPP (various types of traditional or alternative), programs make admissions decisions, admitted individuals make decisions regarding enrollment, the completion of a program depends on the decisions made by enrolled teacher candidates and whether programs judge teacher candidates to have met requirements to remain enrolled and/or to graduate, graduates decide where to apply for first-year teaching positions; schools/districts make decisions about job offers, and teacher applicants make decisions about whether to accept job offers. In other words, any differences in outcomes observed between pathways could reflect the effects of recruitment and selection rather than preparation, or some combination (we return to the various types of selection in Section 3 below).

More recently, studies have begun to link the value-added measures of teachers to the preparation programs granting them credentials (e.g., Boyd, Grossman, Lankford, Loeb, & Wyckoff, 2009; Goldhaber, Liddle, & Theobald, 2013; Koedel, Parsons, Podgursky, & Ehlert, 2015; Mihaly, McCaffrey, Sass, & Lockwood, 2013; von Hippel, Bellows, Osbourne, Lincove, & Mills, 2016; von Hippel & Bellows, 2018). In these studies, in-service teacher graduates are grouped together according to the programs that granted them credentials and then the programs are judged based on how the group from each program performs in terms of impact on student achievement (i.e., value-added measures). These studies reach somewhat different conclusions about the extent to which preparation programs explain meaningful variation in student achievement.[6] Regardless, studies examining differences between programs based upon outcomes of in-service teachers (or their students), like those examining differences between alternative and traditional pathways, are not designed to distinguish the effects of selection from the effects of preparation. Thus, findings about the effectiveness of teachers receiving their credentials from a particular program are not necessarily indicative of the value of the educational experiences that those teachers received while attending that program.

Even were it the case that value-added measures of the effectiveness of teachers from different programs were indicators of the contribution that those programs made to teacher candidate skills, the measures themselves do not provide much in the way of actionable feedback to programs about how they might programmatically change to improve the performance of their graduates. The reason is simple: Value-added measures of programs as a whole do not identify anything about the features of programs that make them effective or ineffective. These studies may suggest that some programs are better than others but not *why*.

Studies Examining the Programmatic Features of Teacher Preparation Programs

More promising for providing programs with information that can be used for improvement are studies about features of teacher preservice training that might be associated with measures of performance and other workforce outcomes. Several such studies now exist, though most have emerged only in the past decade. Boyd et al. (2009), for instance, analyze programmatic features and surveys of new teachers and find that teachers are more effective when programs exert more oversight of student teaching, including more supervision and more alignment with methods coursework; coursework is linked more directly to classroom practice (e.g., covering elements of the district curriculum); and programs require a capstone project that relates student teaching experiences to the training received.

A growing number of studies find that features of student teaching, in particular, predict better outcomes for graduates. Ronfeldt (2012) finds that teacher candidates who student-teach in higher functioning schools (as measured by having a relatively low non-retirement attrition rate, referred to as the "stay ratio") are more effective once they have classroom responsibilities of their own. These findings are thought to be related to student teachers learning more when student teaching takes place at schools with better conditions for working and learning to teach—culture conducive to teachers wanting to remain at those schools (hence a high stay ratio). This explanation is supported by evidence from surveys of student teachers, who reported better working conditions and learning more in schools with lower turnover, and with evidence from Ronfeldt (2015) that teachers are more effective when they complete student teaching in schools with higher levels of teacher collaboration. Finally, Goldhaber, Krieg, and Theobald (2017) find that early-career teachers are more effective when the student demographics of their school of employment are more similar to the demographics of the school in which their student teaching occurred. This finding may reflect the fact that student teachers develop teaching skills specific to particular types of students (e.g., economically disadvantaged) that benefit them in their future classrooms.

Teacher Preparation Program Research Using Instructional Performance as the Outcome

A couple of recent studies link teacher preparation to graduates' performance based on observational ratings, an alternative (or supplement) to value-added measures of teacher quality.[7] Examining all institutions that prepare teachers in Tennessee, Ronfeldt and Campbell (2016) find that about 20% of institutions differed significantly from the state mean in terms of graduates' average observational ratings. Moreover, differences seem meaningful, with graduates from top quartile institutions performing as though they have an additional year of teaching experience relative to graduates from bottom quartile institutions. One aspect of preparation that seems to influence graduates' instructional effectiveness is how instructionally effective their cooperating/mentor teachers (the P–12 teachers supervising student teaching on the district side; hence "mentor") were during student teaching. Ronfeldt, Brockman, and Campbell (2018) demonstrate that teachers receive better observational ratings during their first years of teaching when the mentor teachers who previously supervised their student teaching had received better observational ratings. The authors also find that teachers have higher value-added measures in their first years of teaching when they learn to teach with mentor teachers who had better value-added measures. Similarly, Ronfeldt, Matsko, Greene Nolan, and Reininger (2018) find positive associations between the observational ratings of first-year teachers and the mentor teachers in Chicago that mentored them during their preservice student teaching experiences.

Teacher Preparation Program Research Using Teacher Retention as the Outcome

There are fewer studies that focus on the connections between teacher education and teacher retention, though this is arguably a very important outcome given large estimates of the explicit costs (e.g., advertising, interviewing, and onboarding) associated with replacing a teacher who leaves,[8] and research showing that teacher turnover has a negative impact on student achievement independent of the relative effectiveness of outgoing or incoming staff (Atteberry, Loeb, & Wyckoff, 2017; Ronfeldt, Loeb, & Wyckoff, 2014).

Goldhaber and Cowan (2014) study the extent to which TPPs from which teachers receive their degrees are predictive of teacher attrition and find large and statistically significant differences in the probability of exiting teaching across Washington programs.[9] A few studies focus on the experiences that teacher candidates have while enrolled in TPPs and subsequent retention patterns. Ronfeldt (2012) finds that teachers completing student teaching in a high stay ratio school not only have better student achievement (see above) but also have higher retention rates. And Ronfeldt, Schwartz, and Jacob (2014) find that teacher candidates completing more methods coursework and practice teaching while enrolled in a TPP have higher retention rates; the findings were similar across traditional and alternative TPPs.

All of the above *nonexperimental findings* on teacher preparation are intriguing in that they suggest ways in which teacher preparation might be improved. But, as we have emphasized, the findings need to be interpreted with caution. Because these studies are based on outcomes for in-service teachers who have been matched to particular jobs and classrooms, we need to be cautious about making causal attributions about the contributions that teacher education makes toward the skills of teacher candidates (Boyd et al., 2009; Goldhaber, 2013; Goldhaber et al., 2014).

LIMITATIONS OF CAUSAL INTERPRETATION OF CURRENT EVIDENCE

Nonexperimental data can be used to assess the extent to which teachers' credentials, or preservice experiences, are predictive of performance or retention, but the various types of selection that result in a *match* between teacher candidates and jobs imply that observed associations are not necessarily indicative of a causal impact of programs or experiences. This match entails various forms of selection. Specifically, in the case of the individual teacher candidates: (a) they have chosen to apply for particular TPPs or pathways; (b) they have been selected into TPPs; (c) they have particular experiences, such as student teaching in schools with mentor teachers; and (d) they have graduated and received a teaching credential. Then there is the match that allows researchers to observe outcomes for in-service teachers. We only observe in-service outcomes for those teacher candidates (and their students) that (e) apply for and are offered jobs in particular schools; and (f) are assigned to particular classrooms and students.

Most of the studies described in the above section attempt to address these type of selection issues by including in statistical models characteristics of students, schools, teachers, or the TPPs granting credentials. And indeed, these sorts of statistical controls likely go a long way in addressing the various types of selection as they create comparison groups within the categories of the variables that are included in the statistical model. For instance, models might only compare teachers who are teaching within a particular school system. This would help to account for the possibility that some types of teachers tend to teach in school systems with particularly good curricular materials or a very skilled superintendent (i.e., district-level factors). But statistical controls that utilize available observation data may only go so far. Unobserved factors, such as the motivation of teacher candidates to be good teachers, or the degree to which motivated parents seek out classrooms of skilled teachers (skills that might be important but not captured by the types of variables typically included in administrative data, such as holding a master's degree), may still lead research to misattribute the effects of *unobserved* factors to TPPs or their features.

As an example, take the finding that having a higher-performing mentor teacher appears to increase the performance of teacher candidates who eventually become teachers themselves (Ronfeldt et al., 2018; Ronfeldt et al., 2018). This is a perfectly sensible finding, consistent with the notion that teacher candidates learn more from mentors who are themselves more instructionally effective with P–12 students. Thus, in turn, it suggests that one way to upgrade the skill set of incoming teacher candidates is to find more instructionally effective mentor teachers with whom teacher candidates can complete student teaching.

But it is also conceivable that the finding does not reflect a causal relationship. It may be that teacher candidates who are motivated and skilled seek out more skilled mentor teachers to work with in their internships, and that the finding is simply a reflection of unobserved skills of the teacher candidates (i.e., not related to what the mentor teachers contribute to teacher candidates during student teaching experiences). It's not possible to distinguish between these two possibilities without conducting an experiment. This distinction matters because there may be costs associated with recruiting different types of mentor teachers and/or costs associated with different types of mentor teachers taking time from regular class assignments to supervise student teaching (Goldhaber, Krieg, & Theobald, 2018).

To make this point more sharply, it's useful to review a few features of the teacher pipeline and labor market that highlight why we should be cautious in interpreting the findings from the above section as casual evidence about the value of teacher education.

Features of Teacher Preparation Programs and the Teacher Labor Market

First, TPPs have very different admission standards and likely cater to teacher candidates that differ in clearly observable ways. In Florida, for instance, data from the most recent year of the Title II Report database (school year 2014–2015) suggests some universities require particular measures of candidate quality (e.g., certain SAT or ACT scores, and/or GPAs) for admission to their undergraduate programs, while other institutions do not require any of these criteria (for more on variation between programs see Title II Reporting website https://title2.ed.gov/Public/Home.aspx). In general, there appear to be large differences in the selectivity standards of TPPs (NCTQ, 2017).

Second, teacher labor markets tend to be quite localized (Boyd, Lankford, Loeb, & Wyckoff, 2005) in the sense that teachers find teaching jobs that are close to where they grew up, the institution where they did their training, and/or where they did their student teaching. Goldhaber et al. (2013), for instance, find that over 15% of teacher candidates end up employed in the same schools in which they did their student teaching.[10] In Tennessee, Ronfeldt et al. (2018) find that about 45% of recently employed graduates take initial teaching positions in the same districts in which they completed their preservice student teaching experiences. The localization of teacher labor markets is exemplified in Table 8.1,[11] which shows the distance between the first school district in which teachers are employed, their homes while in high school, and the preparation program from which they received their teaching credentials. Krieg, Theobald, and Goldhaber (2016) find teachers are likely to end up employed near home: nearly two-thirds are employed within 50 miles of where they lived during high school in this particular study. Many are also likely to be employed near the institution from which they graduated: About a third of teachers' first jobs are within 50 miles of these institutions, and nearly 8% end up in the very same school district in which their institutions are located.

As a consequence of differences in the teacher candidates who attend different institutions, along with the localness of teacher labor markets, it is challenging to statistically distinguish whether estimated differences in teacher effectiveness are associated with the individuals who attend different TPPs, the educational experiences they receive, or the characteristics of the schools and school systems in which they are employed (e.g., the effectiveness of their principals).

In some contexts, such as Washington State (Goldhaber et al., 2013) and Tennessee (Ronfeldt & Campbell, 2016), there is enough mixing of teachers across schools that one can employ statistical techniques that try

TABLE 8.1 Distance Between First Teaching Job, Teacher Preparation Program, and Home

First Job District	Teacher Preparation Program	Home
Same district as	7.9%	23.3%
Within 25 miles of	23.2%	54.3%
Within 50 miles of	33.4%	66.6%

Source: Krieg et al. (2016).

to separate the influence of teachers (and TPPs) from the schools in which they are employed. In particular, the comparison of teachers or programs is a "within-school" one.[12] But in other contexts, such as Florida (Mihaly et al., 2013), there is too much funneling of teachers into particular schools or school clusters to enable those techniques.[13]

Importantly, however, even if it is possible to do within-school comparisons, these may not provide a good indication of the quality of teachers. This point is illustrated in Figure 8.1—based on hypothetical data—which shows the distribution of teacher quality from two hypothetical preparation programs.[14] Teachers from Program B (the dotted line) tend to be higher quality than those from Program A (the solid line). The average difference in quality between the teachers from these two programs is the horizontal distance between the vertical lines connected to the peak of each distribution. But now imagine that we only measure quality based on the differences between those teachers who are hired into a particular school (Taft Elementary) and, moreover, that Taft only hires teachers from a narrow range of the quality distribution (represented by the dashed lines between the ellipse).[15] In this case we would be comparing teachers from only the upper end of the distribution of teacher quality from Program A to those from the lower end of the distribution from Program B. And, as a result, the estimated differential (represented by the horizontal shaded portion of the figure) would greatly understate the magnitude of difference between teachers from the two programs.

As the above example, along with the more general discussion in this section of the chapter, illustrates, there are limits to what one can definitively

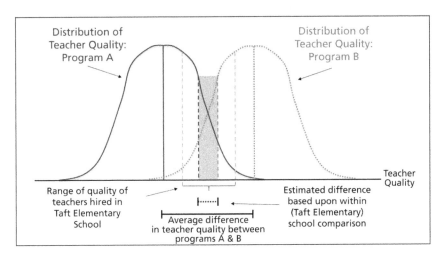

Figure 8.1   Hypothetical example illustrating difficulty of identifying the quality of teachers from different teacher preparation programs.

infer from nonexperimental data. Thus, we are arguing here that *establishing causal estimates of TPPs or features of programs requires experimental studies that randomize the features of teacher preparation within TPPs.* In the next section we describe an example of an experimental study with this type of design.

IMPROVING THE STUDENT TEACHING INITIATIVE EXPERIMENT

Improving Student Teaching Initiative (ISTI) is an initiative designed by us to test key features of the experiences that teacher candidates have during the course of their student teaching. The initiative began with one TPP in the Spring of 2016, and has (as of the beginning of 2018) been implemented in seven traditional (college or university-based undergraduate) TPPs. We believe this is the largest randomized control trial study focused on features of TPPs.

There are two different interventions that we are testing. The first focuses on the identification of effective student teaching placements (the "placement initiative") and the second on the provision of more frequent and contextualized feedback (the "feedback initiative").[16] Importantly, as discussed in the above section, we implement the experiment using within-TPP randomization. As much as possible, we also designed our interventions to align with existing program procedures, as described below.[17]

Ultimately, we plan to assess whether different aspects of student teaching *impact* (here we emphasize causality) the following outcomes: the perceptions of teacher candidates of their student teaching experience and/ or feelings of preparedness to teach, the likelihood that teacher candidates end up in the labor market, teacher performance and value-added effectiveness, and retention.

Implementing Within-TPP Randomization

We sought to work with programs that were able to do within-program randomization for one or both of the interventions (the placement initiative and/or the feedback initiative) we describe below. In theory, we could test these initiatives with a group of programs willing to participate by randomly assigning whole programs to the intervention or control conditions, but we believed this approach would have raised several methodological and logistical problems. First, we were worried about the significant risk of other features of programs being conflated with the treatment status. We could account for this potential problem with enough programs, but recruiting even seven programs has been extremely challenging. This is a particularly significant issue because program-level effects explain relatively little of the variation of teacher quality (Koedel et al., 2015; von Hippel et al., 2016; von Hippel & Bellows, 2018), implying it would take a large number of programs participating in the experiment to have enough statistical power to detect reasonably sized effects of planned variation in program features (i.e., the treatment described below). As a consequence, a study with program-level randomization would be costly and possibly infeasible to get enough programs to participate. By randomly assigning *within* program we ensure that, even in small samples, teacher candidates are receiving roughly equal preparation apart from our initiative changes.

Second, as we have described above, programs tend to funnel teacher candidates into particular school systems and districts. Thus, in a program-level randomization we might still have trouble differentiating whether any observed differences in teacher outcomes/student achievement is causally related to the treatment or the districts/schools into which teachers from programs tended to be sorted.

Third, the placement initiative part of the ISTI experiment involves making judgments about the quality of internships teacher candidates might receive amongst those judged possible by the programs. We could not easily implement this part of the study were we to need to create multiple placements for all teacher candidates in a program, especially since many programs report it challenging to secure even one placement per candidate. Additionally, there might also be ethical concerns with doing so, given that one aspect of the initiative described below entails assigning teacher candidates to mentor teachers predicted to be of higher or lower quality. Randomizing by program would likely mean that all candidates from some programs would be placed with lower quality mentor teachers.

The Placement Initiative

We designed our placement initiative to test the value of the match of teacher candidates to student teaching (internship) schools and mentor teachers. Specifically, to guide the placement of student teachers, we developed an algorithm to rank potential student teaching internships based on evidence from three observational research studies using data from Washington State, New York City, and an anonymous school district (Goldhaber, Krieg, Theobald, 2017a; Ronfeldt, 2012, 2015) that found that school effectiveness (i.e., average school value-added outcomes) and climate (measured by staff turnover) of student teaching placement schools predicted student teachers' later effectiveness as classroom teachers. We included these measures in our placement algorithm and then added measures of the mentor teacher quality (value-added measures, observational evaluations, and experience). Because these findings came from different states with different available measures of teacher and school quality, we aggregated these measures into a single index of internship placement quality. Specifically, we standardized the individual measures (school value-added measures, school turnover, teacher value-added measures, teacher experience, teacher observational evaluations). We then created a teacher index by averaging standardized teacher-level value-added measures, experience, and observational evaluations. We also created a school index by averaging standardized school value-added measures and school turnover measures. We then combined the teacher and school measures, weighting the former at 75% and the latter at 25%. In this way, the measure served as a research-based proxy for how promising a student teaching placement was likely to be, which then guided our randomization procedures, as described below.

Additionally, as much as possible, we designed our randomization procedure to align with the normal placement procedures of programs. Many programs, including those with whom we partnered, considered the geographic needs and preferences of candidates when making student teaching placements. We asked programs to organize their student teachers into blocks according to the geographic preferences (district or county), subject area (e.g., math, social studies, self-contained) and grade level (e.g., elementary grades, high school) of the candidates. We then asked programs to use typical procedures (with some deviations, described below) to recruit potential mentor teachers for each block. To provide flexibility in our placement procedures and to ensure alternates in the case of attrition, we asked programs to recruit more cooperating teachers than the number of student teachers in each block.

After programs returned to us the lists of potential mentor teachers, organized by block, we linked these teachers/schools to administrative data in order to generate placement ratings for each mentor-school combination (there could be multiple potential mentors in the same school) using the algorithm described above. Using the block median as the cutoff, we separated placements into two lists—those with higher ratings and those with lower ratings.[18] We then randomly assigned student teachers to one of the two lists (higher or lower quality placement) but did not actually assign them to a specific mentor-school. Though it would have been simpler, in some ways, for us to have randomly assigned teacher candidates to specific mentor-school combinations, programs indicated to us that they wanted to retain control over making the final placement decisions; running the initiative in this way also ensured that the placement process was as close to business-as-usual as possible while still accommodating our randomization procedures. We returned the two placement lists, as well as the corresponding teacher candidate lists that had been randomized to each placement list. We then asked programs to make the final placements, being sure only to place each teacher candidate with a mentor from the list (high- or low-quality placement) to which s/he had been randomized. If a selected mentor became unavailable to serve, we asked programs to select a different mentor from the same list (either high- or low-quality placement), where possible, to ensure teacher candidates remained in the condition to which they had been randomized.

In order to participate, programs did have to make some changes to their typical procedures; some of these changes created logistical challenges. First, programs found it difficult to recruit more mentors than teacher candidates; in fact, this initiative expectation was the most common reason why programs turned down our requests to participate. Particularly in shortage subject areas (e.g., foreign language), it was sometimes difficult for programs to find even one willing teacher to serve as a mentor teacher, so finding extras could be difficult or impossible. Additionally, programs, especially larger ones, often depended upon local district leaders to help them recruit potential mentors. Since it was already challenging for many districts to meet current placement requests, asking them to over-recruit required them to change procedures and sometimes strained relationships. Given that we needed initial mentor recruitment to occur before we could link mentors to administrative data and run our placement algorithm, this meant asking programs and districts to begin their recruitment procedures earlier than usual, typically between 2 to 4 weeks earlier. Meeting these challenges was especially difficult for providers who had to manage many different districts to recruit potential mentors on their behalf; inevitably, some districts were unable to meet these expedited deadlines, thus delaying the entire placement process.

The placement initiative was especially difficult for programs that required teacher candidates to have more than one student teaching placement during the semester or year. For example, to meet our expedited timeline, programs that did mid-semester placement changes often would have had to begin the recruitment process for the second placement as soon as the first placements got underway. The shorter timeline, combined with more complicated procedures, made the turnaround challenging for programs, districts, and our research team. In particular, we had to facilitate multiple placements for all teacher candidates while ensuring that they remained in their assigned condition (low or high placement rating) across them. Having two placements increased the likelihood that, in at least one of these placements, (a) we would be unable to match a teacher candidates with a mentor in her assigned condition, (b) a recruited mentor would become unable or unwilling to serve, or (c) a teacher candidate decided to request a different mentor mid-placement (e.g., because the match was not working) and there was no viable alternative on her assigned placement list;

because a teacher candidate in any of these scenarios was dropped from the experiment, having multiple placements greatly increased attrition.

The Feedback Initiative

The feedback initiative was designed to leverage and build upon the existing student teaching arrangements and clinical evaluation systems used by programs. As context for the initiative, we begin with a brief description of how programs typically organize student teaching. In most programs, two kinds of teacher educators evaluate and support the development of teacher candidates: (a) university field instructors/supervisors (UFI) who are employees of the university/institution where the program is based and (b) mentor teachers who are full- or part-time P–12 teachers, employed by local schools/districts, who agree to mentor student teachers while allowing them to use their classrooms as student teaching placements for their clinical training. For taking on these additional responsibilities, programs usually offer mentors a small stipend.[19] Typically, UFIs are assigned to supervise multiple teacher candidates and must conduct multiple observations of each teacher candidate during a student teaching placement. After each observation, UFIs usually debrief the lesson they observe and complete an evaluation using the program's observation rubric, which includes numeric scores for performance in different areas/domains of instruction. They then share these written evaluations with program leadership and their teacher candidates. Mentors are also asked to complete formal observations and evaluations of the mentee assigned to their classrooms, though typically fewer than UFIs must complete. In fact, many programs require mentors to complete only a single, end-of placement evaluation, often that is more summative in nature rather than based upon observations of specific lessons.

For our feedback initiative, UFIs and mentors continued to complete their evaluations using the same rubric that the programs would have used in the absence of the ISTI intervention, and mostly the same procedures as before as well.[20] We then requested that evaluators (UFI and mentors) submit their evaluations into an online portal that we created. We created an algorithm that aggregates evaluations for each teacher candidate—across lessons observed and across evaluators—and then compares that teacher candidate's rating in each instructional domain to the average ratings of peers in the same program. At the top of the reports, we displayed a teacher candidate's overall domain ratings next to the median and interquartile range for his/her program. To quickly summarize a teacher candidate's performance, we labeled domains with smiley faces corresponding to his/her level of performance. To avoid the "boomerang effect" observed in other studies with informational interventions, we added one smiley face for teacher candidates scoring in the 50th to 75th percentile and two smiley faces for teacher candidates scoring in the 75th to 100th percentiles (those below the 50th did not receive a smiley face).[21] In the next sections, we compared an individual's performance both to the overall domain ratings (of peers) and to the individual teacher candidate's rating in other domains. Through these comparisons, for each teacher candidate, we identify one instructional domain in which she is performing relatively well (area of strength) and one in which she is performing relatively poorly (area of focus).

Our portal then automatically generates a report that includes both the individualized and program average information, and then sends these reports to each teacher candidate and her evaluators (UFI and mentors) by email. Across student teaching (the timing and length of which can vary by program), our portal regularly generates new reports that are updated as new evaluations are entered. One expectation that was a change from normal procedures for most programs was, at least for one observation, we asked both the UFI and menotr to observe the same teacher candidate lesson, submit evaluations independently, and then jointly debrief with the teacher candidates. We hoped that these joint observations would lead to generative conversations but also give evaluators the opportunity to discuss and reconcile differences in evaluations.[22]

There were of course challenges in implementing the feedback initiative too. In particular, in some cases there was relatively little variation in the ratings that teacher candidates received, making it difficult to identify areas for teacher candidates to focus on for improvement. Evaluators were sometimes tardy in submitting their evaluations so some candidates had little time to adjust their teaching based upon information they gleaned from reports. Finally, in the absence of empirical knowledge about how malleable the different skill sets are that teacher candidates are learning while doing their student teaching, we are not really sure we are identifying good areas upon which to focus for purposes of development.

CONCLUDING THOUGHTS

For decades, reviews of the literature and policy reports have bemoaned limited empirical support for whether and how teacher education makes a difference.[23] In so doing, they have repeatedly called for more large-scale studies linking preparation to graduates' workforce outcomes, including impact on student achievement. As reviewed in the opening section, a new and growing body of research has responded to this call, providing critical evidence that a number of features of preparation predict better graduate outcomes. These include efforts to test the same features of preparation (e.g., having student teaching placements with more effective mentor) across different labor markets, different workforce outcomes, and using different analytic methods (and assumptions), thus allowing scholars to determine whether observed relationships are reproducible or not, and under what conditions.

While this recent body of research has made tremendous strides towards providing a much-needed empirical basis for the effects of teacher preparation, important limitations persist. Namely, prior research is largely correlational in nature. While studies typically adjust for covariates, including fixed effects (e.g., program or school), in order to account for different kinds of selection, so many forms of selection exist that it is challenging to address them all, especially since unobserved factors, such as teacher motivation or preferences, are difficult to measure and often unavailable.

We believe the time is right for teacher education researchers to pursue experimental studies. Only through random assignment, especially through within-program random assignment, can scholars account for the many forms of selection and obtain truly causal estimates. Moreover, the growing correlational evidence has identified specific features of preparation that are promising levers for experimental interventions so that TPPs and scholars interested in assessing potential reforms need not throw darts in the dark.

The ISTI initiatives described in this chapter represent a proof point showing that TPPs are willing and able to engage in this type of experimentation. The placement initiative, for example, draws on existing correlational studies which have identified characteristics of placement schools and mentor teachers that predict better workforce outcomes. By randomly assigning candidates within programs (and specifically within subject-grade-county blocks) to placements that have these characteristics, the initiative assures comparisons are between candidates with similar forms of preparation and backgrounds. If this study finds that candidates assigned to the more promising placements have better workforce outcomes, then it would provide perhaps the best causal evidence that specific features of student teaching make a difference for the preparation of new teachers. It could also offer programs and district stakeholders with a low-cost strategy for identifying promising student teaching placements with information that is now commonly collected in districts and states across the country.

In ISTI, we focused on student teaching as a lever to improve teacher preparation, but there is certainly no shortage of other aspects of teacher educational experiences that we might wish to learn about. For example, it would not be too difficult to randomize aspects of the pedagogical or content focused coursework that teacher candidates are required to complete, particularly since these are aspects of teacher preparation that are fully under the control of TPPs. Or researchers could design similar experiments to test whether or not different forms of feedback on assessments, such as the edTPA, make a difference in teacher candidates' skills.

Though conducting experimental studies like ISTI has much promise, interested researchers also face many challenges. Aside from practical implementation challenges like those described in prior sections, there is a more fundamental challenge—stakeholders in teacher education programs tend to be skeptical about subjecting their teacher candidates to any form of randomization or experiment. As a case in point, in our ISTI work we have faced tremendous challenges in recruiting programs who are willing to partner. There are good reasons for this skepticism. In particular, program leaders are concerned with equity—specifically, that no candidates receive, or are perceived to be receiving, better training than others. At the same time, there is tremendous variation between programs both within and across states in the experiences required of teacher candidates. One explanation for this is that the existing empirical basis for different forms of preparation is such that we really don't know whether certain forms of preparation are better than others; randomization to different forms would help to develop this much-needed empirical basis. Regarding concerns over "experimenting" on candidates, our response is that without a strong empirical basis for the kinds of preparation we are currently giving our teacher candidates, we are already largely experimenting on future teachers. Instead, we are advocating for experimentation that is more deliberate and evidence-based and that may be used to generate evidence to improve teacher preparation.

ACKNOWLEDGMENTS

We thank James Cowan and Nate Brown for their research assistance and editorial feedback, and the Bill and Melinda Gates Foundation for funding the ISTI project that we describe in this chapter. The opinions reported in this chapter are attributable to the authors, and do not necessarily reflect the views of the institutions with which the authors are affiliated. The authors are solely responsible for any and all errors.

NOTES

1. Teacher preparation programs may be traditional (college and university) or alternative (e.g., TFA), but there also may be distinct programs within an institution (e.g., a university may have a traditional program but also train TFA corps members and/or the programs to prepare teachers with different specialties, e.g., special education versus middle school math, may differ from one another). We discuss this more extensively in Section 3.

2. This is based on an assessment of expenditures on tuition by teacher candidates and investments in professional development after teachers enter the profession (Goldhaber, Krieg, & Theobald, 2017b).

3. We focus on studies that have this type of linkage, but there are also studies that link preservice experiences with, for instance, demonstrated subject matter knowledge or feelings of preparedness of teacher candidates. See, for instance, Caprano, Caprano, and Helfeldt (2010) and Bain, Lancaster, Zundas, and Parkes (2009).

4. Though this body of research does tend to find that traditionally prepared teachers stay in the profession longer.

5. By contrast, a small-scale (a total of 90 teacher candidates) randomized control trial study (Konold et al., 2008) finds that teacher candidates with greater pedagogical training produce greater learning gains for students during their student teaching experiences.

6. See a discussion of this in Goldhaber (2019) and von Hippel and Bellows (2018).

7. A potential advantage of observation ratings is that they are direct measures of teachers' instruction, whereas value-added measures infer instructional quality through the performance of teachers' students. Observation ratings have also been found to be significantly and positively related to value-added measures, though correlations tend to be small in magnitude (Kane & Staiger, 2012). However, some studies have raised concern over lack of variation in the ratings that teachers receive in practice, and challenges with rater agreement, training, and bias (Bell et al., 2012; Ho & Kane, 2013; White, 2017). Additionally, a growing number of studies have found observation ratings to be associated with teacher and student characteristics, and other aspects of classrooms beyond the instructional quality they were designed to measure (Campbell & Ronfeldt, 2018; Jiang & Sporte, 2016; Steinberg & Garrett, 2016; White, 2017; Whitehurst, Chingos, & Lindquist, 2014).

8. Barnes, Crowe, and Schaefer (2007) and Milanowski and Odden (2007), for instance, suggest that these costs are generally over $3,000 per teacher hired.

9. The authors estimated, based on data from programs in Washington State, the difference between teachers credentialed by programs with the highest and lowest attrition rates are about 5–7 percentage points (with a baseline level of annual attrition from Washington State public schools of 7%).

10. Similarly, Ronfeldt et al. (2018) find this to be the case for 17% of candidates in Chicago.

11. The data reported in the table are derived from Krieg et al. (2016).

12. This is the estimation of "school fixed effects" models.

13. Research has recognized the problems with selection and tried to address them. For instance, as mentioned above, a few studies (e.g., Clark et al., 2013; Constantine et al., 2009; Glazerman et al., 2006) randomly assign students to teachers within schools, which does protect against one type of selection, (i.e., that more motivated or academically able students tend to be assigned to certain types of teachers—traditionally or alternatively credentialed). But this is only one of the six types of selection we might worry about in trying to

assess the contribution of particular programs or features of programs to the development of teacher candidates.

14. Note that teacher quality is not measured in any particular way so the statistical problem that is illustrated here could affect any method of judging quality.

15. This kind of phenomenon could, for instance, be related to which teacher applicants apply to particular schools or the selection processes used by school to determine job offers.

16. We gratefully acknowledge funding from the Bill and Melinda Gates Foundation for the implementation and study of the ISTI project we describe in this section, including monetary support for partnering programs.

17. In order to support programs in meeting logistical challenges that our initiatives created, and to encourage their participation in spite of them, we offered programs modest monetary incentives. Programs that participated in both the placement and feedback initiative received approximately $125 per participating teacher candidate. Programs that participated in only the placement initiative received $75 per teacher candidate, while programs participating in only the feedback initiative received $50 per teacher candidate.

18. For our largest partnering program during our pilot year, the difference in average placement ratings between those in the higher ($n = 199$) and lower ($n = 189$) groups was about 0.61 standard deviations.

19. In a recent survey of all mentors in Chicago, Matsko et al. (2017) found that mentors received, on average, about $300 for mentoring a student teacher/resident. The highest-paying program was a residency program, which required a year-long residency and more training/responsibilities than most other programs; it offered its mentors $3,000.

20. We asked UFIs and mentors to complete at least one joint observation per candidate, described further below, which, for most programs, was a change from normal procedures. In rare cases, we had to request programs to make small changes to normal procedures in order to meet other minimum requirements for our initiative. For example, we required that all evaluators use identical rubrics so information could be aggregated across raters. At least one program had historically asked mentors to complete only summative evaluations and used a modified rubric for this purpose; we requested that both evaluators use the same rubric so the scores could be aggregated across raters.

21. The boomerang effect refers to experimental results where participants who exceed some target value decline in their performance after receiving reports (Allcott, 2011; Cialdini, Reno, Kallgren, 1990; Schultz, Nolan, Cialdini, Goldstein, Griskevicius, 2007).

22. Note that because the feedback initiative involves multiple potential changes to TPP practices (e.g., the joint observation and the additional reports that student teachers receive), we will not be able to definitively determine the extent to which any treatment effects we might find are attributable to the different aspects of the intervention.

23. Some examples include Greenberg, Pomerance, and Walsh (2011), Grossman, Ronfeldt, and Cohen (2012), McIntyre, Byrd, and Foxx (1996), National Research Council (2010), Wilson, Floden, and Ferrini-Mundy (2002), and Wilson and Floden (2003).

REFERENCES

Allcott, H. (2011). Social norms and energy conservation. *Journal of Public Economics, 95*(9–10), 1082–1095.

Atteberry, A., Loeb, S., & Wyckoff, J. (2017). Teacher churning: Reassignment rates and implications for student achievement. *Educational Evaluation and Policy Analysis, 39*(1), 3–30.

Bain, A., Lancaster, J., Zundans, L., & Parkes, R. J. (2009). Embedding evidence-based practice in pre-service teacher preparation. *Teacher Education and Special Education, 32*(3), 215–225.

Barnes, G., Crowe, E., & Schaefer, B. (2007). *The cost of teacher turnover in five school districts: A pilot study.* Washington, DC: National Commission on Teaching and America's Future.

Bell, C. A., Gitomer, D. H., McCaffrey, D. F., Hamre, B. K., Pianta, R. C., & Qi, Y. (2012). An argument approach to observation protocol validity. *Educational Assessment, 17*(2–3), 62–87.

Boyd, D., Lankford, H., Loeb, S., & Wyckoff, J. (2005). The draw of home: How teachers' preferences for proximity disadvantage urban schools. *Journal of Policy Analysis and Management, 24*(1), 113–132.

Boyd, D. J., Grossman, P. L., Lankford, H., Loeb, S., & Wyckoff, J. (2009). Teacher preparation and student achievement. *Educational Evaluation and Policy Analysis, 31*(4), 416–440.

Campbell, S., & Ronfeldt, M. (2018). Observational evaluations of teachers: Measuring more than we bargained for? *American Educational Research Journal, 55*(6), 1233–1267.

Caprano, R. M., Caprano, M. M., & Helfeldt, J. (2010). Do differing types of field experiences make a difference in teacher candidates' perceived level of competence? *Teacher Education Quarterly, 37*(1), 131–154.

Chamberlain, G. E. (2013). Predictive effects of teachers and schools on test scores, college attendance, and earnings. *Proceedings of the National Academy of Sciences, 110*(43), 17176–17182. https://doi.org/10.1073/pnas.1315746110

Cialdini, R., Reno, R., & Kallgren, C. (1990). A focus theory of normative conduct: Recycling the concept of norms to reduce littering in public places. *Journal of personality and social psychology, 58*(6), 1015–1026.

Chetty, R., Friedman, J. N., & Rockoff, J. E. (2014). Measuring the impacts of teachers II: Teacher value-added and student outcome in adulthood. *American Economic Review, 104*(9), 2633–2679.

Clark, M. A., Chiang, H. S., Silva, T., McConnell, S., Sonnenfeld, K., Erbe, A., & Puma, M. (2013). The effectiveness of secondary math teachers from Teach for America and the Teaching Fellows Programs. NCEE 2013-4015. *National Center for Education Evaluation and Regional Assistance.*

Constantine, J., Player, D., Silva, T., Hallgren, K., Grider, M., & Deke, J. (2009). An evaluation of teachers trained through different routes to certification. Final Report. NCEE 2009-4043. *National Center for Education Evaluation and Regional Assistance.*

Gershenson, S. (2016). Linking teacher quality, student attendance, and student achievement. *Education Finance and Policy, 11*(2), 125–149.

Glazerman, S., Mayer, D., & Decker, P. (2006). Alternative routes to teaching: The impacts of Teach for America on student achievement and other outcomes. *Journal of Policy Analysis and Management, 25*(1), 75–96.

Goldhaber, D. (2013). *What do value-added measures of teacher preparation programs tell us? What We Know series: Value-added methods and applications. Knowledge brief 12.* Stanford, CA: Carnegie Foundation for the Advancement of Teaching

Goldhaber, D. (2019). Evidence-based teacher preparation: Policy context and what we know. *Journal of Teacher Education, 70*(2), 90–101.

Goldhaber, D., Brewer, D., & Anderson, D. (1999). A three-way error components analysis of educational productivity. *Education Economics, 7*(3), 199–208.

Goldhaber, D., & Cowan, J. (2014). Excavating the teacher pipeline: Teacher preparation programs and teacher attrition. *Journal of Teacher Education, 65*(5), 449–462.

Goldhaber, D., & Koedel, C. (2018). Public accountability and nudges: The effect of an information intervention on the responsiveness of teacher education programs to external ratings (Working Paper 182). *National Center for Analysis of Longitudinal Data in Education Research.*

Goldhaber, D., Krieg, J., & Theobald, R. (2014). Knocking on the door to the teaching profession? Modeling the entry of prospective teachers into the workforce. *Economics of Education Review, 43,* 106–124.

Goldhaber, D., Krieg, J. M., & Theobald, R. (2017a). Does the match matter? Exploring whether student teaching experiences affect teacher effectiveness. *American Educational Research Journal, 54*(2), 325–359.

Goldhaber, D., Krieg, J., & Theobald, R. (2017b, November). *The costs of mentorship? Exploring the impact of student teaching placements on student achievement.* Association for Public Policy Analysis & Management Conference Paper. Chicago, IL.

Goldhaber, D., Krieg, J., & Theobald, R. (2018). The costs of mentorship? Exploring student teaching placements and their impact on student achievement (Working Paper 187). *National Center for Analysis of Longitudinal Data in Education Research.*

Goldhaber, D., Liddle, S., & Theobald, R. (2013). The gateway to the profession: Assessing teacher preparation programs based on student achievement. *Economics of Education Review, 34,* 29–44.

Goldhaber, D., & Theobald, R. (2013). *Do different value-added models tell us the same things?* Carnegie Knowledge Network. Retrieved from http://carnegieknowledgenetwork.org/briefs/value-added/different-growth-models/

Greenberg, J., Pomerance, L., & Walsh, K. (2011). *Student teaching in the United States.* Washington, DC: National Council on Teacher Quality.

Grossman, P., Ronfeldt, M., & Cohen, J. (2012). The power of setting: The role of field experience in learning to teach. In K. Harris, S. Graham, T. Urdan, A. Bus, S. Major, & H. L. Swanson (Eds.), *American Psychological Association (APA) educational psychology handbook: Applications to teaching and learning* (Vol. 3, pp. 311–334). Washington, DC: American Psychological Association.

Ho, A. D., & Kane, T. J. (2013). *The reliability of classroom observations by school personnel* (Research paper, MET Project). Seattle, WA: Bill and Melinda Gates Foundation.

Jackson, C. K. (2018). What do test scores miss? The importance of teacher effects on non-test score outcomes. *Journal of Political Economy, 126*(5), 2072–2107.

Jiang, J. Y., & Sporte, S. E. (2016). *Teacher evaluation in Chicago: Differences in observation and value-added scores by teacher, student, and school characteristics*. Chicago, IL: University of Chicago Consortium on School Research.

Kane, T. J., Rockoff, J. E., & Staiger, D. O. (2008). What does certification tell us about teacher effectiveness? Evidence from New York City. *Economics of Education Review, 27*(6), 615–631.

Kane, T. J., & Staiger, D. O. (2012). *Gathering feedback for teaching: Combining high-quality observations with student surveys and achievement gains* (Research paper, MET Project). Seattle, WA: Bill and Melinda Gates Foundation.

Koedel, C., Parsons, E., Podgursky, M., & Ehlert, M. (2015). Teacher preparation programs and teacher quality: Are there real differences across programs? *Education Finance and Policy, 10*(4), 508–534.

Konold, T., Jablonski, B., Nottingham, A., Kessler, L., Byrd, S., Imig, S.,... McNergney, R. (2008). Adding value to public schools: Investigating teacher education, teaching, and pupil learning. *Journal of Teacher Education, 59*(4), 300–312.

Kraft, M. A. (2019). Teacher effects on complex cognitive skills and social-emotional competencies. *Journal of Human Resources, 54*(1), 1–36.

Krieg, J. M., Theobald, R., & Goldhaber, D. (2016). A foot in the door: Exploring the role of student teaching assignments in teachers' initial job placements. *Educational Evaluation and Policy Analysis, 38*(2), 364–388.

Matsko, K., Ronfeldt, M., Greene, H., Klugman, J., Reininger, M., & Brockman, S. (2017, November). *Panel paper: Cooperating teacher as model and coach: A district-wide portrait*. Association for Public Policy Analysis & Management Conference Paper. Chicago, IL.

McIntyre, D. J., Byrd, D. M., & Foxx, S. M. (1996). Field and laboratory experiences. In J. Sikula (Ed.), *Handbook of research on teacher education* (pp. 171–193). New York, NY: Macmillan.

Mihaly, K., McCaffrey, D., Sass, T. R., & Lockwood, J. R. (2013). Where you come from or where you go? Distinguishing between school quality and the effectiveness of teacher preparation program graduates. *Education, 8*(4), 459–493.

Milanowski, A., & Odden, A. (2007). A new approach to the cost of teacher turnover (Working Paper 13). Seattle, WA: School Finance Redesign Project, Center on Reinventing Public Education.

National Council on Teacher Quality. (2017). *State policy yearbook: National summary*. Retrieved from https://www.nctq.org/dmsView/NCTQ_2017_State_Teacher _Policy_Yearbook

National Research Council. (2010). *Preparing teachers: Building evidence for sound policy*. Committee on the study of teacher preparation programs in the United States. Washington, DC: National Academies Press.

Nemko, B., & Kwalwasser, H. (2013, October 23). Why teacher colleges get a flunking grade: Let's give up on education majors. Too much theory, not enough practical learning about teaching. *The Wall Street Journal*. Retrieved from http://www.wsj.com/news/articles/SB100014240527023048645045791439026083329802

Nye, B., Konstantopoulos, S., & Hedges, L. V. (2004). How large are teacher effects? *Educational Evaluation and Policy Analysis, 26*(3), 237–257.

Rivkin, S. G., Hanushek, E. A., & Kain, J. F. (2005). Teachers, schools, and academic achievement. *Econometrica, I*(2), 417–458.

Ronfeldt, M. (2012). Where should student teachers learn to teach? Effects of field placement school characteristics on teacher retention and effectiveness. *Educational Evaluation and Policy Analysis, 34*(1), 3–26.

Ronfeldt, M. (2015). Field placement schools and instructional effectiveness. *Journal of Teacher Education, 66*(4), 304–320.

Ronfeldt, M., Brockman, S., & Campbell, S. (2018). Does cooperating teachers' instructional effectiveness improve preservice teachers' future performance? *Educational Researcher, 47*(7), 405–418.

Ronfeldt, M., & Campbell, S. (2016). Evaluating teacher preparation using graduates' observational ratings. *Educational Evaluation and Policy Analysis, 38*(4), 603–625.

Ronfeldt, M., Loeb, S., & Wyckoff, J. (2014). How teacher turnover harms student achievement. *American Educational Research Journal, 50*(1), 4–36.

Ronfeldt, M., Matsko, K. K., Greene Nolan, H., & Reininger, M. (2018). *Who knows if our teachers are prepared? Three different perspectives on graduates' instructional readiness and the features of preservice preparation that predict them* (CEPA Working Paper No. 18-01). Retrieved from http://cepa.stanford.edu/wp18-01

Ronfeldt, M., Schwartz, N., & Jacob, B. (2014). Does pre-service preparation matter? Examining an old question in new ways. *Teachers College Record, 116*(10), 1–46.

Schultz, P. W., Nolan, J. M., Cialdini, R. B., Goldstein, N. J., & Griskevicius, V. (2007). The constructive, destructive, and reconstructive power of social norms. *Psychological Science, 18*(5), 429–434.

Steinberg, M. P., & Garrett, R. (2016). Classroom composition and measured teacher performance what do teacher observation scores really measure? *Educational Evaluation and Policy Analysis, 38*(2), 293–317.

U.S. Department of Education, Office of Postsecondary Education. 71892 (2014, December 3). Teacher preparation issues, proposed rule, 79 Fed. Reg. 71819. Retrieved from https://www.federalregister.gov/articles/2014/12/03/2014-28218/teacher-preparation-issue

von Hippel, P. T., Bellows, L., Osborne, C., Lincove, J. A., & Mills, N. (2016). Teacher quality differences between teacher preparation programs: How big? How reliable? Which programs are different? *Economics of Education Review, 53*, 31–45.

von Hippel, P. T., & Bellows, L. (2018). How much does teacher quality vary across teacher preparation programs? Reanalyses from six states. *Economics of Education Review, 64*, 298–312.

White, M. (2017). *Generalizability of scores from classroom observation instruments* (Doctoral dissertation). Retrieved from https://deepblue.lib.umich.edu/handle/2027.42/138742?show=full

Whitehurst, G. J. R., Chingos, M. M., & Lindquist, K. M. (2014). *Evaluating teachers with classroom observations*. Washington, DC: Brown Center on Education Policy at Brookings Institute.

Wilson, S. M., & Floden, R. E. (2003). *Creating effective teachers: Concise answers for hard questions* (addendum to the report *Teacher preparation researcher: Current knowledge, gaps and recommendations.*). Washington, DC: American Association of Colleges for Teacher Education.

Wilson, S. M., Floden, R. E., & Ferrini-Mundy, J. (2002). Teacher preparation research an insider's view from the outside. *Journal of Teacher Education, 53*(3), 190–204.

Xu, Z., Hannaway, J., & Taylor, C. (2011). Making a difference? The effects of Teach for America in high school. *Journal of Policy Analysis and Management, 30*(3), 447–469.

CHAPTER 9

SUPPORTING THE USE OF EVIDENCE IN TEACHER PREPARATION

Considerations and Next Steps

Cara Jackson
Bellwether Education Partners

Jennifer E. Carinci
American Association for the Advancement of Science

Stephen J. Meyer
RMC Research

Improving the use of evidence in teacher preparation is one of the greatest challenges and opportunities for our field. The chapters in this volume explore how data availability, quality, and use within and across preparation programs shed light on the structures, policies, and practices associated with high-quality teacher preparation. Chapter authors take on critical questions about the connection between what takes place during teacher preparation

Linking Teacher Preparation Program Design and Implementation to Outcomes for Teachers and Students, pages 237–247
Copyright © 2020 by Information Age Publishing

and subsequent outcomes for teachers and students, illustrating a variety of approaches and related challenges. In this concluding chapter, we highlight themes across the chapters, including issues of data availability and quality, the uses of data for improvement, priorities for future research, and opportunities to promote evidence use in teacher preparation.

COLLECTIVE RESPONSIBILITY FOR DATA AVAILABILITY AND QUALITY

Recurring themes across chapters are the lack of available data and issues of data quality, suggesting the importance of collective responsibility to ensure data availability and quality. For example, as Pivovarova, Viga, and Barnard note in Chapter 7, private schools are not required to report employment data to the state education agency (SEA); therefore, their analyses are restricted to teachers employed in public schools in the state. While SEA data systems include information about teachers in public schools, the information they contain is limited. In Chapter 1's discussion of work across multiple state education agencies to improve data related to teacher preparation, Warner, Allen, and Coble identified several shortcomings and significant challenges that remain to be addressed (including developing valid and reliable assessments of candidate or completer outcomes, standardizing definitions and implementation within and across states, creating meaningful reports, and assisting stakeholders in understanding limitations and how to use data for improvement purposes). In addition, several authors noted the challenge of following program graduates who took teaching positions out of state. Finally, Goldhaber and Ronfeldt made the critical distinction in Chapter 8 between emerging data from recent studies exploring associations between preparation programs and outcomes versus desperately needed data to understand the causal impact of teacher preparation disentangled from various selection effects.

Data Availability: Potential Role for State and Federal Agencies

State agencies are particularly well positioned to bring coherence to the available data about teachers and students that may be used to understand the effects of teacher preparation and inform program improvement. State agencies typically play a role in determining both what types of measures are included in teacher evaluation systems, as well as the extent to which measures are consistent across districts. For example, as Warner and colleagues note in Chapter 1, some states require all districts to use the same evaluation instruments, while others allow districts to develop their own.

The absence of common measures for beginning teachers impedes the ability of preparation programs to learn from the outcomes of graduates in a variety of districts. Because data are rarely shared across state lines, opportunities to examine outcomes for teachers who are prepared in one state and teach in another are limited. Collaborations across SEAs, such as the Multistate Educator Lookup System (MELS) being developed by the National Association of State Directors of Teacher Education and Certification (NASDTEC), are necessary to provide teacher preparation programs (TPPs) and SEAs better information for examining program completer outcomes. While states have expressed interest in examining the performance of program graduates to guide improvement efforts (Meyer, Brodersen, & Linick, 2014), they often have limited resources to build data infrastructure and capacity, and lack clear guidance about the particular data elements that best inform accountability and program improvement efforts.

Thus, researchers must partner with SEAs and practitioners to take on investigations designed to inform such guidance to push the field towards collection and use of more meaningful data to drive a more evidence-informed profession and accountability system. Developing, and iteratively testing, instruments that produce reliable and valid data—that can meaningfully distinguish performance within and across programs—are critical steps ripe for researcher support. While there has been some movement since NRC 2010, as illustrated by the TPP-, researcher-, and state-led efforts described in this volume, without more of these types of investigations (especially those designed to ascertain causal relationships, as called for by Chapter 8 authors), we will not have sufficient empirical evidence regarding how TPPs can best develop effective teachers.

In some cases, data are available, but TPPs lack access due to privacy issues (Data Quality Campaign, 2017). Data sharing between TPPs and the schools or districts where program graduates teach has potential to benefit both parties. For TPPs, information about the performance of their graduates as beginning teachers can inform continuous improvement efforts. Schools and districts may also benefit from more information-rich hiring processes, if given better access to information collected on teacher candidates during their preparation about their program experiences and individual strengths (Carinci, 2016). Data sharing between TPPs and school districts could be encouraged by state or federal agencies, through guidance about data that may be shared or protocols regarding data privacy. Models of ethical data collection and data sharing could have value for the field of education research more broadly.

Fostering the consistent collection, analysis, and reporting of data about TPPs and their outcomes may hinge on increased guidance and involvement of state and federal agencies, as well as programmatic accreditors and specialized professional associations. For example, states are better positioned than individual TPPs to collect data on teachers in private school settings, and federal agencies could play a role in facilitating data sharing across state lines. As states and TPPs are increasingly called upon to collect data about the implementation and outcomes of teacher preparation—through requirements for accreditation and federal reporting requirements, for example—states and federal agencies have opportunities to provide guidance and resources that support more consistent data collection. One such area, the definition and measurement of placement diversity, was identified in Chapter 5. Further, as data are collected more consistently, state and federal agencies may be able to better promote data quality, through the identification, development, and shared use of measures with evidence of reliability and validity. Provision of more consistent and meaningful data with relevant comparisons would allow for more appropriate and consistent program approval and accreditation decisions, and reduce duplication of effort within and across TPPs and states.

Data Quality: Ensuring Adequate Validity and Reliability

Throughout the chapters, data quality is also a recurring concern. In Chapter 1, Warner and colleagues note the significant variability in the validity and reliability of measures employed, as well as flaws in the design of measures that compromise validity and reliability. In Chapter 7, Pivovarova and colleagues acknowledge that they cannot determine whether the measures used in their study are sufficiently free of rater bias. Lewis, Rivero, Musson, Lucas, and Tankersley note in Chapter 4 that the limited availability and use of validated instruments has been a perennial issue in studying teacher preparation; because some teacher evaluation instruments are inappropriate for use with preservice teachers, they cannot be used to assess changes in instructional practice between preservice to in-service teaching. Reflecting on the need to work diligently at identifying valid and reliable sources of data, Weitzel, Merk, Waggoner, Carroll, and Hetherington (Chapter 3) comment on the importance of ensuring that data used for decision-making are valid, reliable, and confirmed through multiple measures.

If states attach strong accountability consequences to program performance scores of questionable quality, the combination of strong accountability and weak performance measures may undermine stakeholder confidence in the accountability system, and yield inaccurate judgments of program performance. For example, a recent study found that estimates of differences between TPPs based on value-added to student test scores are too small to support effective policy decisions (von Hippel, Bellows, Osborne, Lincove, & Mills, 2016); a reanalysis of six states' TPP evaluations found little variation across TPPs, even in states where substantial differences had been reported previously (von Hippel & Bellows, 2018).

Effective use of data, whether for accountability purposes or for program improvement, is predicated on the assumption that data are part of an integrated system that is valid, reliable, and fair (Worrell et al., 2014). Attention to the reliability and validity of measures, and development of validated measures that reflect the goals of TPPs, could enable more accurate identification of program strengths and weaknesses. As Warner and colleagues caution in Chapter 1, the quality of the measures influences the efficacy of the program performance review system.

COLLECTIVE RESPONSIBILITY FOR RECOGNIZING THE MULTIPLE INFLUENCES ON TEACHER OUTCOMES AND FOR CONTINUOUS PROGRAM IMPROVEMENT

Another theme that arose throughout the chapters is that teacher outcomes are jointly produced by TPPs and the contexts of the schools where student teaching is completed and where program graduates work as teachers of record. As Goldhaber and Ronfeldt note in Chapter 8, the extent to which teachers are non-randomly assigned to schools complicates the attribution of teacher effectiveness to specific preparation programs. Several chapters illustrate the competing influences on teacher outcomes. For example, Unal, Bodur, and Unal (Chapter 5) find that the diversity of student teaching placements is associated with both teacher candidate performance and program graduate outcomes, and Preston (Chapter 2) notes that mentoring, induction, and school climate may contribute to teacher effectiveness.

Since many teachers end up teaching in schools that are close to where they are prepared (Mihaly, McCaffery, Sass, & Lockwood, 2012), TPPs might consider how evidence may be used to support better alignment between preparation programs and school districts. For example, TPPs might seek to better align the measures used to evaluate teacher candidates with those of local district teacher evaluation systems and use that alignment as the basis for collecting more coherent information about program candidate and completer performance. In addition, alignment between TPPs and local districts around curriculum, assessments, and norms may facilitate a successful transition to the workplace, at least for those individuals who end up teaching in a nearby district. School districts, in turn, should recognize the advantages of partnering with local universities to prepare teachers and the importance of aiding researchers in efforts to identify practices that produce effective teachers.

Authors emphasized the responsibility of TPPs to move beyond a compliance mindset and make use of data to continually self-assess and improve. Both Weitzel and colleagues (Chapter 3) and Unal and colleagues (Chapter 5) noted the role of the Council for the Accreditation of Educator Preparation (CAEP) accreditation standards in fostering an ethos of improvement. The use of data for improvement was tied to CAEP's accreditation process, which calls on TPPs to use a suite of measures to examine the results of teacher preparation where they matter most—in classrooms. Through the application of rigorous standards that insist that all educators be prepared to meet the needs of increasingly diverse PreK–12 learners, national accreditation can be used as a lever to improve the effectiveness of instruction.

The chapters in this volume provide examples of how TPPs can use data to reflect on the quality of preservice teaching experiences and assess whether those experiences are associated with desired outcomes. In Chapter 2, Preston exploits variation across TPPs to examine the relationship between program features and teacher outcomes. In several chapters, the authors look within a single program to identify whether programmatic inputs led to desired outputs; these chapters shed light on the importance of placement diversity (Unal and colleagues, Chapter 5), subject matter knowledge (Lewis and colleagues, Chapter 4), and signature teaching practices (Collett, Dubetz, Fayne, Marshall, and Rothstein, Chapter 6). By examining longitudinal data, TPPs can ascertain whether short-term gains are sustained over time—an approach illustrated by Collett and colleagues (Chapter 6), who find that teacher candidates learn signature practices, but don't necessarily implement them consistently. Clearly, thoughtful use of data can generate multiple forms of knowledge that can be used to develop next steps for program improvement.

In the process of using data for improvement, TPPs may discover that certain structures, policies, and practices require making tradeoffs. For example, in Chapter 5, Unal and colleagues find that placement diversity is associated with greater satisfaction of both graduates and employers, but lower ratings of candidates' practice. In Chapter 4, Lewis and colleagues call for research-based certification, including strengthening requirements around subject matter knowledge, but acknowledge that doing so may come at the expense of efforts to diversify the teaching profession. In keeping with the theme of collective responsibility, researchers making policy recommendations should try to anticipate potential unintended consequences and be clear about the trade-offs while emphasizing nuances and limitations of study findings, and policymakers will need to ask themselves if a proposed legislative solution might improve one desired outcome at the expense of another.

PRIORITIZING THE USE OF RIGOROUS RESEARCH DESIGNS TO CONTRIBUTE TO THE KNOWLEDGE BASE AND PROVIDE CONTEXTUALIZED EVIDENCE TO GUIDE PROGRAM IMPROVEMENT

Teacher educators can benefit from a variety of research approaches that allow them to better understand how program graduates are performing and start to consider what factors are related to variation in performance. Studies designed to investigate causal relationships between specific preparation experiences and outcomes for graduates and their PreK–12 students, as discussed in Chapter 8, are a critical step toward identifying evidence-based practices for teacher educators and preparation program designers. Over time, this sort of research has tremendous potential to fill gaps in the knowledge base, providing information about the extent to which various approaches have a causal impact on teachers' effectiveness.

In the interim, however, various stakeholders must collect and use information to make decisions about programs, monitoring progress and making improvements as needed. As noted by Worrell et al. (2014), these "decisions should be made with the best evidence that can be obtained now, rather than the evidence we might like to have had, or that might be available in the future" (p. 4). Based upon a convening of various stakeholders, DeMonte (2017) suggested that the most beneficial research to inform program improvement would be nuanced, actionable, formative, and contextualized. The studies in the present volume align closely with these characteristics, as indicated below.

Nuanced

Nuanced research focuses on specific aspects of programs, taking a fine-grained approach and examining multiple sources of data. The mixed methods approach used in Chapter 6 by Collett and colleagues focused on signature practices emphasized in preservice, and examined how and to what extent these practices were present once program graduates became teachers of record. In Chapter 8, Goldhaber and Ronfeldt describe an experiment designed to answer questions regarding whether certain features of student teaching are causally related to outcomes. Such research gives TPPs valuable insight as to the efficacy of specific program features.

Actionable

"*Actionable* is a quality of research that is valid and purposeful to a variety of constituents who are willing to take risks to use the findings to understand impact and implement change" (DeMonte, 2017, p. 3, emphasis in original). In Chapter 5, Unal and colleagues demonstrate the actionable approach in their exploration of tracking teacher candidates' practicum placements. Faculty used the placement diversity data for the specific purpose of improving decision-making about the sufficiency of placement diversity. Likewise, Chapter 4 exemplifies the principle of actionability through the comparative approach used by Lewis and colleagues in assessing the subject matter knowledge, science misconceptions, self-efficacy, and instructional practices of two TPPs. As a result of the study, the university added a course in teaching English language learners to the TPP and restricted program admission to candidates who had completed science coursework. Chapter 1 describes Teacher Preparation Analytics' desire to create a wide-ranging, transparent group of outcome measures to be useful to various stakeholders (including various states, the concerned public, and TPPs) for program improvement and accountability.

Formative

In Chapter 3, Weitzel and colleagues describe ongoing use of evidence to support the continuous improvement model used by the TPP. The authors embraced the iterative nature of improvement science, cumulatively gathering evidence and deliberately applying experience with each implementation cycle to inform refinement of design aspects. For example, they refined assessments and increased response rates over time. The authors of Chapter 6 not only investigate the extent to which the signature practice of formative assessment is utilized by their graduates, but also model this practice in their utilization and continued monitoring of changes suggested by their findings.

Contextualized

Several chapters reflect the importance of considering context. For example, in Chapter 2 Preston highlights the fact that research findings from one setting don't always replicate in others; unlike prior work, she did not find that more math courses were associated with higher student achievement. This suggests that increasing certain inputs (such as coursework) may be more beneficial in some contexts than others. In Chapter 7, Pivovarova and colleagues recognized the contextual nature of the program examined and encouraged replication attempts in other settings. Furthermore, as Weitzel and colleagues noted in Chapter 3, results must be considered within the context of the expectations of program graduates as they enter teaching positions.

In sum, TPPs may benefit from various types of research that may be used to shed light on aspects of program implementation and outcomes. Identifying aspects of preparation that are associated with desired outcomes can help TPPs determine which practices are most promising to explore in a more rigorous fashion. To better understand which practices cause improved outcomes for teachers and students and generate knowledge that is generalizable beyond a single TPP, we should continue to press for stronger research designs. Per Goldhaber and Ronfeldt's suggestion in Chapter 8, researchers might focus on what we can learn from experimenting with program features. For example, a TPP (or a consortium of TPPs) could randomly assign a year of student teaching to half of the teacher candidates and a semester of student teaching to the other half and examine whether outcomes differ as a function of length of student teaching.

OPPORTUNITIES TO PROMOTE USE OF EVIDENCE IN TEACHER PREPARATION

The chapters in this volume highlight various efforts to examine connections between teacher preparation and outcomes for teachers and students, suggesting several approaches that TPPs, researchers, state agencies, and PreK–12 stakeholders may consider to better evaluate and promote effective approaches to teacher preparation. One opportunity suggested by this work involves coordinating the various actors into collective action. As Bryk, Gomez, and Grunow (2010) argue, "The field suffers from a lack of purposeful collective action. Instead, actors work with different theories of the same problem, activities are siloed, and local solutions remain local" (p. 4). Individual TPPs have a responsibility to purposefully experiment, appropriately adjust programs based on evidence, and measure progress; however, research from individual TPPs is unlikely to yield results that drive widespread implementation of effective practice. State and federal agencies, policy makers, researchers, teacher educators, and PreK–12 administrators and teachers must work together to foster coherence, build on lessons learned, and seek opportunities for synergy among related efforts. Teacher preparation cannot transform into an evidence-based profession with a culture of continuous improvement unless valid and reliable data are intentionally collected and used in consistent and meaningful ways to better understand outcomes of teacher preparation and to inform program improvement.

Despite the absence of common data, many programs are going beyond collecting and reporting data for accountability purposes and are using data to support research and continuous improvement efforts. A robust quality assurance system ensures continuous improvement by relying on a variety of measures, establishing performance benchmarks for those measures, seeking the views of all relevant stakeholders, sharing evidence widely with both internal and external audiences, and using results to improve policies and practices in consultation with partners and stakeholders (Ruben, 2010). Adding to the profession's knowledge base and repertoire of practice, deploying what is learned throughout the organization, and quickly developing and testing prospective improvements (Langley, Nolan, Nolan, Norman, & Provost, 2009) are some of the benefits continuous improvement systems afford programs. Bryk et al. (2010) found that research and development can deepen the knowledge of existing best practices and provide models of emerging innovations to transform teacher preparation. Contrary to common practice, data for accountability, improvement, and research need not be mutually exclusive; effort invested upfront to anticipate questions of interest for several purposes can cut down on data collection burden and capitalize on opportunities to steward resources towards data collection, analyses, and use by multiple stakeholders to maximize impact.

The collaborative approach to problem solving between TPPs and researchers called for by Goldhaber and Ronfeldt in Chapter 8 offers an optimal venue for strengthening the methodological rigor of research. While more rigorous research designs may require disruptions to how business is typically conducted, generating knowledge that strengthens teacher preparation ultimately benefits the broader PreK–12 education community. As such, federal and state education agencies should consider structures and incentives to both encourage TPPs, schools, and researchers to collaborate on rigorously designed studies and inspire TPPs to adopt evidence-based strategies as part of their shared responsibility for student outcomes. To the extent that these investigations yield information that can be used to increase the quality of teacher preparation, this could be used as a proof of concept to encourage others in the broader PreK–12 education community to engage in similar partnerships to further evidence-based teacher preparation and ultimately more effective outcomes for teachers and their students.

REFERENCES

Bryk, A. S., Gomez, L. M., & Grunow, A. (2010). *Getting ideas into action: Building networked improvement communities in education.* Stanford, CA: Carnegie Foundation for the Advancement of Teaching. Retrieved from http://www.carnegiefoundation.org/spotlight/webinar-bryk-gomez-building-networked-improvement-communities-in-education

Carinci, J. E. (2016). *Investigating pre-service teachers' competencies and beliefs in relation to their hiring outcomes.* (Unpublished doctoral dissertation). Johns Hopkins University, Baltimore, MD.

Data Quality Campaign. (2017, August). Using data to ensure that teachers are learner ready on day one. Washington, DC: Author. Retrieved from https://dataqualitycampaign.org/wp-content/uploads/2017/08/DQC-EPP-primer-08032017-1.pdf

DeMonte, J. (2017). *Fostering a new approach to research on teacher preparation: Results of the first convening of researchers, practitioners, and K–12 Educators.* Washington, DC: American Institutes for Research.

Langley, G. L., Nolan, K. M., Nolan, T. W., Norman, C. L., & Provost, L. P. (2009). *The improvement guide: A practical approach to enhancing organizational performance* (2nd ed.). San Francisco, CA: Jossey-Bass.

Meyer, S. J., Brodersen, R. M., & Linick, M. A. (2014). *Approaches to evaluating teacher preparation programs in seven states* (REL 2015–044). Washington, DC: U.S. Department of Education, Institute of Education Sciences, National Center for Education Evaluation and Regional Assistance, Regional Educational Laboratory Central. Retrieved from http://ies.ed.gov/ncee/edlabs

Mihaly, K., McCaffery, D., Sass, T., & Lockwood, J. R. (2012). *Where you come from or where you go? Distinguishing between school quality and the effectiveness of teacher preparation program graduates* (CALDER Working Paper No. 63). Washington, DC: National Center for Analysis of Longitudinal Data in Education Research.

Ruben, B. R. (2010). *Excellence in higher education guide. An integrated approach to assessment, planning, and improvement in colleges and universities.* Washington, DC: National Association of College and University Business Officers.

von Hippel, P. T., Bellows, L., Osbourne, C., Lincove, J. A., & Mills, N. (2016). Teacher quality differences between teacher preparation programs: How big? How reliable? Which programs are different? *Economics of Education Review, 53,* 31–45.

von Hippel, P. T., & Bellows, L. (2018). How much does teacher quality vary across teacher preparation programs? Reanalyses from six states. *Economics of Education Review, 64,* 298–312.

Worrell, F., Brabeck, M., Dwyer, C., Geisinger, K., Marx, R., Noell, G., & Pianta R. (2014). *Assessing and evaluating teacher preparation programs.* Washington, DC: American Psychological Association.

ABOUT THE EDITORS

Jennifer E. Carinci is a program director for STEM education research at the American Association for the Advancement of Science (AAAS). Her project portfolio includes the NSF Robert Noyce Teacher Scholarship Program and investigating innovations in preservice STEM teacher education. Dr. Carinci most recently was the inaugural Director of Research, Innovation, and Data Strategy at the Council for the Accreditation of Educator Preparation (CAEP) where her role involved shaping and implementing an ambitious agenda to advance educator preparation. Previously Jennifer served as an Institute of Education Sciences (IES) pre-doctoral training fellow with a background as a middle and high school art teacher in Baltimore City. She has evaluated students, interns, programs, and prospective and current teachers. Distinctions earned include Maryland Art Education Association's New Middle School Art Teacher of the Year, Fulbright Teacher Scholar, and a past member of the AERA Council. Jennifer holds a BFA from Maryland Institute College of Art (MICA), as well as a Master of Science in education and a doctorate in teacher development and leadership from Johns Hopkins University.

Stephen J. Meyer is a director at RMC Research. Currently, Dr. Meyer serves as a researcher for Regional Education Laboratory (REL) Central at Marzano Research leading research and technical assistance activities in the seven-state region. Dr. Meyer leads studies of educator mobility and attrition, and technical assistance activities for state education agencies to support use of data and research related to educator preparation and certification, and teacher shortage prediction. Dr. Meyer also directs an evaluation of

Linking Teacher Preparation Program Design and Implementation to Outcomes for Teachers and Students, pages 249–250
Copyright © 2020 by Information Age Publishing

TeachDETROIT, an urban teacher residency program and impact studies of various interventions focused on improving student literacy, mathematics, and social and emotional learning skills. Dr. Meyer's background includes training in quantitative and qualitative research, evaluation, and statistics. Dr. Meyer is a certified What Works Clearinghouse reviewer and received his PhD in education-measurement, evaluation, and statistical analysis from the University of Chicago.

Cara Jackson is an associate partner with Bellwether Education Partners, focusing on issues related to evaluation and planning, research design, survey research, and quantitative data analysis. She provides technical assistance and supports capacity building related to program evaluation and quasi-experimental analysis for a variety of projects. Cara also teaches research methods at American University's School of Education. Previously, she designed and conducted studies to inform district policies for Montgomery County Public Schools, developed teacher evaluation systems as the assistant director of Research and Evaluation for Urban Teachers, and conducted studies of federal education policy as a senior analyst at the U.S. Government Accountability Office. Earlier in her career, Cara taught in New York City. She is a certified What Works Clearinghouse reviewer and earned her PhD in education policy and an advanced certificate in education measurement, statistics, and evaluation from the University of Maryland. Her master's degree is from the Harvard Graduate School of Education and she is an alumna of Harvard's Strategic Data Project Fellowship.

ABOUT THE CONTRIBUTORS

Michael Allen is a nationally known education policy researcher and consultant who has written or co-written numerous publications over the last 20 years on teacher preparation and teacher quality. He is a founding partner of Teacher Preparation Analytics, and he previously coordinated the four-state REL Appalachia Higher Education Consortium, served as a senior consultant to the Association of Public and Land-grant Universities (APLU), and was a senior program officer at the National Research Council. Dr. Allen's education policy career began at the Education Commission of the States, where he ultimately became director of the teacher quality program and worked with education leaders across the United States. Prior to that, he was a philosophy professor and ethics consultant, having earned a PhD and AM in philosophy from Boston University, an MEd in research methods from Australia's Charles Sturt University, and a BA from the University of Colorado at Boulder.

Wendy Barnard is an assistant research professor and director of the College Research and Evaluation Services Team (CREST). Dr. Barnard received her PhD from the University of Wisconsin-Madison, where she focused on the impact of early education experiences and parent involvement on long-term academic achievements. Her research interests include evaluation methodology, longitudinal research design, and the impact of learning opportunities on teacher performance. Currently, she works on evaluation efforts for U.S. Department of Education grants, National Science Foundation grants, local foundation, and state grants.

Linking Teacher Preparation Program Design and Implementation to Outcomes for Teachers and Students, pages 251–259
Copyright © 2020 by Information Age Publishing
251

Yasar Bodur is a professor of elementary education and assessment coordinator in the College of Education at Georgia Southern University. He received his doctorate degree in elementary education from Florida State University. His research interests include different pedagogies in teacher education, and teacher education for diversity.

Jennifer E. Carinci is a program director for STEM education research at the American Association for the Advancement of Science (AAAS). Her project portfolio includes the NSF Robert Noyce Teacher Scholarship Program and investigating innovations in preservice STEM teacher education. Dr. Carinci most recently was the inaugural director of research, innovation, and data strategy at the Council for the Accreditation of Educator Preparation (CAEP) where her role involved shaping and implementing an ambitious agenda to advance educator preparation. Previously Jennifer served as an institute of education sciences (IES) pre-doctoral training fellow with a background as a middle and high school art teacher in Baltimore City. She has evaluated students, interns, programs, and prospective and current teachers. Distinctions earned include Maryland Art Education Association's New Middle School Art Teacher of the Year, Fulbright Teacher Scholar, and a past member of the AERA Council. Jennifer holds a BFA from Maryland Institute College of Art (MICA), as well as a Master of Science in education and a Doctorate in teacher development and leadership from Johns Hopkins University.

James B. Carroll has been at the University of Portland since 1992. He has written in the areas of assessment in teacher preparation and educational technology. He teaches courses in educational research and has co-authored a book on that topic.

Charles Coble was professor of science education for 23 years and for 13 years was dean of the School of Education at East Carolina University. He served for 6 years as vice president for the 17-campus UNC System and for 3 years vice president for policy studies and programs for the Education Commission of the States in Denver, CO. Dr. Coble was co-director of the Science and Mathematics Teacher Imperative (SMTI) with APLU in Washington, DC for 7 years. Dr. Coble has directed over $12M in grants/contracts and is author or co-author of 10 books and over 80 published articles. Dr. Coble holds undergraduate and advanced degrees from UNC-Chapel Hill.

Jennifer Collett is an assistant professor of literacy instruction and development in the Department of Early Childhood and Childhood Education at Lehman College of the City University of New York. She holds a PhD from the University of California, Berkeley. Her research looks at the intersection of identity and literacy development for emergent bilinguals in elementary school. She has published several articles in the *Bilingual Research Journal, Journal of Language, Identity and English*, and the *Journal of Multilingual Education Research.*

Nancy E. Dubetz is a professor of childhood education in the Department of Early Childhood and Childhood Education at Lehman College, City University of New York. Her research interests include the study of teachers' theories of practice, teacher advocacy for English language learners, school/university partnerships, and English as a foreign language instruction in Latin America. She has published several book chapters on preparing teachers of English language learners and professional development school partnerships and has published articles in *Action in Teacher Education, Bilingual Research Journal, The Journal of Research in Education, English Language Teaching*, the *Journal of Multilingual Education Research,* and *Issues in Teacher Education.*

Harriet Fayne is a professor in the Department of Counseling, Leadership, Literacy and Special Education at Lehman College, City University of New York and principal investigator, MATH UP (USDOE sponsored urban residency project). From 2011–2016, she served as dean of Lehman's School of Education. She has authored or co-authored articles and book chapters that focus on teacher education redesign and presents her work at international and national conferences. Dr. Fayne holds a BA with a major in American studies from Barnard College, a MAT in social studies education from Harvard University, and a PhD in educational psychology from Columbia University.

Dan Goldhaber is the director of the Center for Analysis of Longitudinal Data in Education Research (CALDER, caldercenter.org) at the American Institutes for Research and the Center for Education Data & Research (CEDR, cedr.us) at the University of Washington. Both CALDER and CEDR focus on using state administrative data to do research that informs decisions about education policy and practice. Dan's work speaks to issues of educational productivity and reform at the K–12 level, the broad array of human capital policies that influence the composition, distribution, and quality of teachers in the workforce, and connections between students' PK–12 experiences and postsecondary outcomes. Dan previously served as president of the Association for Education Finance and Policy, an elected member of the Alexandria City School Board, and as co-editor of *Education Finance and Policy.*

Brandon Helding received his PhD from Arizona State University in 2010. During and after a postdoctoral research fellowship he began work at Boulder Language Technologies. His research interests include hierarchical linear and nonlinear modeling, scalable research designs, modeling of complex systems, and program evaluation (with requisite measure development).

Randy Hetherington is an assistant professor in the School of Education at the University of Portland, in Portland, Oregon. He served for 34 years in the P–12 system in Canada with the last 17 as principal at the elementary and high school levels. He teaches in the Doctor of Education and Master of Education programs in school and district leadership, curriculum development and reform, and educational foundations. Randy also serves as a clinical supervisor and child development instructor for preservice teachers. Research areas include school and district governance, school leadership, and teacher education.

Cara Jackson is an associate partner with Bellwether Education Partners, focusing on issues related to evaluation and planning, research design, survey research, and quantitative data analysis. She provides technical assistance and supports capacity building related to program evaluation and quasi-experimental analysis for a variety of projects. Previously, Cara designed and conducted studies to inform district policies for Montgomery County Public Schools, developed teacher evaluation systems as the assistant director of Research and Evaluation for Urban Teachers, and conducted studies of federal education policy as a senior analyst at the U.S. Government Accountability Office. Earlier in her career, Cara taught pre–K and kindergarten in New York City. She is a certified What Works Clearinghouse reviewer and earned her PhD in education policy and an advanced certificate in Education Measurement, Statistics, and Evaluation from the University of Maryland. Her master's degree is from the Harvard Graduate School of Education and she is an alumna of Harvard's Strategic Data Project Fellowship.

Elizabeth Lewis is an associate professor of science education in the Department of Teaching, Learning, and Teacher Education at the University of Nebraska-Lincoln. Dr. Lewis has been the principal investigator of two National Science Foundation Noyce (Track I, Phase I & II) grants that have supported 80 preservice science teachers and a longitudinal study of beginning science teachers and their reformed-based instructional practices. Findings from this project have been disseminated by her research group through many conference presentations at NARST, ASTE, and ESERA, several dissertations, and will be highlighted in other publications in addition to this volume's contribution. Dr. Lewis is a former geologist with her master's degree in geological sciences and taught high school Earth and space in Maine and Massachusetts. She also investigates geoscience education issues that have been published in the *Journal of Geoscience Education*.

Lyrica Lucas is a postdoctoral research associate in the School of Natural Resources at the University of Nebraska-Lincoln (UNL) where she studies inquiry-based learning strategies and students' use of computational models for complex systems in introductory biology courses. Previously, she was a research assistant on a longitudinal study on the development of secondary science teachers and a university supervisor to preservice science teachers in local school districts. Dr. Lucas completed her PhD in Educational Studies at UNL, earned her master's degree in physics at the University of the Philippines-Diliman, and continued her studies in science education at UNL as a Fulbright scholar. As a former physics instructor, she is also interested in physics education research particularly in the use of multiple representations for problem-solving and modeling.

Anne Marie Marshall is an associate professor of mathematics education in the Department of Early Childhood and Childhood Education at Lehman College of the City University of New York. She received her PhD in curriculum and instruction from the University of Maryland—College Park. As a former third grade teacher in the Milwaukee Public School District, she is devoted to developing skillful preservice teachers to educate historically underserved students in urban settings. Her current research interests focus on equity in mathematics education and preservice mathematics teacher education. She is interested in how equity focused mathematics teacher preparation impacts the knowledge and dispositions of prospective teachers.

Hillary Merk is an associate professor in the School of Education at the University of Portland, in Portland, OR. She taught elementary aged students for several years in Los Angeles County, CA and continues to find opportunities to stay engaged with K–8 schools. Hillary received her PhD in education with an emphasis in classroom management and diversity, and a specialization in cultural studies and social thought in education from Washington State University in Pullman, WA. She researches in the area of classroom management, cyberbullying, diversity, new teacher development, and teacher education.

Stephen J. Meyer is a director at RMC Research. Currently, Dr. Meyer serves as a researcher for Regional Education Laboratory (REL) Central at Marzano Research leading research and technical assistance activities in the seven-state region. Dr. Meyer leads studies of educator mobility and attrition, and technical assistance activities for state education agencies to support use of data and research related to educator preparation and certification, and teacher shortage prediction. Dr. Meyer also directs an evaluation of TeachDETROIT, an urban teacher residency program and impact studies of various interventions focused on improving student literacy, mathematics, and social and emotional learning skills. Dr. Meyer's background includes training in quantitative and qualitative research, evaluation, and statistics. Dr. Meyer is a certified What Works Clearinghouse reviewer and received his PhD in education-measurement, evaluation, and statistical analysis from the University of Chicago.

Aaron Musson earned his doctorate at the University of Nebraska-Lincoln (UNL) in educational studies in August 2018. His research has focused on the assessment and discourse practices of beginning physical science teachers. As a 20-year science teacher, Dr. Musson has taught mostly chemistry, but also physics and biology, in Nebraska secondary private and public schools, and in the University of Nebraska-Omaha's chemistry department. Dr. Musson earned his master's degree in education in curriculum and instruction from Wayne State College. While at UNL he worked as a lecturer and science teacher educator coordinating and teaching a two-semester science teaching methods course and supervised and oversaw preservice teachers' clinical experiences. He currently teaches in Omaha Public Schools.

Margarita Pivovarova is an assistant professor in the Mary Lou Fulton Teachers College at Arizona State University. Margarita's research interests include educational policy in the area of teacher quality and evaluation, and teacher mobility. She has published in educational, statistical, and education policy journals such as *Journal of Teacher Education, Statistics and Public Policy,* and *Educational Policy.* Margarita received her PhD in economics from the University of Toronto.

Courtney Preston is an assistant professor of educational leadership and policy in the Department of Educational Leadership and Policy Studies. Dr. Preston holds a PhD in leadership and policy studies from Vanderbilt University's Peabody College of Education and Human Development and a master's in English education from Georgia State University. Dr. Preston studies teacher education and novice teachers, recently focusing on STEM teacher preparation for high needs schools and novice teacher labor markets. Dr. Preston teaches courses on school and teacher policy. Her work has recently appeared in *Teachers College Record* and *Journal of Teacher Education.*

Ana Rivero is a clinical assistant professor in STEM education in the Department of Teaching, Learning, and Social Justice at Seattle University. Dr. Rivero has a master's in education and organizational development from the University of Monterrey and completed her PhD in educational studies with a focus on science education at the University of Nebraska-Lincoln. Her dissertation study investigated beginning science teachers' knowledge and experiences of metacognition and reflective practices for teaching secondary science. Dr. Rivero has collaborated with Dr. Lewis's research group on projects about the efficacy of teacher education programs developing beginning secondary science teachers' inquiry-based teaching practices. Dr. Rivero is a former high school chemistry teacher, science department chair, and was a curriculum supervisor in a private higher education institution in Monterrey, Mexico.

Matt Ronfeldt is associate professor of educational studies at the University of Michigan School of Education. He earned his PhD from Stanford University, where he concentrated on teacher education. Ronfeldt was an IES postdoctoral fellow in the Institute for Research on Educational Policy and Practice (now CEPA) at Stanford, focusing on large-scale quantitative research. He previously taught middle-school mathematics and science for 7 years. Ronfeldt seeks to understand how to improve teaching quality, particularly in schools and districts that serve marginalized students. He positions his scholarship at the intersection of practice and policy and focuses on how preservice teacher education and aspects of school organizations (esp working conditions) are related to teaching quality and other workforce outcomes. He is principal or co-principal investigator on investigations of teacher preparation supported by the Tennessee and U.S. Departments of Education, the Bill and Melinda Gates Foundation, the Spencer Foundation, and the Joyce Foundation.

Anne Rothstein is a professor in the Department of Early Childhood and Childhood Education at Lehman College of the City University of New York. She received her EdD from Teachers College—Columbia University. She has served as a department chair, associate dean of professional studies, and associate provost for sponsored program research. Since 1985 Anne has written over 400 grant proposals, receiving more than 300 awards. She has also directed many grant-funded programs for K–12 students, teachers, and for college students. Her current research interests focus on college access and readiness, impact of college readiness program dosage on student success, high school graduation and college enrollment and role of college student support in increasing 4-year graduation rates. Her most recent book, *Creating Winning Grant Proposals: A Step-by-Step Approach*, will be out in Spring 2019.

Amy Tankersley is a doctoral student in the Department of Teaching, Learning, and Teacher Education at the University of Nebraska-Lincoln. Ms. Tankersley currently works as a research assistant on a longitudinal study of beginning teachers and their reformed-based instructional practices. She also works as a university supervisor with preservice science teachers in local school districts. Ms. Tankersley is also a former biologist with her master's degree in microbiology from the University of Central Oklahoma as well as a biology and environmental science teacher who worked with local and state agencies in Oklahoma on curriculum and reform-based teaching practices.

Aslihan Unal is an associate professor at Georgia Southern University. She earned her doctorate degree in elementary education from Florida State University. Her areas of research are assessment, distance education, and teacher education.

Zafer Unal is an associate professor and assessment coordinator at USF St. Petersburg. He earned his doctorate degree in elementary education from Florida State University. His areas of research are teacher education, educational technology, and assessment of teacher candidate learning and online portfolios.

Robert Vagi is an independent research consultant and most recently held the position of research associate at the Center for Applied Research and Educational Improvement at the University of Minnesota. His research spans a variety of topics and has been featured in several academic and popular media outlets including PBS's *Horizon, The Arizona Republic,* and the Brookings Institution's *Brown Center Chalkboard.* Prior to earning a PhD in educational policy and evaluation at Arizona State University, Robert spent 6 years as a public-school teacher in Phoenix, Arizona.

Jacqueline Waggoner is a tenured professor in the School of Education at the University of Portland in Portland, Oregon. She received her bi-university EdD from the University of Oregon and Portland State University in public school administration and supervision and has worked in higher education and public P–12 education for over 25 years. Research areas include teacher education, measurement, instrumentation; assessment; and data-driven decision making. Additionally, Jacqueline co-led the School of Education's 2013 successful NCATE and State of Oregon accreditation efforts, receiving commendations in Standard 2, Assessment and Standard 4, Diversity.

Saroja Warner is currently senior director on the learning innovations team at WestEd where she supports states and local school districts in their work to build and maintain an effective educator workforce. Before joining WestEd, she was the director of Educator Workforce Initiatives at the Council of Chief State School Officers (CCSSO) where she directed two cross-state initiatives focused on strengthening the educator workforce: the Network for Transforming Educator Preparation (NTEP) and the Diverse and Learner-Ready Teachers Initiative (DLRT). Prior to joining CCSSO, she was the chief of Educator Preparation Program Approval and Assessment at the Maryland State Department of Education. She began her career as a high school social studies teacher in Maryland where she taught for 15 years and was twice certified as a national board certified teacher. She continues to serve as a member of the graduate faculty at the University of Maryland, College Park where she works in teacher preparation to ensure candidates are ready to support equity in classrooms, conduct action research to better their practice and student learning, and actively act as agents of school change.

Bruce Weitzel is an associate professor and the associate dean of the School of Education at the University of Portland. He teaches in both the Master of Arts in teaching program and in the administrative licensure program, specializing in secondary classroom methods and management, and in leadership for school change. Licensed as an Oregon teacher and administrator, he brings over 20 years of experience as a secondary school principal and change agent to his research interest in student learning gains.